Sweet F.A.

Sweet F.A.

GRAHAM KELLY
with Bob Harris

CollinsWillow
An Imprint of HarperCollins*Publishers*

First published in 1999
by CollinsWillow
an imprint of HarperCollins*Publishers*
London

The HarperCollins website address is:
www.**fire**and**water**.com

1 3 5 7 9 8 6 4 2

A CIP catalogue record for this book
is available from the British Library.

ISBN 0 00 218928 3

Printed and bound in Great Britain by Clays Ltd, St Ives plc.

Photographic acknowledgements
All photographs supplied by Graham Kelly with the exception of the following:
Action Images plates section pp 6t, 6br, 16t; Allsport 2, 4b, 11t;
Colorsport 3t, 4t, 5t; Empics 3c, 5b, 12b, 16c; PA News 9tl, 9tr,
9c, 12c, 13 (all), 14t, 15t, 15c, 16b; Rex Features 6bl.

Contents

Sweet F.A.

Prologue

It was Friday 12 February, just two months after I had been forced to fall on my sword as Chief Executive of the Football Association, when BBC Radio 5 Live called me at my Cambridgeshire home to ask for my reaction at being cleared by FIFA, football's world governing body, of any impropriety in what had come to be known as the 'Cash for Votes' scandal.

My reaction, in fact, was to be totally stunned. I was taken aback because not only had I received no information, I did not even know that FIFA had been conducting an investigation into the whole affair which had led to my departure from Lancaster Gate!

I welcomed the news to say the least, albeit from such an unexpected source. The next question was even more of a surprise when I was asked whether I would be invited back by the Football Association as Chief Executive. I replied that there were pigs flying over the Cambridgeshire countryside as I contemplated that possibility. There was no way 'New FA' would be seen to be going back, having been at such pains to justify my removal over the previous weeks.

But while making light with the interviewer, I felt an overwhelming sense of relief come over me. It was one thing to lose your job and quite another to be accused of corruption. I was, and still am, very grateful to the men in Zurich. It would have been difficult, however, for them to have reached any other conclusion as I was following the advice of *their* most senior officials, not to mention our own Government.

The story began at the start of 1998 when Alec McGivan, the director of the World Cup 2006 campaign, persuaded the FA Executive Committee to support the principle of giving aid to foreign associations, particularly in places where it would improve our chances of securing the World Cup, although of course it should have been obligatory for any association the size of England to be helping smaller nations and that was the thrust of his and my argument.

In early March of the same year Keith Wiseman and I had lunch with FIFA President Joao Havelange and General Secretary Sepp Blatter in Paris before an International Board meeting and they impressed on us the urgent need to replace David Will on the FA Executive Committee with FA Chairman Keith Wiseman. Indeed, they stressed that it was absolutely crucial for our World Cup bid. Will, a Scot, had occupied the British seat on FIFA for eight years after succeeding Northern Ireland's Harry Cavan, who had been there for the previous 30 years. England, the home of football and one of the world's strongest footballing nations in economic terms, had, unbelievably, been out in the cold for nearly 40 years. Sir Stanley Rous had, of course, presided over FIFA before Joao Havelange, but that position demands that the incumbent represents the entire world of football rather than his country of origin.

Little did I realise at the time that before the year was out, I would be out of a job myself, on the grounds of exceeding my authority.

Those two months between my dismissal and the all-clear from the world ruling body had been the hardest of my life, beginning on the morning of 15 December 1998 when I arrived at my office at my usual time of 7 am. Keith Wiseman was in thirty minutes later to discuss the fall-out from the Executive Committee meeting the previous evening which, significantly, we had not been invited to attend.

Neither of us could contribute an iota of information and we could not even speculate on what had happened as, unusually, there had been no rumours!

We did not have to wait long. The bombshell exploded an hour later when FA Vice-Chairman Geoff Thompson walked purposefully into my office, removed his papers from his briefcase and said that he was sorry to have to tell me that it was the unanimous view of the Executive Committee that there were sufficient grounds for dismissing me. He added that the decision would be confirmed at the Executive Committee meeting later that day, previously a routine meeting that I had been preparing for prior to his arrival.

There was not a lot of room for doubt or discussion as Thompson told me that I would be suspended from duty. The Committee did not have the power to implement the decisions themselves, but they would be making a recommendation to the FA Council.

I expressed my surprise as I recovered from the shock and warned him that I would contest the decision, asking at the same time what was happening with Keith Wiseman. Thompson responded that it was very much the same and that the Executive Committee wanted him to resign but he had already said that he would not. Keith was determined to present his case personally to the full Council.

On Thompson's instructions Nic Coward, the FA Company Secretary, had previously outlined a procedure whereby my case would be heard first by the Executive Committee and secondly by a special Appeals Board comprising three Council members. This seemed to have vanished into the ether during the intervening days.

I was in a complete daze as I changed into my suit. I was aware that there were a few members of the Council who had been after me for some months, but it was still a total surprise. It was always in the back of my mind that it could come to the ultimate conclusion, but when it actually happened it was still a massive blow. It was so terminal, so final.

Fortunately a sense of foreboding had prompted me to take legal advice the previous month after Keith Wiseman had told me that there might come a time when we each needed to look after our own interests. My worst fears realised now, I rang my solicitor and he immediately telephoned Nic Coward to point out that I could not be suspended without a hearing. The response was to arrange a second meeting with Geoff Thompson, who, by then, was at the Kensington Park Hotel.

My solicitor let me know that the FA planned a press statement for that afternoon and that he had suggested there should be a 24-hour delay. He had also started to talk to the FA about a deal and by midday they had come back and offered to pay me a year's salary to leave, their offer being open until 3 pm when there would be a press conference.

It was faceless and impersonal. All the discussions came through the solicitors with me not even knowing who was sitting in the Kensington Park Hotel deciding my future. Eventually I was called over to meet Geoff Thompson, arriving at the Kensington Park Hotel at 12.55 pm.

I pointed out to Thompson that he was not complying with the terms of my contract. As it was a disciplinary issue, the matter had to be raised in a formal way and progressed through the proper channels. He claimed I had acknowledged that it was a disciplinary matter at a previous meeting of the Executive Committee on 1 December, but I argued that it was quite the opposite. I had given a full explanation and had stated that it had been given without prejudice to the terms of my contract.

Thompson then counter-claimed that Clause 14 of the contract was not relevant and that I could have attended the Executive Committee meeting that morning – even though he had made it perfectly clear to me earlier that same day that I was not wanted and neither was Keith Wiseman.

He backed down and wanted to start the discussions under Clause 14 there and then, but I insisted that my solicitor was present and by the time the talks started both parties had their legal aides at their sides, with Christopher Osman of Clifford Chance representing the FA.

The FA produced a long letter which they had been intending to send to me. It was read out and effectively said that they were terminating my contract for exceeding my authority. It was a letter that was never handed over as we embarked on a discussion to see if there was a way of concluding the matter without them formally dismissing me. They said yes – but not at any price.

My official termination notice was three years, but they insisted on one year and the haggling went on until around 4.30 pm. I was in a near impossible situation. I had three options. The first was to receive the letter and fight the Executive Committee decision by seeking to overturn their recommendation in the Council. Unlike Keith Wiseman, I did not want to go to the full Council. It would have been asking the Council to go against the Executive Committee. On a charge of this magnitude I did not think I had a cat in hell's chance of persuading them, because the one thing I was being accused of was an issue which was very close to their hearts. They desperately wanted to preserve their authority. The Council were jumpy enough if the Executive Committee themselves exceeded their authority, never mind a mere paid servant.

The second option was to go to law. However, I did not have unlimited resources, even though my solicitor said that there was a fair chance of winning as I had the backing of the Chairman throughout. But as they were getting rid of him too, it might be touch and go. In any event it would be an expensive gamble I could not afford to take.

While it was nice to be lauded in the media for taking the third option, resigning honourably, there were, in truth, not a great many alternatives left open to me.

We then had an argument about the FA press statement which I felt was unnecessarily long. It referred to the FA 'moving forward with integrity' which I thought was rather too damning of both Keith Wiseman and me. Their lawyer also wanted to include waivers about sex discrimination and race relations, which hardly seemed relevant.

The entire scenario was awful. I was closeted away in a basement room in the hotel and had to walk what seemed like a mile just to use the mobile telephone, so I didn't speak to anyone other than Geoff Thompson and the solicitors throughout the entire day. I had earlier spoken to my wife-to-be, Romayne, before 9 am, to inform her of the situation. She had not realised that the Executive Committee had been meeting the previous evening and was stunned to hear that I was on my way out of a job. I told her that I was speaking to my solicitor but, because of the circumstances, it was much later before I spoke to her again. It must have been a long day for Romayne as well.

I finally agreed to leave my position for a pay-off of £375,000 plus being allowed to keep my car. The FA were clearly in a hurry as their statement appeared on the BBC's 'Six O'clock News' even though I did not actually sign the contract until an hour and a half later! The financial terms were to remain confidential, but informed guesses soon appeared in the newspapers when Thompson, Chelsea Chairman Ken Bates and Sir David Hill-Wood, the Chairman of the Finance Committee, made disparaging remarks about me.

I wandered down Kensington Gore with a strange mixture of feelings. There was an immense weight lifted off my shoulders, yet the future looked completely uncertain. I had secured a pay-off which many would regard as eminently reasonable, but I faced heavy financial commitments including steep mortgage repayments incurred when I moved to the South of England at the height of the property boom and a not insubstantial tax bill.

I bumped into Nic Coward and Michael Cunnah, the FA's Finance Director, at Lancaster Gate. Nic was at pains to ensure that I should not depart in a rush but was to go back and see them for a proper farewell. Michael pointed out that I would have to come in for the log book of the car.

I cleared my desk, talking to Press Officer Steve Double, who thanked me for my support, before taking a call from my former deputy Pat Smith who asked me to join her and her husband Mark Day for dinner at the Concordia Italian restaurant. After a hasty meal I did my duty in front of the cameras, repeating that what I had done was, and had always been, in the best interests of the FA.

I finally headed off home at 10 pm thinking that after thirty happy years in football, I was suddenly out in the cold. The drive back to Cambridgeshire gave me plenty of time for reflection.

CHAPTER ONE

Cry Foul

In a matter of hours, it seemed, my business life had become totally unravelled. Clearly it was no overnight decision by the Football Association to dispose of me, and just as transparent was the fact that there was more to it than the 'Cash for Votes' scandal that had ousted both Keith Wiseman and me.

As I contemplated the reasons on the drive up the A1 it became evident that there were three seemingly diversified strands which had merged into that final reason for my departure.

Central to the issue was the Football Association's bid for the World Cup in 2006. It was a long and expensive process and, according to all the advice from FIFA downwards, the key was to have our Chairman Keith Wiseman in a senior position with the world governing body.

There was also the crucial vote for the Presidency of FIFA, the most powerful position in Planet Football. I had become embroiled by having to publicly take sides, much to the chagrin of certain members of the FA Executive who had originally given us *carte blanche* to decide between Lennart Johansson and Sepp Blatter.

Finally, but definitely not least of all, was the power struggle within the corridors of power at Lancaster Gate where the increasingly powerful chairmen of the Football Association Premier League were working towards assuming control of the game in England. That was something both Wiseman and I were ready to fight until the end.

Unfortunately the end came rather quicker than either of us ever anticipated!

I recalled that there had been a fair amount of sniping over the previous months. It is difficult to say what started it off or where it came from, but I had the distinct and unsettling feeling that there were those on the Council who wanted me out. It began when I received a telephone call while on a short break in Chester during the previous August, tipping me off that Harry Harris from the *Daily Mirror* was enquiring about a move to get rid of me. Keith Wiseman had answered the call and shrugged it off.

I rather gained the impression that it was coming from somewhere within the Premier League but I could not pin it down. I went to see Ken Bates in Monaco at the end of that month while we were there for Chelsea's European Super Cup Final against Real Madrid. We engaged in a rather desultory conversation about changing the FA and having a Board instead of an Executive Committee. But, in truth, I had gone specifically to try and tease out of him exactly what this problem was that I was facing. All I could get from him was that 'knowledge was power' and that I needed to know that there were one or two in positions of power who wanted me out. It didn't tell me much but at least it confirmed that something was afoot. One? Two? Ken Bates himself? It was impossible to tell.

Certainly the abrasive Bates and the cultured Sir David Hill-Wood had formed an unlikely alliance on the National Stadium Shadow Board. Bates was Chairman but, during his absence on holiday, Hill-Wood had nominated himself deputy in order to try and raise the necessary finance in the City. Bates was later to launch a vain attempt to change the rules to allow Hill-Wood to be appointed Vice-President.

There was what proved to be a significant Finance Committee meeting on 9 September. I usually made a point of attending these but, unfortunately, Hill-Wood, who represents Australia with the FA, had arranged the date at the end of the previous meeting in July which had been allowed to overrun, causing my early departure. I wasn't particularly pleased at missing the meeting, but it would be paranoid to think that the timing was deliberate.

It was then that the Welsh issue first surfaced. Hill-Wood had got hold of an invoice from the Welsh FA for £400,000 which should never have been sent to the FA but to the Football Trust. He made it clear that he was not going to sanction this payment and was going to refer it to the Executive Committee.

I was more than a little cross when I heard about it for it was clear that Hill-Wood had made some strong criticisms of the staff, including me, while I was absent, which I thought unethical. I did not learn about what had happened at the meeting until my return from the Turkish FA's 75th Anniversary celebrations the following Saturday when I bumped into Noel White, Chairman of the International Committee, at West Ham United's game against Liverpool.

I had also been under pressure over Glenn Hoddle's *World Cup Diary* – another factor lurking in the background – and we were discussing the England manager's new contract. We had a meeting on 16 September where Noel White and Dave Richards, the Sheffield Wednesday Chairman, expressed some criticisms but not particularly strong ones. Noel complained that he did not know that the players and their wives had gone out for dinner in London during the build-up to the World Cup, nor had he been notified about a private practice game in Caen until the last minute, a match on which we imposed a news blackout because of security.

Keith Wiseman was bemused. They were niggling, petty matters viewed in isolation but, put together and added to the fact that David Hill-Wood had written a letter to Keith Wiseman criticising me, they showed that the thunderclouds were beginning to gather.

It was ironic that Hill-Wood should be proving to be the thorn in the side of both myself and Keith Wiseman, because Keith had bent over backwards to keep him on the Council two years earlier when the Chairman of the Australian Federation wanted to replace Hill-Wood at Lancaster Gate with Terry Venables.

It is, of course, odd in itself that, at a time when many Australians do not want our monarch, the Australian Soccer Federation even have a representative on the FA! We had decided some years ago that when the present holders of the positions of Australia and New Zealand finished for whatever reason, they would not be replaced, and had it not been for Keith allowing the Australians time to think again, Hill-Wood would certainly have been off the Council.

Hill-Wood brought the arrangement with Wales to the Executive Committee's attention by a letter complaining that he did not think we should help the Welsh at all and added a postscript saying that they (the Executive Committee) should not *'allow the wool to be pulled over their eyes '*. That slur did not please me a lot.

The agreement with the Welsh was originally made on Cup Final day, 16 May 1998. Keith Wiseman had failed in his attempt to be elected to the UEFA Executive Committee when UEFA held their Congress in Dublin in April and immediately afterwards we decided to write to the other three British Associations suggesting that Keith should take over the FIFA British Vice-Presidency from Scotland's David Will. We explained that we had been advised in our World Cup campaign visits that it was crucial for us to be directly represented around the table and that we could not lobby through another person, David Will, even though he had always been fair to us and had been an efficient representative. The obvious fact was that we needed to have a direct presence. This was how South Korea had persuaded FIFA to share the 2002 World Cup with Japan.

David was also perceived to be in the Lennart Johansson UEFA camp in the battle for the FIFA Presidency not least because he, Will, was the sole declared candidate to succeed Johansson at UEFA, had the Swede been successful against Sepp Blatter in the FIFA elections in June. Our perception was that David would not be pulling up any trees on behalf of England, because he would be keen to ensure smooth relations in UEFA who were, of course, backing Germany for 2006 and definitely not England. He was not one for making waves.

We had to get in touch by letter, as a meeting was out of the question with the Scottish representatives in the USA and the other Associations' representatives flung all over the globe. We knew we desperately needed to replace David Will if our ambitions to stage the World Cup were to be realised, and after an internal discussion at the FA with the management team it was recommended to Keith Wiseman that, if necessary, we should offer to help either the Welsh or the Irish with their development programmes in return for their support to have him as the British representative and to assist us in strengthening our voice generally in the international corridors of power.

The management team included Pat Smith, Nic Coward, David Davies, Director of Public Affairs, Mark Day, the retiring Finance Director, Michael Cunnah and Alec McGivan, director of the 2006 bid.

Keith and I had a meeting with Jim Boyce, the Irish President, and David Bowen, their Secretary, on the evening before the Cup Final. We took them to the Royal Garden Hotel and enjoyed an amicable evening, but Jim Boyce made it clear that he would be unlikely to be shifted in his support for David Will. He felt that it was not right to remove him so suddenly, though he promised to think about our request.

On Cup Final morning we had a meeting in the Wembley boardroom with David Collins, General Secretary of the FA of Wales.

The Welsh had never had a turn at the FIFA position in living memory and, although they would have liked it for themselves, they came to realise that they did not have a strong candidate who was acceptable to the other British in the same way that Keith Wiseman might be. Collins had previously asked me if there was any reason why a General Secretary should not be appointed and, while it was true that FIFA would have no objections, it was extremely unlikely that the Home Nations would support a paid official for the role.

It was at that meeting of the three of us that we reached the position, as recommended by our management team to Keith Wiseman, that we would help the Welsh FA financially.

David Collins told us that he was worried about the Football Trust money which was no longer due after the Trust was reconstituted following the advent of the National Lottery. He was also concerned that our television payments to Wales would cease with the increasing interest in the subject of the European Commission. The FA allocated money to Wales from the television contract because English matches were shown in Wales. He asked if we could ensure that they would continue to get the money from both sources up to 2006. The television money was due to run out in 2001, so they wanted a guarantee for the extra five years which, legally, we might not to have to pay them. We also promised to help them continue with their payments through the Football Trust by trying to negotiate a partnership with the Welsh Sports Council.

We said we would use our best endeavours with the Welsh Sports Council, and if it didn't happen we would underwrite the payments on their behalf.

Both payments were £400,000 per year at that time so we were looking to pay them £400,000 a year plus inflation until 2006 for television and then pay a similar amount to the Football Trust to be available for use in Wales. We were hoping that £200,000 per annum would be paid by the Welsh Sports Council from the National Lottery and we would then match that.

Because of the uncertainties, it was a variable sum. At worst from our point of view it could amount to a few million pounds over eight years, set against many, many millions of pounds due to us from television and sponsorship, and at best it could be very much less than that. In the circumstances a gamble well worth the risk, we judged.

We attended the FIFA Congress in Paris in June, but the representatives from Scotland and Northern Ireland did not attend the pre-conference dinner at Versailles and thus were unable to discuss the British Vice-Presidency with us at that time. Scotland, not unnaturally, wanted David Will to carry on and Northern Ireland supported them, while Wales backed us in trying to have Keith Wiseman elected.

There was also a question of whether David Will was up for re-election anyway. He had served eight years but the Scots argued that he took over Harry Cavan's two years of unexpired tenure in 1990 and was not up for re-election anyway in 1998. It was complete deadlock.

I put in a hand-written letter to FIFA saying that the position was unresolved so it was never brought up at the Congress. That upset the Scots who asked what right I had to write to them off my own bat. I explained that I just wanted to make sure that the position did not go by default.

There were two further meetings in July and August, but we could not persuade the Scots and the Irish to shift their position, although they did agree that it would be reviewed in a year's time, possibly giving Wiseman the last nine months to lobby FIFA on behalf of 2006. At the first meeting it became quite hairy because no one was going to back down and Jim Farry, the Chief Executive of the Scottish FA, started quoting the FIFA rule book at us, saying that the dispute would have to go to an arbitration hearing under FIFA's procedures.

This was akin to litigation and the prospect startled both David Collins and me. I said: 'Hang on, we are supposed to be talking among friends here. We have a difference of opinion, but we don't want to ventilate it outside in that way.'

Jim said that he was just doing his homework and showing that this was what might happen if we could not agree the matter between us. In other words, back off!

It certainly stoked up the tension that was already present with the two versus two situation and it became clear that we were not going to get anywhere. The best we could hope for was a compromise where Keith Wiseman could take over later from David Will, who had said this would be his last term. That would have let Keith Wiseman in for the last nine months. It was all to no avail, and after Keith and I left the FA made their peace with David Will. His term was extended until 2002 – and then FIFA brought forward the 2006 decision from June to March 2000! Subsequently they moved it back again to July.

In fairness to David Will, the position was clearer as he assured us that he was no longer standing for any position in UEFA, meaning that there was no reason why he could not play a full part in the English campaign for 2006. Obviously it would have been better for us to be directly represented – that was why we were going through all of this rigmarole!

The irony was that our greatest adversary in the discussions, Jim Farry, was to go soon after me, removed because of delays in registration of a transfer. I chuckled when the bookmakers had me at a good price as one of his likely replacements. It showed that the bookmakers do not always have the best advice, but it did seem that I had started something of a trend!

When questions started to be raised in September, I spoke to David Collins in Wales again and told him we had a problem with a number of our members being unhappy about the deal we had set up, and we agreed to knock off the last three years and simply take it up to 2003 and then do our best to do more at a later date. I admitted to him that it had become an embarrassment to Keith Wiseman and me.

The Executive Committee had Hill-Wood's report at their meeting on 6 October but deferred discussing it as Keith Wiseman was in Lisbon for a meeting on the threatened European Super League with UEFA.

It gave me time to talk to Wiseman about the entire situation, especially as Hill-Wood seemed to have a personal agenda and was making all sorts of complaints against me, arriving at the sudden conclusion that he did not think that I was a good man for the job after ten years during which time the FA had gone from strength to strength. Wiseman said that Hill-Wood's letter to him was disgraceful and that we should concentrate on the real issues and 'haul him back into line'.

It had taken me some time to become used to working with Keith Wiseman, who certainly set himself a punishing schedule, but, at this stage, we were getting on very well. We had had a long chat in Casablanca in May when he had just had his proposal to remunerate the Chairman and the Vice-Chairman of the Football Association rejected. He thought that the FA were moving forward extremely well and was upset that the Annual General Meeting of shareholders had not ratified the previous decision of the Council to make the Chairmanship a remunerated position.

I also had an annual appraisal and after my previous one on 1 September 1997, Wiseman had said that the FA were highly satisfied with me at that time, indicating that the problems which arose, whatever they were, came about very quickly indeed.

My gut feeling is that some of the high financiers in the Premier

League did not want someone who might oppose their ambitions. Neither, I am sure, did it help that I was not the sort of person to spend much time cultivating those in high places. I always preferred to play it straight down the middle, and when push came to shove, I simply did not have enough people to say: 'Hold on, let's go a little more deeply into this', rather than lose a Chief Executive who, in most respects it seemed, was held in reasonable esteem. I regarded all of the Council members as equal, whilst most of them valued my total commitment to all levels of the game.

Wiseman thought that it was a conspiracy and part of a Premier League push for power to get rid of the Chairman and the Chief Executive in order to destabilise the FA. He cited conversations which he had heard about.

The problem was that he and I were inextricably linked in this. We were at the meeting with the Welsh together and we had supported each other throughout. It became apparent that he was no longer flavour of the month with a few influential members of the Council, despite having been re-elected unopposed at the summer meeting in July at Eastbourne. There was some residual feeling against him, presumably because of the way he won the Chairmanship when he outflanked Dave Richards, who was the Premier League's choice. He had originally lost the support of the Premier League when he addressed them while suffering with a raging toothache while Richards gave them a bit of Northern homespun philosophy on how he would sort out the FA.

Wiseman, even though he had lost his place as one of the FA Premier League's representatives on the Council to Coventry City's Bryan Richardson, refused to lie down and went to Bryan Moore of Yeovil Town, a regional representative on the FA, and did a deal with him to replace him as Group Eight representative, with the agreement that if Wiseman won the vote as Chairman it would create an automatic place for Moore's return. If he failed, he would immediately stand down.

Wiseman beat Sir David Hill-Wood, Geoff Thompson and Dave Richards to win the election of Chairman, but that sort of slick deal does not go down awfully well with some of the rank and file. There was still some feeling about it, even though it happened two years earlier. It also rankled with some that he had stood for re-election in 1997 and then immediately afterwards had written a long letter to the Council, telling them that they should recompense his firm for the time he spent on FA business. Irrespective of the feelings of the Council on the first issue, I can see why they did not like the way he handled the second, though to be fair to Keith, he had raised this matter with Sir Bert Millichip, the previous Chairman, in August 1995, long before he took over. He pointed out to Sir Bert that this was an issue that needed to be faced by the FA because they were restricting their choice of the man to lead them, confining themselves to retired or wealthy candidates, and that the ordinary guy with a living to earn was being precluded from the chairmanship.

Under the FA's constitution the Chairman merely chairs a number of important meetings. However, in reality, the job is full time, involving a great deal of foreign travel and high level lobbying. Most Council members recognised this, but not enough to convince the requisite 75% of shareholders.

Keith had every right to feel aggrieved. Nobody had opposed the remuneration proposal in Council, but some members did absolutely nothing to convince the shareholders in their constituencies.

Keith had this credibility problem at the same time that mine was surfacing. He also found out that David Sheepshanks, the Chairman of the Football League, was being touted for the Chairmanship by Sir Bert Millichip, who had gone to people saying that the Ipswich man cut the right sort of figure and would represent their best choice.

We had a meeting of the Council on 28 September soon after Ken Bates had been quoted in the newspapers criticising Hoddle. He had written to Wiseman about the recently published *World Cup Diary* and the controversial faith healer Eileen Drewery. Bates went to the *Daily Mail* on the Saturday before the meeting with six complaints about how the FA were getting it all wrong and wrote a letter to the FA with nine questions asking for details of Le Tournoi in 1997 and the World Cup in 1998, questions which took an inordinate time to research and answer with such minor queries as to how many FA staff had gone to Le Tournoi. Not very many, as I recall!

He stood up at the meeting and demanded to know about the appointment of a 'Sleaze Buster' by the FA and asked, why did he have to read about it in the newspapers before he and the Council had been officially informed? I suppose I could have pointed out that it was no different to him going to the press before coming to the meeting, however, there was no need as I simply pointed out that it was in the minutes of the Executive Committee, already approved by the Council that we were to appoint a Compliance Officer and it was hardly our fault if the media decided to interpret this as a Sleaze Buster!

Undeterred by the facts, Bates forcefully suggested that we needed a working party of back benchers to sort things out at the FA. He then went on to ask why we were thinking of giving Glenn Hoddle, his former manager at Chelsea, an extension to his contract, and how had the FA's Director of Public Affairs David Davies, had time to write the *World Cup Diary*? Moreover, having done so, 'was he fit to continue in his position?'

Keith responded that a sub-committee had been appointed to look into all of these matters and then wrote a strongly worded reply to Bates' earlier letter, saying it was unacceptable for him to criticise David Davies in public and that his entire approach before and at the meeting had been wrong. I felt that Keith, in trying to show he was a fair and democratic Chairman, allowed Ken far too much latitude to dominate the meeting.

I went to see Sports Minister Tony Banks to try and get him to use his influence to raise money through the Welsh Sports Council in the same way he had done with the English and Scottish Sports Councils for the Football Trust. I pointed out that there was a commitment in the Labour election manifesto that the Football Trust would be a United Kingdom-wide body, whereas it was only operating in England and Scotland. He promised to try and help.

One of the reasons for the issue arising in the first place was the pressure from the Government, in the form of Banks, to press home England's case for the World Cup in 2006 by replacing David Will on the FIFA Executive Committee with Keith Wiseman. Banks had been quick enough to support Prime Minister Tony Blair over the removal of England coach Glenn Hoddle, but I waited in vain for him to support me in my hour of need. In fact, not only did Banks not support me publicly, neither he nor his department made any contact personally and that disappointed me. I was not surprised, though, for Banks was paranoid about the press and would have fretted over the media reaction to such a move.

I recalled that on one trip promoting 2006 he was telephoned by his office to be told that the *Daily Telegraph* wanted to interview him. He spent the entire trip worrying about whether to grant the interview, because he felt he had been so badly treated in the past. I eventually prevailed upon him to speak to the journalist concerned for a feature based on World Cup 2006, and the result was highly favourable both to the minister and to the FA's campaign.

Despite the backing of the Chairman, the Minister for Sport and

FIFA, I suppose that in strict terms I do not think I could claim to have the authority to negotiate contracts like that with the Welsh without a committee's approval.

My problem was that I had gone straight from that meeting with the Welsh to seek out Mark Day, the then Finance Director, in the Wembley banqueting hall before lunch and told him that the Welsh wanted help with the Sports Council and the television payments. I asked him to contact the Welsh to finalise the details and put the arrangement into proper form. Following discussions with David Collins, he drafted a letter for me which we sent to the Welsh FA on 26 May.

The Welsh agreed and promised to support Keith Wiseman but the letter, looked at with hindsight, should have been couched in different terms. The way it was written, it promised them the full amount of money while, in actual fact, I was hoping to limit the exposure to the FA by getting money out of the Welsh Sports Council. That letter, signed hastily as I was preparing for the AGM, the trip to Morocco and, importantly, the World Cup, sealed my fate seven months later.

The lines of authority at the FA have always been blurred and I had always taken the view that, providing I got on with the job and reported back fairly frequently, all would be well. Unfortunately, and while not attempting to shift the blame, it was my assumption that Mark Day would speak to his Finance Committee chairman and put it through the books of the FA, just as he had done on previous occasions when we first agreed to make the TV payments to the Welsh and the Irish. Those certainly did not go through the full Council until later. Also, when payments were made to the Professional Footballers' Association out of our television money, I delegated it to the Finance Director who again piloted the arrangement through the system. Those were the precedents which had been set and to which I was working. There are other things which you become paranoid about when you hear that your position is under threat. I had a conversation with Dave Richards in October when he asked what it was that I really wanted, pointing out that I was well respected within UEFA and FIFA while Peter Leaver, the Chief Executive of the Premier League, was not that well known abroad. It was as if he was suggesting if there was a job I could do for English football within UEFA or FIFA. Then Peter Leaver had on two previous occasions asked me who would be the next General Secretary of FIFA, intimating, to my mind, that I should think seriously about a job which had clearly been earmarked for

Michel Zen-Ruffinen, Sepp Blatter's deputy. It seemed strange at the time that they should both be asking these questions.

On the other hand, I also asked myself at the time whether the target was really Keith Wiseman and if I had been brought down along with him by association.

He gave me his backing over the Welsh issue, even though it was mainly my agreement with the Welsh and not his. He had not gone into the finer points of it and he had assumed that it would be put through the system in the usual way.

He had become particularly supportive of me after I told him of the difficulties of the past when Sir Bert Millichip had cast doubts on my ability to outsiders. It was very dispiriting trying to convince your own boss of your ability all of the time as I had to do with Sir Bert, just as my predecessor, Ted Croker, had to do with Sir Harold Thompson.

Keith Wiseman sent our report to the Executive Committee in October. In his memorandum Keith pointed out that there appeared to be a number of hidden agendas and added pointedly that it was an insult for David Hill-Wood to suggest that we would try to pull the wool over their eyes. He also told them that they had to '*grow up and live in the real world*', a phrase he used often and which increasingly grated upon them. In the circumstances it was probably not the wisest thing to say, and he was soon to realise this.

Keith was trying to emphasise that we needed to have proper representation on UEFA and FIFA and start to punch our weight again. I do not think the Executive Committee realised that we had been involved in such high level discussions, lunches with President Havelange and flying to Zurich to discuss matters with Sepp Blatter before he was elected in June. The one crucial factor which came through time and time again was that if we were to be successful in our bid to stage the World Cup, we must be represented on the FIFA Executive Committee.

In retrospect it is hard to believe that those who wielded the power in the Football Association could not understand the seriousness of the matter. It was staring them in the face that we needed to replace David Will with Keith Wiseman if our costly campaign to stage the World Cup was not to be wasted. Instead of supporting their Chairman, Chief Executive and senior management, they offered a sympathetic ear to those who complained about our more aggressive style of lobbying for influence.

At the FIFA Executive meeting in March the UEFA group had tried to force Sepp Blatter to stand down as General Secretary because he was rumoured to be canvassing for support as President. When asked by FIFA President Havelange to give a ruling as head of the legal committee, David Will could not do so because he was committed to the UEFA camp. Almost everyone of authority we met – people like Dr Mong Joon Chung, the President of the Korean FA and another FIFA Vice-President; Jack Warner of Trinidad and Tobago, the longest serving FIFA member; and Abdullah Al-Dabal, a member from Saudi Arabia – said to us: *'Get yourselves there.'*

Keith Wiseman pointed out to our Executive Committee that he was happy with the agreement we had made with the FA of Wales. We had just signed a contract worth £35 million with Umbro and we were due to sign a new TV contract in 2001, so it wasn't as if we couldn't afford the money to the Welsh. One or two made the point that we were depriving English kids to further our political ambitions in football, which was a load of hypocrisy.

We had a meeting of the Executive Committee on 11 November when Hill-Wood spoke about his report criticising me and our deal. Despite our arguments, the committee were unwilling to ratify the agreement we had made with the Welsh. Geoff Thompson said he was saddened that he had not been consulted at the time and that the issue was not raised with the Finance Committee. He stressed that the game in England had its needs and while he wanted to support what we had done, did not feel that he could. Frank Pattison, of the Durham FA, also said that he would like to support the Chairman but could not. Barry Bright of the Kent FA was concerned about the financial commitments of the FA quoting money that was needed for small-sided football, while Hill-Wood denied that he had a separate agenda.

The Committee dispatched us to Wales to tell them that the Executive didn't like the agreement. I wrote to Peter Hain at the Welsh Office to see what he could do to help raise the money for the Welsh FA and then went down to Cardiff on the Sunday. That was the day that the story broke in the national press and I had the unpleasant task of showing Keith Wiseman the report across a couple of pages which vilified him and accused him of being power hungry. It had clearly been leaked from within the committee, who had met only days earlier.

Keith had been pretty deflated after the Executive Meeting but Pattison, a shrewd lawyer whom many rank and file members of the Council looked up to, assured him that it was not a resigning matter.

Keith was no fool, though, and he sensed the mood of the Executive Committee when he found that David Dein, the vice chairman of Arsenal, seemed unwilling to chat with him. David was an inveterate gossiper and would talk about football and football issues all day long. When Keith found that David suddenly had to dash off, he sensed that something was very much amiss.

He was also depressed at the attack on him in the Sunday newspaper, particularly when it said that Wiseman had failed to convince the Executive Committee of the honourable intent of the deal. This was very damaging to him in his profession as a solicitor and immensely hurtful to his family. He was described as *'power hungry, cunning and would drive hundreds of miles to open a biscuit tin if it were to be noticed by the Counties,'* and he had *'blatantly exceeded his powers.'*

We had our meeting with the Welsh and reported back on the day of the match against the Czech Republic on 18 November. The Executive Committee again refused to ratify the agreement and sent three of their number, Geoff Thompson, David Sheepshanks and David Dein, to negotiate with the Welsh. It was clear at our meeting with David Collins that the Welsh felt that they had a binding agreement with us and while they sympathised with the position we were in, they did not want to do anything about it, not unnaturally.

There was some misunderstanding about the power of the three Executive Committee members and Nic Coward had to point out to them that they were not an investigating committee, but merely empowered to re-negotiate the deal with the Welsh. Collins told the press that they had opposed David Will because he was one of those who had tried to sack Sepp Blatter in March.

We had another Council meeting on 19 November where Keith Wiseman made a statement that someone who wanted his job had caused him and his family immense hurt, referring to the article in the Sunday paper and the inside information it had contained. Hill-Wood retorted that Keith was merely trying to push the thing under the carpet and endeavouring to seek sympathy.

There was no reason at all why we should not have helped Wales then or in the future. We have their best players in our League and it is a tradition in football that the bigger nations help the smaller ones. Had the spirit of mutual co-operation disappeared completely with the abolition of the Home International Championships?

UEFA themselves were helping African nations financially at the same time as they were canvassing support for Lennart Johansson for the FIFA election. I had spoken to one member of the committee in November and he told me that there were a lot of different agendas, but even he did not know who had been pulling the strings. He felt even then that Keith Wiseman's position was untenable, but my name had not been mentioned. It is startling to think that my reputation had been tarnished so quickly between the Executive meeting on 1 December and 15 December when I left.

The 1 December meeting had been called to receive the report from the sub-committee who had visited the Welsh FA. They had negotiated the payments down and the committee were very pleased with the job they had done. Then they turned to Keith and I to hear our explanations. Keith spoke for about an hour and went through it all again. When my turn came I asked that the staff leave the room and gave my story. I told them that I had acted with the chairman at all times in the best interests of football; how we had been under pressure from within FIFA; explained the situation with David Will and the precedents for what had happened. I referred to the reasons we had for helping the Welsh FA. The meeting at the Park Court Hotel finally concluded at 7 pm.

It was to no avail. I do not think that they were interested in listening to reasons and even less in accepting them. I believe that their minds were made up before we even addressed them.

After that experience I knew right from the start of the fateful last day that I would not have the opportunity to try and win over the Executive Committee, it was a question of getting the best result I could, whether it was a stay of execution or whatever. It was a sickening blow but it was not completely out of the blue.

On the day I was too preoccupied. I felt devastated. I managed not to show it, but over the next two days I was very angry to have lost my job despite not doing anything wrong.

The Football Association had not appreciated what I had done. I thought it would have been better for both sides to have resolved it a different way. The Executive Committee could have dealt with the matter internally, but somebody ambitious had leaked it to the press in a shameful way.

David Dent, the Secretary of the Football League and Gordon Taylor, Chief Executive of the Professional Footballers' Association, both phoned that evening to express concern at what had happened. The first call taken by the FA the following morning was from Paul Gascoigne;

after two or three checks they established that it really was Gazza conveying his support for me! Among others, Alex Ferguson, with whom I have crossed swords on more than one occasion, said how sorry he was. There were many letters of support. I appreciated the messages, but they were not going to get me reinstated to a job I had loved and lost.

My resignation attracted massive media interest and to escape the constant ringing of the telephone, I went for a long run on the morning after the night before, arriving back home to find the news cameras outside the house. I had a brief chat with the reporters and they departed.

The staff at headquarters had remained supportive with Nic Coward again urging me to attend the staff Christmas Party at the Copthorne Tara in Kensington. Graham Noakes, Head of Regulations and Competitions, was the only one pleased to see me go because it gave him the chance to claim the number nine shirt on the staff football team!

There was no reason why I should keep a low profile in the circumstances and I went to watch Nottingham Forest on the Saturday and did a radio interview with Brian Alexander on Sunday. I had no reason to hide.

Keith Wiseman and I inadvertently provided any number of people with a collectors' item in the form of an official FA Christmas card signed by both of us and arriving through most people's letter boxes the day after our fate was sealed. We had lunch together in Oxford on New Year's Day in a Pizza Express at a site called the Golden Cross Inn where, in the mid 16th Century, Protestant Bishops Cranmer, Ridley and Latimer were held prisoner before being burned at the stake. An apt choice of venue considering that Keith was to face his hearing before the FA Council on 4 January.

All in all it was a long Christmas with all the rubbish coming out in the press and with Ken Bates having his usual two pennyworth, claiming that the FA staff committee had voted themselves loans. He did not understand that the staff committee were in fact not members of the staff but a committee of Council members who dealt with staff matters. They gave modest taxed loans to the staff for things like home improvements at low interest rates in the way that many large companies do. This was just one of the many niggles to surface after the event, none of them very helpful to anyone.

When the Council meeting took place early in the New Year, Keith Wiseman gave a strong account of himself, reasoning that if they wanted to change their Chairman they should put somebody up against him at the summer meeting.

However, virtually all the Executive Committee members had been primed to speak against him and nobody else felt able or willing to challenge the party line. Who knows how the vote of no confidence would have gone, for Wiseman quickly reached the view that all the enjoyment had gone out of the job and, thoroughly disillusioned by the lack of loyalty he expected from those he had come to regard as friends, he resigned.

I was let down at the time, but I do not harbour any feelings of resentment now. I do not feel any bitterness and I do not become angry when I think about it any longer. There is no point destroying myself over something I cannot alter. I cannot put the clock back and bitterness, I know, can be a very destructive emotion.

I feel it is the FA's loss. I really do believe that I was good at the job, the right man for it and certainly good for a few more years.

CHAPTER TWO

2006 And All That

It was at a meeting in London on 23 September 1996 that retiring Football Association Chairman Sir Bert Millichip reminded us that we had discharged our duty in terms of our promises to the French to stay out of the bidding for the 1998 World Cup and that we were now free to pursue our ambitions to stage the 2006 Finals.

His comments, which fly in the face of the UEFA claim that he had done a private deal with the Germans, were noted and minuted and then, unfortunately, forgotten in the dusty files and thousands of words which have poured out on the subject ever since.

I have no doubts in my mind that Sir Bert, a member of the UEFA Executive Committee from 1988 to 1996, in all goodwill had sometime and somewhere said something to somebody which supported a German bid, but there are no minutes or record of any such agreement either with UEFA or at the FA. Indeed, our own intention to bid was minuted at Lancaster Gate as far back as 1993.

Strange that something which began back in 1991 should prove so significant in my career, something which would have looked good on a curriculum vitae but ended with my demise.

It was then that we at the FA were considering a bid for the World Cup which was subsequently and successfully held in France. We were running neck and neck and had comparable bids for 1998 but we decided to go for the European Championships in 1996 instead, leaving the French clear for the World Cup. We made a deal to support each other's bids, they agreed and both sides honoured that agreement. In May 1992 we were duly awarded the European Championships, beating the other contenders Greece, Austria, Portugal and Holland for the honour.

Germany launched their bid for 2006 at the World Cup draw in Las Vegas late in 1993. It was not until after the successful organisation of Euro 96 that we decided to forge ahead in competition for the World Cup. When we received a letter from FIFA President Joao Havelange congratulating us on Euro 96, I officially responded to the effect that we would be bidding for the next World Cup, announcing it publicly on the day after Germany had beaten the Czech Republic in the European Championship finals at Wembley Stadium at a time when the world's media were present and working. Sir Bert's final Executive Committee meeting a week later endorsed the decision.

We felt we would rarely be in a better position. Our credentials could not have been stronger as we listed our main reasons for going for it: our superb new stadiums; the tearing down of the fences; the excellent, trouble-free atmosphere at Euro 96; the successful administration of the competition; the fact that England was considered worldwide the home of football; and, last but not least, the English tourist industry which would be capable of handling and entertaining the supporters who would be attracted.

To set the ball rolling we immediately appointed Alec McGivan, Media Relations Manager of Euro 96, as Campaign Manager for 2006.

The Germans, who were in London in force for the Final, were clearly aware of our intentions and, indeed, Wolfgang Niersbach from the German Federation launched an attack on Wembley Stadium in response to our declaration, saying it would be a hopeless venue for the World Cup and that, in any case, Dr Havelange had promised the World Cup to Germany back in 1993.

The FIFA President was, of course, fairly liberal in his promises, often depending on where he was and to whom he was talking at the time. The Germans were aware of this and after Havelange had visited 10 Downing Street, met Prime Minister Tony Blair and inevitably endorsed England, Niersbach commented wryly: 'There aren't too many more to go. Dr Havelange will be awarding the World Cup to Malta next!'

We were not interested in a slanging match with the Germans or anyone else as, if we were to stand any chance at all, we had to put in a lot of work and find the necessary and enormous funding to follow up a bid of this nature. We received the backing of the English Sports Council and the Premier League who both pledged to contribute a third towards offsetting the estimated cost of £9 million, but not without a minor hitch. The Premier League wanted strings attached and, through Peter Leaver, expressed the opinion that if we then went on to secure commercial sponsors for the bid, as we subsequently did with British Airways, Umbro, Nationwide and Marks and Spencer, the sponsors' payments would be taken off the Premier League share of the bill. I felt that that was not the understanding we had reached and I couldn't see a sponsor coming in to underwrite the Premier League's donations. That did not stack up with me at all and I rejected it out of hand.

The other difficulty we had was that the Government were very keen on grounds in Wales and Scotland being used in the bid. They were under pressure from Scottish and Welsh MPs and we had to fight hard to show that it was England's bid. We appreciated that there were fine grounds in Scotland, but we could only start thinking about taking matches outside England if and when we were successful with the bid by asking FIFA at the time. We could not prejudice the bid at that stage because it would be seen as a sign of weakness, that we didn't have enough grounds in England.

I called a meeting, our first, on 23 September 1996. I wanted our English representatives on the various UEFA and FIFA committees to be talking with one voice when they attended their various committees and matches around the globe. There was a need for everyone to know what the priorities were in so far as English football's agenda was concerned.

There were only a handful of English representatives to start with, especially with FIFA where we had only Sir Bert Millichip who was on the World Cup Organising Committee. Graham Taylor had been on FIFA's Technical Committee but he resigned when he left the England job in November 1993 and we never managed to replace him.

Our numbers on UEFA were not a lot better and I decided there and then that it was a priority to work on increasing our representation. Our target was FIFA General Secretary Sepp Blatter and I explained to him that if he expected our backing, then he was obliged to help us, especially as the Germans had half a dozen representatives in key positions. By the time I left the FA we had five people with FIFA and a total approaching twenty on the two organising bodies together.

But, at the time, we were thin on the ground. I was on a couple of committees, Rick Parry was involved, while Charles Hughes, our Director of Coaching, was a member of the UEFA Technical Committee. It was at this meeting that Sir Bert Millichip personally reminded us of the deal we had done with the French five years earlier saying: 'Remember, you did a deal with France five years ago, so now you are free to go ahead with a bid for 2006.' There was no mention of any deal with the Germans by him or anyone else and, if the facts were to come out, surely that would have been the moment?

The first we knew of this contentious, so-called 'Gentleman's Agreement' was when UEFA suddenly told us to back off on 29 January 1997. Our campaign had already been running for about six months, having been announced on 1 July 1996. It could not have been more public and, indeed, following the European Championship Final Lennart Johansson himself was quoted in a television interview that day, saying that England had a good chance because of the way Euro 96 had gone.

We had enjoyed a busy and productive six months, recruiting staff and pressing our claims by inviting FIFA Executive Committee members to 10 Downing Street to meet John Major on the day of the World Cup qualifying match against Italy on 11 February. Two of these invitations went to Per Ravn Omdal of Norway and Senes Erzik of Turkey, both European members of the FIFA Executive. They casually informed the rest of the UEFA Executive in Lisbon on 29 January 1997 that they had been given the invitations – and then the balloon went up.

The General Secretary Gerhard Aigner was instructed to write to me pointing out that UEFA had already committed themselves to supporting the one candidate, Germany, by virtue of the so-called 'Vision' document in 1995*.

Where had these people been for the past six months? Didn't they read the newspapers, watch the television or talk to each other? How could they not know that England were making a serious bid?

Aigner's fax was received at Lancaster Gate late on Friday and immediately it struck us as strange that the German Federation

---

* 'Vision' was UEFA's proposal to change the way many important decisions were made by FIFA. It envisaged the rotation of the World Cup around the continents and the restriction of one bid per continent. The FA, like all UEFA's national associations, had committed itself to 'Vision', but there was never any suggestion that Germany had already been selected as the chosen candidate.

President Egidius Braun was upset, not because England were campaigning for the World Cup but, as Chairman of Euro 96, he had not been invited to meet John Major!

That, however, was all that was amusing about this latest serious development. Perhaps they expected us to doff our caps, sack our staff, return the money and say sorry. No chance. We came out with a very strong statement the following morning and prepared to do battle in the best possible British way.

We were joined by no lesser person than the Leader of the Opposition, Tony Blair, who complained about a cosy stitch-up in UEFA, prompting UEFA to immediately attempt to saddle Sir Bert Millichip with the responsibility for having made a 'Gentleman's Agreement' on behalf of English football.

They claimed he had been present in Las Vegas when Germany launched their campaign. Aigner said that it was unfortunate that a former Vice-President of UEFA forgot that he was present at meetings in which everyone endorsed Germany. This, as far as I was concerned, was disloyal to Sir Bert, who was their special advisor by that time.

In actual fact, they were trying to hold us to 'Vision 95' which never actually went before FIFA because, amongst other things, UEFA were preoccupied in challenging the contracts FIFA had made over television coverage for the next two World Cups.

We clearly upset UEFA by issuing such a strong press statement and going on the offensive against them. They instantly sent three people, Aigner, Erzik and Omdal, to London to talk to us, presumably to make us see sense! We met in another Kensington hotel on 7 February 1997 and Keith Wiseman started by asking whether the 'Vision' document was still alive. He never received an answer. They said they deplored the tone of our press comments and mysteriously added that we should have told them that we were campaigning for 2006.

Not only had we announced it publicly and drawn comments from Johansson but we had also referred to it in their presence on a number of occasions, including the retirement party for Sir Bert Millichip in September 1996 at the Hilton Park Lane after he left the chair of the FA. In my speech I mentioned the fact that Sir Bert's efforts had done a lot to win us the vote for Euro 96 and left us in a prime position to bid for the World Cup in 2006.

Subsequently Egidius Braun hosted a thank you dinner for the Football Association staff in Geneva for their efforts in Euro 96. Again I spoke at that dinner and referred to the friendly rivalry between ourselves and Germany for the World Cup. Braun must have been impressed with my speech, for he promised he would invite me to speak at one of the dinners he was arranging in Germany – an invitation which, incidentally, did not materialise.

The three wise men accused us of by-passing 'Vision' and of breaking the so-called 'Gentleman's Agreement'. But as hard as I pressed them, they were unable to quote any dates or times as to when it was made. I was at pains to point out to the Germans that our quarrel was not with them. Our dispute was with UEFA and I hoped we would remain on friendly terms.

It is difficult to analyse where and how the agreement was made through Sir Bert. Jeff Powell of the *Daily Mail* swears that Bert told him about the agreement when it was made, but I cannot find anyone who can vouch clearly for any agreement between England and Germany. Maybe it was the French deal which was confusing the issue. That was the only gentleman's agreement we made to my knowledge and we naturally honoured it. I can only think that this German candidacy was something which was mentioned regularly in UEFA circles and because Sir Bert never objected to it – he had no reason to – it was always assumed that he and, by extension, England were supporting Germany. This was never the case, as an examination of FA minutes will show.

Nevertheless it has to be said that whenever we talked about the World Cup bid in front of him, Sir Bert was a little uneasy. But I don't think he made any commitment which should have bound the FA in any way at all. When our Executive Committee confirmed our bid in 1996, it was his last meeting and he endorsed it without any objections. That would have been the time for him to stand up and to say: 'Hold on, we are committed to Germany.'

I put the controversy down to a combination of factors. I do not think UEFA dreamed the whole thing up, but to try to decide such an important issue on the basis of a cosy chat somewhere which was never minuted nor communicated to the member associations is quite wrong. We are talking about such a major issue here, the second most important sporting competition in the world, and to subject it to an intimate chat between friends is out of order.

The answer, of course, would be for UEFA to publish their minutes and, indeed, on another subject I once suggested it, pointing out that their communications would be improved, but they weren't listening. Why not? Who knows.

At the meeting in February, Erzik agreed that there had been a lack of communication and asked for a letter of application from us. I was not quite sure why the European ruling body should want us to apply to them to stage the World Cup as it was FIFA we were asking.

We adjourned for our own private discussions, and when they came back they agreed to open it up to competition. They were still keen to avoid the sort of bidding war between Japan and Korea for 2002 when it became an embarrassment to their members to be continually doorstepped by so many people bearing gifts. They were adamant that they would make a decision and only one should apply from each continent. We responded that we would need to see what the rules were going to be before we entered any competition and asked how it could be fair when they had already decided who the winner was.

We eventually agreed to meet in Geneva on 17 April to try and find a procedure which was fair to both. Unfortunately a week later Aigner was saying in public that UEFA still favoured Germany. He had been irritated by the English press who had written that UEFA had climbed down at the meeting in London. His response was to state that they had not changed their stance and that they were still supporting Germany. Lennart Johansson echoed this.

Germany, in the meantime, had done their chances little good outside the Continent when they upset a number of the FIFA people by backing out of the Confederations Cup to be held at the end of December 1997, a decision which cost everyone a great deal of money and face.

The friction between the UEFA and FIFA was, by then, tangible. President Joao Havelange, in Britain for the International Board meeting in Belfast in March, stirred up the pot when he confirmed that England had every right to bid and was a strong candidate. He added, to UEFA's chagrin, that the restriction of one candidate per continent was unfair to national associations.

Sepp Blatter even believed that England would win the European nomination if it went to the vote of the associations in UEFA, but I disagreed because I could not see how we could overturn the UEFA Executive Committee's recommendation. Germany had made plenty of friends in the new emerging nations of the former Eastern bloc. Blatter pointed out to me that these countries would soon be getting money from FIFA and that the UEFA money and influence would be less important. I personally didn't relish a battle with Germany at a congress of all 51 nations but Blatter persisted, adding significantly that Europe wouldn't get the World Cup if they put forward the wrong candidate.

Sir Bert confirmed that, irrespective of the meeting in February, UEFA's decision was already made and, despite my information to the contrary, FIFA would back the one bid per continent proposal. He was also staggered at the costs we were contemplating and told the Council that we should not spend another penny until we saw which way the wind was blowing.

The Germans were upset and were pushing for a decision, because they needed a commitment in order to confirm investment from their government for stadium building and refurbishment, particularly those in the former East Germany. Our position remained unaltered as we felt that there was nothing wrong with healthy competition, providing it was kept within proper bounds.

It was against this background that we went, with some misgivings, to the meeting at the Hotel La Reserve on the shores of Lake Geneva where we fielded a team of Keith Wiseman, David Davies, Pat Smith, Alec McGivan and me while the Germans lined up with Egidius Braun, General Secretary Horst Schmidt, their former great captain and manager Franz Beckenbauer and Wolfgang Niersbach. Lennart Johansson chaired the meeting and opened by frustratingly referring to the so-called 'Gentleman's Agreement'. He found it difficult to accept that Sir Bert had not told us about it.

UEFA thought the Germans were well equipped by virtue of their past experience and organisational capacity. We responded that they had precluded themselves from conducting a democratic, open and objective selection process and asked why nobody said anything between July and January when they knew we were campaigning.

UEFA Press Chief Fritz Ahlstrom claimed that they had not minuted their support for Germany, because they assumed that they would be the only European candidate and there had been no objections. It seemed to give a clear indication of what had happened, even though he had not been there himself. Braun followed up by saying that we had gone back on our word and should not be awarded 2006 so soon after staging the European Championships. He lectured the meeting about the united Germany and said fans from the former eastern block would all be able to attend the World Cup for the first time.

David Will attended UEFA Executive Committee meetings as an observer. He suggested the matter should be placed before the full UEFA Congress, but we disliked that idea and the meeting drew to an unsatisfactory conclusion.

The last thing I wanted afterwards was a joint press conference or statement, as I preferred to wait until we heard what UEFA had to say for themselves before responding. That decision did not sit well with Johansson and he replied angrily: 'Just do what you want.'

David Will assured us afterwards that he had battled for us in Lisbon when the problem had arisen, but UEFA still came out and said that they noted with surprise that we did not know of the 'Gentleman's Agreement' despite being represented on the Executive Committee by Sir Bert at the time. They added that they would submit the one bid per continent to the FIFA Congress in 1998, while we said we would carry on with our campaign. Braun said in the German statement that the campaign money could be put to better use but, for some reason, seemed to get a rough ride from the German reporters. He retreated in high dudgeon to his bedroom, refusing to join the rest for dinner. It needed Johansson to ask David Davies, who was staying on for another meeting the following day, to get the sulking Egidius to come down.

Germany were clearly disappointed that UEFA had declined to come out in their favour. Franz Beckenbauer had been led to believe that they were going to do that and said so. Sir Bert told the press that he *had* told us UEFA were supporting Germany and Beckenbauer criticised UEFA for sitting on the fence.

As far as we were concerned it was one step forward and two backwards. Little or nothing had been achieved with this high profile meeting and it had, if anything, widened the chasm between us and both UEFA and Germany.

A year later we decided in the week leading up to the FIFA Congress that we would support Sepp Blatter for the FIFA Presidency rather than Johansson. We had given our own Executive Committee a full briefing and they had authorised Keith Wiseman and I to proceed as we thought fit. We thought that Blatter was the better candidate; he knew more about the game worldwide and we felt no desire to follow the party line in Europe.

I suppose we could have kept quiet and let both candidates think we had voted for them as others did, but that was not my style. Moreover, I felt that would have been letting down the people who were backing us in various parts of the world if we did not go along with them and vote for Blatter. It seemed illogical, even crazy to vote for Johansson, albeit he was traditionally a good friend of English football and indeed an Arsenal fan, when he maintained his support for Germany for 2006. It would have given out all of the wrong signals and dealt a very severe blow to our World Cup hopes. We did not relish the prospect of being governed by a FIFA President who so determinedly opposed the English bid. Also, he was the leader of a block of Europeans all backing Germany. It was critical, therefore, for England to maximise support elsewhere.

Alec McGivan, unsurprisingly, was the keenest advocate for Blatter when members of the senior management discussed tactics with Keith Wiseman four days before the Paris vote. Pat Smith was initially unwilling, because she was still smarting from her problems with FIFA over the inadequate allocation of World Cup tickets for our fans. Blatter had made it clear to me throughout that UEFA might be guilty of arrogance in assuming that 2006 would come to Europe in any case. He was zealous in his wish to take the World Cup to the African continent at the earliest opportunity. However, should the African nations make insufficient progress by 2000, I was absolutely confident that Blatter, if he became President, would prefer England to Germany.

There was always a danger that 2006 and all that went with it would become all-powerful and that every decision would be reached with that in mind, and I tried to be careful in balancing that and tried to look at every issue in the round and on its merits, rather than just how it affected the campaign.

It was inevitable, however, that we would be caught up with the bitter battle for the FIFA Presidency and it was increasingly essential that we looked after our own welfare.

Originally there was little doubt that we would be supporting Lennart Johansson and, for a while, it looked as though he would be the only candidate. Johansson had announced his manifesto at a UEFA Congress in Helsinki in September 1997 with Dr Antonio Matarrese of Italy, eulogising him and publicly criticising Denmark for being the only European association not to support Johansson. Denmark were miffed because their man, Poul Hyldgaard, had lost his seat on the FIFA Executive Committee for supporting Havelange.

The President-elect told us in Finland that he wanted to come to London to sort things out as he did not want to leave unfinished business if he went to FIFA.

We felt that it would be more correct if the meeting was in Stockholm, rather than him being seen to attend on us. So we travelled to Sweden in January 1998 and Johansson started off in a somewhat negative fashion by warning us not to spend too much money on our campaign, but then backed off somewhat because he thought the

Germans were causing him some embarrassment by their stridency. He also warned that the British Vice-Presidency could be in danger in the not too distant future and he said he would try and get one or two people to help Keith Wiseman gain a place on the UEFA Executive Committee.

Lars-Ake Lagrell, the President of the Swedish FA, did initiate some moves, but support for Keith was disappointingly low in the event. He had been a thorn in the side of UEFA over the faltering Intertoto Cup. By going out on a limb on behalf of the Premier League clubs who were being threatened with sanctions if they did not enter, he made himself unpopular in the UEFA committees, whose members had grown accustomed to Sir Bert Millichip's ready co-operation.

A few days after the trip to Stockholm we moved on to Gent in Belgium for the draw for the qualifying rounds of the 2000 European Championships. It was sickening the way Johansson and his cronies put on a staged press conference with prepared questions from the press department of the four members on the top table, Senes Erzik, Antonio Matarrese, Egidius Braun and Per Ravn Omdal. Fritz Ahlstrom asked each one a question in turn, giving them the opportunity to endorse Johansson and cast doubt upon Blatter who, by that time, was rumoured to be standing.

It was not a surprise to me that Blatter might be challenging, for I had been given the information in the West Indies on one of our campaign trips that there was a strong move afoot to persuade Blatter to stand in opposition to Johansson.

After the draw in Gent, daggers were drawn between these two powerful men and the tussle between England and Germany was put to one side for the greater war between Johansson and Blatter. Matarrese fired the first salvo when he wrote to Blatter, saying that he hoped he was committed to his job, ensuring security in France during the World Cup, and ensuring the fairness of any election for the FIFA Presidency. Blatter gave a bland reply and referred the matter to Havelange.

Matarrese then wrote to all European associations, complaining of evasive replies, and requested a special FIFA Executive Committee meeting where they argued for four hours. But when David Will, who was also FIFA's legal advisor, declined to offer a legal opinion, Havelange banged the table, said: 'Meeting adjourned' and walked out. UEFA were saying that Blatter should declare his intentions to stand and, if he did, to step aside as General Secretary.

Having said earlier that we wanted to support Johansson, we were now very unhappy at the way things were going, particularly with the 2006 World Cup. As far as we were concerned, the race was well and truly on when Sepp Blatter announced that he would compete for the Presidency and asked to be allowed to stand down from certain of his duties.

I went to see Blatter in a little restaurant in the mountains above Zurich. It was my turn to pay for dinner but, unfortunately, the restaurant did not acknowledge any of my credit cards and, embarrassingly, it ended up with him paying for his own meal. He claimed that he had 100 votes pledged at that stage, enough to secure his election. I collected Joao Havelange at Heathrow next day on his way to Dublin for the UEFA Congress and he told me that he thought Blatter had 104 committed votes.

How far-reaching the effects were could be gauged by the fact that two marketing giants had become involved with TEAM, who marketed the Champions League, strongly for Johansson, while ISL, who looked after both the World Cup and the European Championships, were in the Blatter camp.

It was all becoming unseemly and there was another tacky affair at the Congress in Dublin where Johansson came into the room to the strains of Frank Sinatra's 'My Way' and followed it up by showing a video of Pele endorsing him. I found the campaign oppressive. They kept chanting on like a mantra, '*Solidarity, democracy, transparency*', and yet as far as I was concerned they had not treated England with fairness.

It helped little that the Italian Matarrese was elected chief sycophant and he once again stood up to give oodles of praise to Johansson. He was the wrong man to do it. He had lost his position in the Italian FA and was only there on the sufferance of the Italians. Indeed, I suspect the Italian FA subsequently gave their vote to Blatter! Lennart, having said that he would resign his position with UEFA to stand for FIFA, changed his mind. Perhaps the fact that Jack Warner from Trinidad claimed Blatter was now assured of 115 votes had something to do with that!

The European campaign was not working. France declared in favour of Blatter, prompting another UEFA press release saying that it was surprising that France had become a 'victim' of Blatter's campaign, and how terrible it was after Europe had unanimously supported France for the World Cup in 1998 that they were now voting for the non-European candidate. France, claimed UEFA, would be isolated.

When Havelange visited Tony Blair, it provoked Johansson to declare his support for Germany again. We wrote asking him how he could support Germany at this stage with the decision still two years away and the competition eight years away. Keith Wiseman, as blunt and honest as ever, told him his campaign was coming over badly and that he was hysterical over Blatter's challenge when he should be concentrating on his own strengths.

To give him credit, Johansson wrote back to say he was sorry and would try and avoid mentioning 2006 in future and that it was stupid to react to Havelange and Blatter the way he had done. He claimed he had told his team to work for him rather than against Blatter, but he spoiled it by adding that whatever he did, he attracted criticism from the FA and then, again, he implied that there was a deal over Euro 96.

If he had stopped to think for a moment, there could not have been any collusion when we had gone into competition with Austria, Holland, Portugal and Greece in 1992 to get the Championships. What would those four contenders have said if they thought it was all cut and dried and a deal done before the vote? The timing was all wrong for we had been given Euro 96 before Germany launched their campaign for 2006.

The so-called 'Gentleman's Agreement' would have constituted a conspiracy against these nations, two of whom, Holland and Portugal, were themselves represented on the Executive Committee.

The Johansson campaign was fast going down the drain and Marco Casanova, Johansson's personal assistant, didn't help his master's cause when he castigated Keith Wiseman for attending the May CONCACAF Congress in Antigua. Casanova scarcely endeared himself to Keith when he demanded: 'What are you doing here?' Keith had, in fact, been personally invited by Jack Warner, the head of the North and Central American and Caribbean Confederation.

Everything was pointing to our vote going to Blatter and that was what we decided. After we announced our intentions three days before the election, he rang from Paris to thank us and to say that he now had pledges for 110 votes. I took advantage of the moment to ask him to remind Havelange to speak to Jim Boyce about the FIFA British Vice-Presidency. He not only promised he would, but also advised us that once the decision was reached we would not have to wait until a Congress but that it could be implemented at any time.

Although we had been given *carte blanche* by the FA, our decision to go with Blatter did not meet with universal approval. We tried to persuade Geoff Thompson to support us, but he wanted to stay with Johansson despite our long explanation. The upshot of that unsuccessful meeting was a call from David Dein, a powerful figure on the Executive Committee, who had received an urgent call from Aigner. The Arsenal Vice-Chairman was agitated that we had committed ourselves to what he thought was the wrong man and that Aigner was, not surprisingly, in an even bigger state.

Thompson had apparently told Des Casey of Ireland about our intentions and he, in turn, tipped off Aigner. It was possible that the Premier League thought their interests would be better served by keeping in with UEFA. However, we had consulted fully with Peter Leaver whose own information, gathered from the major European Leagues, pointed to a Blatter victory.

The repercussions rumbled on like thunder when we arrived at the FIFA Congress in Paris. Sweden made their feelings known in no uncertain manner and told us that we were perpetuating corruption by voting for Blatter. I thought that a little strong, to say the least. Where was the evidence? Not being privy to the inner workings of UEFA or FIFA, England had no way of assessing these claims. The Dutch representative Dr Mathieu Sprengers was a lot more considered. He said he understood what we had done but could not agree. However, many Africans and the Spanish President Angel Villar Llona supported us, so we assumed they were in the same camp.

Johansson reacted badly and announced that Keith Wiseman had only recently promised him his support. This was untrue, as Keith had written to him in April, telling him those home truths, and had also told Casanova not to count on England's support in view of their recent comments and attitude towards us.

The voting took a little over two hours on Monday 8 June with Blatter scoring 111 to Johansson's 80. There was a dramatic pause while the delegates waited for the result of the second vote, but it quickly became clear to Johansson that he could not possibly win and he came back into the room to concede generously to Blatter, apparently on the advice of Matarrese.

Corinne Blatter, Sepp's daughter, shed copious tears of joy. Her father, the most influential man in world football, had become the most powerful. Like another powerful figure I had observed at close quarters, Alan Hardaker, the Secretary of the Football League, Blatter had an ego, an acute awareness of the status of the body he led and, above all, an innate feeling for the game. He, more than anybody at

FIFA, had pioneered the measures which had made football a more attractive game, less prey to the brutality and cynicism that had earlier prevailed. The finer points of the laws of the game did not trouble him – the spirit was much more important.

The aftermath followed like a whirlwind. Sir Bert Millichip was furious with us, considering that we had let him down with his friends in Europe. He later told the Council he was ashamed to be English. There was one humorous diversion, however, when one of the ladies we had met on our campaign trail, the wife of the Costa Rican representative Isaac Sasso Sasso, told us that she had been looked after so well in London on her last visit that next time she would like to take lunch with the Queen at Buckingham Palace! We passed on the request, tongue-in-cheek, to poor Alec McGivan who, to his chagrin, was expected to fix everything. That one, however, may prove beyond him!

The Congress was not a good one for the Germans as they lost their place on the FIFA Executive with Gerhard Mayer-Vorfelder being defeated by Joseph Mifsud from Malta, and the resolution for one World Cup bid per confederation was defeated, winning only 87 votes, way too few.

UEFA were naturally upset and there were a few toys thrown out of the pram when they said that Blatter had sought their help in trying to oust Havelange in 1994. Havelange had held on to become king maker for Blatter.

The election for the FIFA Presidency, then, was a critical factor in our quest for the World Cup. Our campaign, meanwhile, was becoming a fascinating journey. The first stop was Trinidad and Tobago where we met the influential and experienced Jack Warner, who advised us that some parts of the world still resented British imperialism. He displayed the fact that he had the ear of the mighty when he informed us, correctly, that Blatter was to stand for the Presidency and he also encouraged us by complaining about the Germans pulling out of the Confederations Cup. He informed us that no way would Havelange quietly fade away and as if to show us he knew what he was talking about, he took our delegation on a visit to the Joao Havelange Centre of Excellence in Trinidad.

Politics reared its head in this unlikely spot when the Trinidad and Tobago Minister for Sport complained bitterly about our government's policy on bananas in the ongoing row with the USA, a row which they were destined to lose. Tony Banks, for once, was lost for words.

But for drama you could not beat our visit to Saudi Arabia on 12 December 1997 when we flew straight into a desert storm which promised consequences which could seriously affect our World Cup planning and even embroil the Government in a damaging trade row.

We arrived late in the evening in Riyadh where the British Ambassador quickly informed us that Tony Banks was in a state of great agitation after learning that we were being accused of going back on our word because Glenn Hoddle did not want to play the Saudis at Wembley in May 1998 as part of his World Cup build-up.

The Saudis felt that Alec McGivan had promised that England would invite Saudi to play England on that date. I had spoken to Glenn about it and he swore that he had made no firm commitment and did not see Saudi as the ideal opponents so close to the World Cup. We talked through the dilemma until 3.30 in the morning in Riyadh before we eventually agreed between myself, David Davies, Alec McGivan and Keith Wiseman that David should fly back to London immediately to speak to Glenn Hoddle to try and explain that our Saudi friends did not accept the usual football logic. Glenn had been happy for England to play them, but not in the immediate build-up to France. The trouble was that the fast of Ramadan precluded them from playing in February and there was no other date available.

Our difficulty was that the powerful and proud Princes had announced to the press that the game would be at Wembley in May. It is definitely not politic to argue with the Saudi Princes and we thought they suspected a plot to keep them out of the limelight.

We had our Government putting added pressure on us, as they were saying that the two British nurses under the threat of death for the alleged murder of one of their colleagues would be prejudiced by our stance. This was according to the Ambassador, so it was difficult to dispute. Not only that, but British trade and other sports contacts with Saudi would be in danger if we failed to fulfil what they saw as an agreement. They would see it as a massive political snub if we failed to deliver.

Poor Alec McGivan was on the spot and had been of the opinion that Glenn had cleared the match, subject to the draw in Marseille on 4 December keeping the two teams apart. I had discussed this particular situation with Glenn on a couple of occasions and I actually feared that he might resign as England coach if he was told that he had to play in the national interest. I was much relieved when he eventually accepted the position. I assured him that we would never normally overrule him on playing matters like that.

It was the sort of incident that a manager would resign over. They tend to be obstinate in that respect, and rightly so, but we had reached that decision in the early hours that the match had to go ahead for the national interest, rather than just our own concerns. The Embassy officials were on tenterhooks as they saw it as the biggest potential row between the two countries since the controversial television documentary *Death of a Princess*. Glenn's co-operation was very welcome.

Poor David Davies. It was his only trip with us on the campaign and he had hardly left the airport before he had to fly home again on such a critical mission.

We continued with our visit and invited the FIFA representatives, Johansson, Per Omdal, Charlie Dempsey, Jack Warner and Sepp Blatter to lunch at the house of the British Charge d'Affaires. Politically, it was a very good attendance for us which I am sure was entirely unconnected with the fact that alcohol could be served in the diplomatic quarters.

The visit was to coincide with the Confederations Cup. We were seeing two games a day for four days and drinking a lot of sweet Saudi Arabian tea in the meantime. I also took the opportunity to persuade the FIFA party to play an *ad-hoc* four-a-side game early one morning in the hotel grounds involving Sepp Blatter, FIFA Technical Director Walter Gagg and Leon Walker, former Swiss national coach. The Confederations Cup was of little interest to anyone locally, apart from when the Saudis themselves were playing. I flew back from Riyadh with quite a shopping list. Egypt wanted a friendly match against England, Nepal asked for a couple of places on a coaching course, and Thailand required a coach for their national team. Michel Platini, lined up alongside Blatter in the prospective leadership battle, was worried about the Germans succeeding to three of the top four posts in UEFA and FIFA. He foresaw Braun taking over from Johansson and Horst Schmidt moving into Blatter's job, with Gerhard Aigner already General Secretary of UEFA.

When the Saudis came over to us in May, we had a glittering dinner at the Guildhall hosted by the Football Association and the City of London. Our President, the Duke of Kent, was host and welcomed everyone as they arrived in a private reception room before the main event. We were waiting for the Saudi princes to arrive from the Dorchester Hotel. There must have been about fifteen who came into the room in a flash, completely destroying any preparations we had made for the formal introductions. That hardly mattered as we had seen them three or four times already.

However, in the middle of all these bigwigs, I spotted the diminutive figure of ITV's Pat Gregory who had been swept along in the crowd, shaking hands with the host. The penny suddenly dropped that she was in the wrong room and had to find a way of extricating herself. Her face was a picture as she realised women do not usually occupy such a prominent position in Saudi society.

The next stop was Paraguay with Tony Banks, Sir Bobby Charlton and Alec McGivan. Our first port of call was to see Dr Nicolas Leoz, President of the South American Confederation. We went into an office which he had just built in Asuncion where we could have comfortably played an eight-a-side game. There were so many meeting sections within the one office, it was the biggest I have ever seen. They had the television cameras present, as they often do in South America, and he was very amicable.

Invariably our hosts would be delighted that we had taken the trouble to visit their home territory. I would not mind having Alec McGivan's Air Miles at the end of the campaign!

Tony Banks caused something of a difficulty when he reacted warmly to a suggestion from the Jamaican FA while we were in Trinidad that they come to England and play as part of the World Cup build-up if they won through their final qualifying match. When this did not take place, the Jamaicans were quite upset, and it was very difficult to persuade them that it was not a snub by the FA. We could hardly explain that Glenn Hoddle had already had Saudi Arabia thrust upon him in May and this did not increase the prospect of them obtaining a fixture. In the event they played a friendly at QPR's Loftus Road ground, but not against their preferred opponents!

We then went down to Buenos Aires and attended a number of receptions and functions involving the President of the Argentine FA Julio Grondona, the FIFA member, who turned out to be very anti-David Will. We also went to see President Menem, who endorsed the English campaign, and his sports minister, former rugby international Hugo Porta, a delightful man. We were invited to take in a Boca Juniors game where we were put into an executive box with the club president who could not quite understand what I was doing when I asked everyone to pick a name out of a hat for the first goalscorer, collecting $2 each for a sweepstake. He soon cottoned on when the player he had drawn lined up to take a penalty. Here was the president, a multi-millionaire who owned half the city, becoming quite excited at winning $50 – sadly for him, his player shot past the post and the game finished 0–0. Although it was goalless, the game gave us an idea of the fanaticism of the Argentine supporters.

They, like many others on our trips, all knew about English football and our players and we discovered that the first thing they wanted to talk about was the Premier League and how their favourite teams were getting on. It was heartening to observe first hand the growing interest in our bid. We tend to forget that Britons took football to so many countries in the last century.

At one of the receptions we came across the former Argentine captain Antonio Rattin, sent off against England at Wembley in the 1966 World Cup when manager Alf Ramsey was provoked into calling his rivals 'animals '. Bobby Charlton told him that his name was still used to frighten children in England and if they weren't good their fathers would send for Rattin. Nothing could have been further from the truth as he turned out to be another charming man, destroying another of my preconceptions.

When we arrived back from Buenos Aires in the early hours of Sunday morning, it was to learn of the death of Fulham fan Matthew Fox at Gillingham. A sharp return to reality and an unhappy landing.

Tony Banks, who had built himself somewhat of a reputation for putting his foot in his mouth in his first few months as Sports Minister, was excellent on all of these trips and fully redeemed himself after a sticky start in June 1997 at Le Tournoi, the tournament England won prior to the World Cup.

We held a lunch at the British Embassy in Paris and Tony Banks and I found ourselves sitting at a table with three of the FIFA Executive members, Slim Aloulou from Tunisia, Issa Hayatou from Cameroon and Jack Warner. Completely unprompted, Banks, who had been in office only a matter of weeks, wondered aloud why Britain didn't have just one team as it would give us a much better chance of winning the World Cup.

Having fought for years to maintain our individuality and the power base it provided, I hastily had to step in and say that it would not be a subject his hosts wanted him to pursue at that particular moment. In other words – shut up!

Like Banks, I was keen for Britain to be represented at the Olympic Games. However, the other Home Nations, worried about losing special status enjoyed by the British at FIFA, declined to let the highest placed British team in the UEFA Under-21 Championships go on to represent Britain at the Olympics.

Our World Cup bid had been something of a turnaround for Tony as, when a member of the opposition, he publicly supported the World Cup claims of South Africa against England. It is not something you can hide when you are quoted in *Hansard* and he had to skirt around the fact. He always referred to his friendly relations with the Minister for Sport in South Africa, saying he hoped for strong but friendly rivalry.

After his initial blunder in Paris he was fine. He would prepare his speeches very thoroughly on his shorthand pad. He was very hard working and would always say the right thing, sticking to his brief and never saying too much or too little, simply emphasising that the bid was supported by the Government in every way from the Prime Minister downwards and that all the necessary security and diplomatic guarantees would be given at the right time.

He would then leave the way open for Sir Bobby Charlton to speak from the heart as he always did about the merits of the case and of English football. Bobby was brilliant; he would always have an anecdote concerning the country we were visiting, always something relevant.

It was always a tight schedule and Alec McGivan and I often felt guilty as we would only be in the country for a couple of days, combining the political and the diplomatic aspect with the public relations side, leaving Bobby to work from seven in the morning until ten in the evening, coping with all the people he had to meet, including the many media requests. We would consciously try to restrict him a little bit, but he always wanted to do more and never said no. He had a football shirt or a souvenir for every occasion.

The messy business with the International Olympic Committee over money and gifts paid to delegates raised the question of whether there were bribes and inducements offered in the bids for the World Cup. I can honestly say that in my experience it was not an issue. Our generosity extended to a beautifully bound book containing signed photographs of great English players through the ages, while our hospitality rarely exceeded lunch or dinner.

FIFA threatened to issue some guidelines on bidding. They never came out while I was at the FA, but I did see a draft copy and they were all about letting FIFA know if a national association was going to visit a member so that they were not snowed under. Needless to say excessive gifts and money were forbidden. The proposed guidelines came out soon after the IOC problems and I was worried that they would be unnecessarily restrictive in preventing us meeting people, even those who were passing through London.

There was never any suggestion made to us that we should give them inducements. There are only 24 who vote. Some are from less developed areas in the world and they made it clear they need support for their individual projects, rather than for themselves. That is why, when the representative from Thailand, Worawi Makudi, wanted a coach for the national team, it was incumbent on a big player in the game like England to try and find someone to go out there and maybe subsidise his visit as we did with Peter Withe, the former Aston Villa and Nottingham Forest striker.

That is helping football in the country as opposed to giving backhanders to people to exercise their influence. One would assume that Germany have been doing that for years in places like Africa.

CHAPTER THREE

Sweet FA

The FA is a unique organisation because it is governed by 92 people, all members of the Council elected from various parts of the game, and amazingly enough, all holding directorships in the Football Association Ltd.

People rise to positions of influence in the Football Association and these posts can carry considerable power and recognition in such a high profile game. Those with ambition, and there are always a number looking for the glory, seek to be elected to the Executive Committee which, in theory at least, is akin to the Board of Directors of a normal company.

At the time of my departure those with power on the Executive were David Dein, Vice Chairman of Arsenal, David Sheepshanks, Chairman of Ipswich Town and David Richards, chairman of Sheffield Wednesday. They all carry considerable sway in the corridors of power and in the running of the FA but, even so, these powerful representatives of the professional game still have to sit alongside others such as David Henson of Devon, Frank Pattison of Durham, Terry Annable of the Nottinghamshire FA, Ray Kiddell of the Norfolk FA and, of course, Geoff Thompson from the Sheffield and Hallamshire FA, who stepped into the breach when Keith Wiseman followed me out of Lancaster Gate. It was the lack of support from the county members which so dismayed Keith Wiseman when he resigned as Chairman.

The terms of reference of the various committees at Lancaster Gate are sometimes ill defined, with distinctions between one committee and another often blurred. I tried on a number of occasions to divest the Council members of their directorships so as to appoint a modern Board of Management comprising of a smaller number of representatives from the different areas of the game.

This was not a revolutionary concept and, in fact, it had been recommended by a consultancy who had been commissioned to produce a report for the future shortly before I moved from the Football League to the FA in 1988. The report was designed to make the Football Association a more streamlined and businesslike organisation.

PA, the outside company involved, recommended that the Chief Executive should have a vote on the Board of Management and, sitting at the summer meeting in Plymouth in 1988 as the report was debated, I was thrilled when the recommendation to give the Chief Executive a vote on the Board of Management was passed by 38 votes to 37, albeit a narrow squeeze.

But here started the first lesson in FA wheelings, dealings and the all-important conservation of power. The debate went in such a way that 20 minutes later it was decided not to have a Board of Management anyway, so my powers of influence at Lancaster Gate were curbed before I had even started. No one likes to surrender their power and authority.

Other members of Council can exercise influence without the need to be elected to the Executive Committee. Noel White of Liverpool has been the Chairman of the International Committee since succeeding his friend, the former Chairman of Manchester City Peter Swales, in 1994. After the position of Chairman of the FA, this is the ultimate high profile position, responsible for appointing the England coach and overseeing the affairs of the English national team. These are two areas of responsibility which command attention and ensure a high profile in the media.

The distinguished academic Sir Norman Chester, in his first report in 1968, recommended that the FA set up an Executive Committee. They did actually follow his advice, but never gave the committee any real power. Members on the Executive Committee in the years before I went to Lancaster Gate complained that they were the dustbin; everything that did not go to one of the standing committees went to them, and they finished with all the scraps and no real issues to deal with.

They had a series of special meetings and were instantly unhappy about a scheme called *Friends of Football* which my predecessor Ted Croker had introduced through a company called Shandwick. There were shades of modern times and of my own removal about it, as no one admitted to authorising the appointment of the firm.

Suspicion and mistrust were rife in both the Football Association and the Football League in those days and, as a consequence, the relationship between the two bodies often suffered.

Bill Fox of Blackburn Rovers had taken over as League President when Philip Carter of Everton was ousted in October 1988 and he was so keen to avoid a recurrence of the debacle earlier that year when the big five clubs in the top division forced the ITV contract through that he became at odds permanently with the big clubs, rather than heal the scars caused by what had happened in October.

It was very messy and I was annoyed when the League started rearranging league matches for live television just before international matches. They conjured one up in April 1989, three days before a World Cup match against Albania after doing exactly the same thing the previous month before our match with Greece, claiming then that it was a one-off. Our Chairman Bert Millichip complained to the League, but to no avail.

Shortly after I left the League, Sir John Smith, the highly respected and normally diplomatic chairman of Liverpool, even went as far as accusing the League staff of deliberately drawing up the fixtures against the interests of ITV and the big clubs.

The politicking was every bit as intense then as it is now with the game so much more buoyant and powerful. Liverpool threw their weight behind Robert Chase of Norwich City for Presidency of the League, then Chase was eliminated at the first hurdle and the big clubs switched their vote to Aston Villa's Doug Ellis, known throughout the game as 'Deadly'. Gordon McKeag of Newcastle went out in the second ballot. Then came the clincher when Bill Fox said he would appoint Gordon Taylor, the highly respected Chief Executive of the Professional Footballers' Association as Chief Executive and consequently beat Ellis by 31 votes to 28 and a half.

However, Fox ran into problems with the appointment. It was the only known case of the PFA Management Committee objecting to a recommendation from Gordon Taylor as they said 'No', while Fox also had trouble with his own Management Committee, where he was unable to find a seconder for Gordon's lucrative ten year contract. The

PFA took advantage of the moment and said that as there was dissent in the League, they had better keep Gordon Taylor.

Then the League had problems with the company they were using to find the Chief Executive. Arthur Sandford, a local government officer from Nottingham, eventually took the job, but when his name was leaked in the early stages, Michael Squires, the head-hunter, said: 'It is the worst search I have ever been involved in as the goalposts keep moving.

'Jack Dunnett briefed me and then resigned. Bill Fox then told me he had Gordon Taylor and then it was back to square one. The Management Committee couldn't decide on the job specification, they had gone back on their word and changed their mind. I have never known such leaks, arguments and in-fighting.'

There was another argument between the League and the FA over the television facilities fees payable for FA Cup matches. League matches were allocated £195,000 to be shared between the clubs participating in live transmissions while FA Cup matches earned only £120,000 from the central contract. But the difference was that 75% of the Football League television money went to Division One clubs, whereas the Football Association wanted to spread their revenue throughout the game.

The League wanted to claim half the FA's money themselves so that they could distribute it. But they had forgotten that the FA had to pay 25% to Wembley and sustain the grassroots and we faced uncertainty with the impending publication of the Taylor report. If our year end produced a profit, we preferred to make payments to the Football Trust for the wider benefit of the game.

The situation needed to be improved generally for the sake of football in the future and for the England team in particular. These tensions were a root cause of the Premier League when I saw a way of ending the power struggle.

One of the problems with the Football Association is the number of people involved. There was always this strain between the Council members and the full time staff. The Council members often had time on their hands while the staff invariably had too little time. I often used to say that the FA usually found the right answer after exhausting all other possibilities. Gossip was the bane of Lancaster Gate. Staff had a right to privacy in their contractual matters, but salaries commonly became general knowledge to those who knew the right questions to ask.

There were petty complaints, such as the one when, at Umbro's request, we used the legendary former England goalkeeper Gordon Banks to promote a match. Most of the surviving members of the 1966 World Cup-winning team became highly marketable names in the nineties boom. However, Banks was coming towards the end of a long ban on receiving Cup Final tickets because the company bearing his name refused to co-operate with an FA black market tickets inquiry and this prompted one Council member to complain bitterly at our involvement with Banks.

I went for the job of FA Chief Executive for the very simple reason that I knew I could do it well. I had the enthusiasm, the qualifications and, most importantly, a deep love of the game. I was overjoyed when I landed it, much to the surprise of many observers as I had quite clearly come through on the rails. My aim was to make the FA a fully professional and modern outfit, capable of providing leadership for the game, rather than being swept along on a tide of events.

There were three internal candidates for the job of Chief Executive in 1988, Adrian Titcombe, Charles Hughes and Glen Kirton. Pat Smith felt she would do a good job as Deputy Chief Executive because. being a woman who had never played football, she had no aspirations whatsoever for the top job.

Sir David Hill-Wood told me after Pat retired that he found her involvement in staff matters stultifying, not an opinion he had advanced during her many years at Lancaster Gate. I could not see his point as I had always found her fair in dealing with the staff who, by and large, were very well looked after.

I became disenchanted with Hill-Wood, first after he gate-crashed an Executive Committee dinner when he was candidate for Chairman in 1996, and secondly when he departed from his brief as Finance Committee Chairman at the Annual General Meeting in 1997. Then, when Phil Carling of Arsenal applied to succeed Trevor Phillips as Commercial Director, Hill-Wood prematurely alerted the Highbury Board, thus causing potential embarrassment for our employee.

But any problems I might have had with Council members, certainly until my final days at the FA, paled into insignificance compared with those of my predecessor Ted Croker. Sir Harold Thompson, chairman from 1976–81, was as good as his word in staying for only five years. However, he managed to cram sufficient activity into those five years to make Croker's life a total misery.

When I arrived at Lancaster Gate I found the files stuffed with memos from Thompson to Croker, always starting off, 'Dear Croker', which instantly revealed a great deal about their relationship. Thompson, a distinguished academic and scientist, obviously did not understand the offence this unnecessary formality would cause. These memos ran from anything to thirty, forty or fifty items of instructions. I can quite easily see how relations between the two were so patently strained. This was apparent to anyone who knew or were involved with the FA at that time.

Ted Croker, a former professional player, had run a successful business and I doubt whether he took kindly to receiving such memos, nor indeed to being referred to as 'boy' when he was at a lunch with other people at the age of 55. Sadly, I was not there to record it nor his response in person, but I saw the effects of it.

Harold Thompson had an unexpected ally in Alan Hardaker, the prickly overlord of the Football League, who used to delight in winding up Croker because he got on tolerably well with Thompson. It still baffles me as to why. Other fellow Yorkshiremen, like abrasive manager Brian Clough, columnist and personality Michael Parkinson, and Fulham chairman Ernie Clay all felt the length of Hardaker's tongue. Perhaps he could see a common cause with Thompson, knowing he could wind Croker up something rotten.

Power tended to be a shifting thing at the Football Association. Bert Millichip was very clever, for he promoted a number of people to reasonably influential positions but they never became strong enough to challenge him for the chairmanship.

Nothing ever happens at the FA without a committee being appointed. The committee members do invaluable work and it was always rewarding to experience their dedication at first hand, but the structure makes progress excruciatingly slow. Moreover, confusion can arise over the slightest issue. The Premier League wanted to put their referees in green shirts and it was two Football League men, Barry Taylor of Barnsley and John Reames of Lincoln City, who sided with some of the county people to raise objections over this trivial matter at a time when referees in many other countries were adopting a sleeker, more modern look.

There was even a Committee specifically set up to appoint committees, which I found amusing. This was the Officers' Committee, with senior officers like the Vice-Presidents joined by four rank and file members of the Council on a rota basis. They have a meeting every June to appoint the Committees and that is when the lobbying is seen at its most effective and virulent.

Sadly, they never seemed to know whether they were supposed to be changing people around so that they could gain experience of the various areas of work, or whether they should leave them on committees to use the experience which they have gained in that one specialised area.

The lobbying even continued after the committee had concluded its deliberations. Ian Stott kicked up a fuss after he lost his place on the International Committee following Oldham's relegation from the Premier League; Paul Kirby, the New Zealand representative, was kicked off the Publications Committee after a word was put in the right ear – or wrong ear, from his point of view. Both came back.

There is a tradition for new members to be appointed onto the Rules Revision Committee which is one step up from purgatory, involving going painstakingly through the rules of the FA. This is one which everyone tries to escape from as soon as they possibly can.

The two plum committees are, without doubt, those dealing with international football and the FA Cup. Keith Wiseman had gone to enormous lengths in his final season to make sure that the Premier League and the Football League were well represented on the committees that count; International, FA Cup, Finance and Commercial were strengthened by the addition of League people. The Leagues' biggest complaint was that they were under-represented until Keith redressed the balance, and yet he still found himself needing friends at the end of the year.

Influence is very much with the full-time staff. Pat Smith was there for thirty years and she could be very persuasive in committees. She always had a strong grasp of her subject and an innate feeling of what was right for the game and for the FA. Whenever issues like Cup Final tickets were being discussed she always put in a very strong plea for what she felt was the most she could obtain for the supporters and invariably her judgement was correct. She was a stickler for fairness and the correct protocol in all matters.

I promoted her to Deputy Chief Executive in 1995 because she had done everything at Lancaster Gate. She knew the place inside out and backwards. She argued cases impressively, handling the media well when she had to, and she was a big loss when she retired in 1998. She ran so many Cup Finals from behind the scenes that I pushed her in front of the cameras to assist the Duke of Kent in presenting the Cup to Dennis Wise on her last official visit to the Final.

We invariably exchanged knowing glances in meetings when, with tea and coffee going cold in the pots, Pat volunteered to serve the men. Neither she nor I minded helping the others to their refreshments, but we both resented the assumption that a female should pour. Similarly, despite my guidelines for FA matches at League grounds, the club chairmen sometimes opened a private room to which the men gravitated for a tot. All our guests should have been treated equally, but those wearing trousers were accorded more equal treatment than those in skirts. Pat would raise the matter diplomatically later; my approach was blunter, as this perpetuation of outdated values angered me intensely.

Like Glen Kirton, director of Euro 96, before her, Pat was deservedly appointed OBE on her departure from the FA.

Such was the transient nature of authority that it was hard to put your finger on the power and authority, although when I left it seemed to be a distinct group with the acting Chairman Geoff Thompson, David Dein, David Sheepshanks, Dave Richards and David Davies. Those five seemed to guide things through from the moment I departed. It evolved out of the Executive Committee at the time when Keith and I were having our difficulties.

Almost before Keith and I had cleared our desks, there were election speeches going on with Thompson clearly angling for the Wiseman role, and Davies as interim Executive Director ideally placed for mine. It was almost like the hustings.

Thompson, a committed Christian and man who chose his ties well, surprised his colleagues in one meeting when he was offended by the phrase 'singing from the same hymn sheet'. On another occasion he insisted on the retention of the title 'Christian name' on a registration form, even though many non-Christians now play under the FA's auspices.

His main rival, David Sheepshanks, commenced a programme of one-to-one meetings with members from the County Associations to ascertain the likely level of support before announcing he would challenge Thompson for the chairmanship. On the face of it, he presented a strong case, having successfully brought an element of stability to the Football League. But he faced an uphill struggle to dent the grassroots support of Thompson, who relied heavily on the presentational skills of David Davies and was fond of the maxim 'Nobody gets lost on a straight road.' Moreover, it would have been wrong for Sheepshanks to assume he could unite the professional vote. The Premier League, if they could not secure the election of their own man as in 1996, were capable of allying with Thompson.

Ken Bates, after prefacing his criticism the previous September with the assurance that he wasn't interested in the top job, made a short-lived appearance in the press, seeking it for a 'short period' whilst reforms were pursued.

But the politicking was nothing new. There had certainly been some strange times over the years. There was a leak to the *People* one year about my salary negotiations. They had it down to the last penny after my talks with the FA in 1991. I complained to the Staff Committee about it and asked, how could we rebuild trust if people were going to talk outside? Far from investigating where the leak had come from, they were upset with me that I had even raised it. They do not like anybody rocking the boat. They even suggested that it could be a member of staff, but that was nonsense because there were never any staff members present at the negotiations. I had my suspicions who the culprit was. It was a time of high tension over the formation of the Premier League so maybe it was a way of undermining me by implying publicly that I was overpaid.

It was my job to ensure that delays did not arise, to co-ordinate the work of the committees so that we did make decisions and didn't wait weeks for Council meetings. There was a way of making it work: the FA worked well despite the system, not because of it.

After my departure there was widespread amazement at the speed of the FA's decisions over the dismissal of Glenn Hoddle and the rearrangement of the Arsenal FA Cup tie against Sheffield United. The new men were trying to impress, to show the world that they could move swiftly. There was never any reason why decisions could not be taken quickly. If the staff have a view and a clear recommendation, they have only to ring the committee. Even so, I must admit that both matters were resolved with remarkable alacrity.

Delays occur in disciplinary cases because, by rules, players are allowed a fortnight in which to prepare their case. The original charge is a different matter and I charged Eric Cantona within a few hours of his escapade at Crystal Palace, so things hadn't changed that much. It annoyed me that I was suddenly being portrayed as the stumbling block to progress. It was a case of 'The King is dead – long live the King.'

With the removal of Hoddle, the procedure, had I been there, would have been similar. We would have had a small committee, discussed it and come to a decision, although whether it would have been with the same result is a different matter.

As for Arsenal, that would have been much the same decision. In fairness to those involved, it was unprecedented for a manager to turn down a victory. Once agreement between the two clubs had been ascertained, it was then solely a case of getting in touch with the FA Cup committee and confirming the decision.

I advocated transferring power from the Council because they could not be expected to know what was going on in an organisation the size of the FA. There were various schemes, all on the same theme of giving more power to the Executive Committee, who could take an overview and co-ordinate all the activities of the FA.

Back in 1990 I told the FA Council: 'What I believe the Association needs is a little more accountability, less supremos and more Indians.' It is still the case and in truth there were, and still are, too many of both.

The ambitions have still not altered and what they are hoping to do is to mimic the Labour Party. For New Labour, read New FA. The Labour Party had to rid themselves of the infamous Clause Four while New FA are now trying to persuade the Council that there is a better way of running the FA.

It is the only way in which they can drag the Association into the new millennium. The structure is not modern and major surgery is the only answer.

The Premier League is an enigma. In reality they enjoy virtual autonomy. But because their clubs and players bring in most of the money, they are constantly wanting more power over the way the whole of football is run.

By contrast the Football League have one big problem and that is viability. Their clubs are paying the players too much but Richard Scudamore wanted them to be more realistic and live within their means. Within the FA they still exercise influence and have a reservoir of goodwill. They certainly have the sympathy which the wealth of the Premier League has engendered for them.

CHAPTER FOUR

Corridors of Power

The long shadow of Sir Bert Millichip followed me down the corridors of power at Lancaster Gate and through Europe long after he resigned his position as Chairman of the Football Association. Many would argue, myself amongst them, that he should have ceased to be an issue long before he finally bowed out after the success of Euro 96.

There had been considerable speculation as to who would replace Sir Bert Millichip as FA Chairman two years earlier. In 1996 he sent a letter to the Council saying that it was not his intention to carry on after the European Championships. Immediately the books opened on his successor. Sir John Hall, the man with the money behind Newcastle United, was mentioned, as was Alan Sugar of Spurs, Jimmy Hill, Geoff Thompson, Dave Richards and Keith Wiseman. Sir Bert had served the FA well for 15 years. He said at the time of his election in 1981 that, like his predecessor Sir Harold Thompson, he did not believe in long terms of office and would serve only five years at the most. But I suppose that there is never a right time to bow out.

Five years would have taken him to just after the Heysel disaster and ten years would have taken him to just after the Hillsborough tragedy, so there was always some major issue which made a change difficult.

But he upset the Scots, the Irish and the Welsh early in 1996 when he effectively told them that it was every man for himself in the elections for the UEFA Executive Committee as he did not necessarily see that he was representing the four British Associations on the Executive Committee.

He said he was persuaded by Johansson to let his name go forward for the 1996 elections in London. The Irish and Welsh also put forward the names of Jim Boyce and Brian Fear because there were a number of vacancies that year. In the event both Fear and Boyce polled low after Sir Bert had pulled out of the election at the last minute, having been promised an appointment by Johansson as special advisor to UEFA. The Irish, Welsh and Scots were understandably furious and they thought he had let them down badly. There was a possibility that, even at the age of 82, Bert would have been re-elected, especially with the election being held in London on the back of a successful European Championship, but he declined to take the risk.

To his credit he refused to reconsider his decision to stand down as chairman of the FA. Frank Pattison asked him to delay his retirement for another year while steps were taken to find a successor and Dave Richards and Rick Parry came from the Premier League with a similar request. The Counties in the South West also wanted Bert to stay on.

In reality Bert Millichip damaged his reputation by staying around too long. Like Lord Denning, who was Master of the Rolls until the age of 84, he should have retired earlier. Football, even more than the law, is a young person's game, and by clinging to office too long he jeopardised his reputation for integrity and threatened to overshadow all his achievements, like the liberalisation of the offside law for which he campaigned for many years.

The upshot of all this was that next time the election came round for UEFA in 1998 Keith Wiseman, although he had worked diligently and successfully to restore relations with the British Associations, polled only 16 votes in an election which saw the return of all the sitting members. There were no vacancies for England to take advantage of.

We had no one ready to take over from Sir Bert on UEFA in 1996. He always had the best interests of the FA and the game to heart and was a real gentleman as Chairman of the Council. But I did not enjoy the easiest relationship with him. He tended to speak off the cuff to the press which sometimes caused us problems. A classic example was when he effectively gave England manager Bobby Robson the elbow in March 1990 on the eve of the World Cup by publicly casting doubt on his chances of getting a new contract.

I also overheard him complaining and casting aspersions to Lennart Johansson about me. He said the FA would come to a halt if Pat Smith left but could quite easily cope if I was not there. It would probably upset Pat more than it upset me. Then he moaned to Chris Willcox, the Vice Chairman, when I thought I should stay in London to prepare for the first televised FA Cup draw under the new format, rather than accompany him to a meeting in Belfast.

Bert was a good Chairman of the Council, but he was never one for making decisions which could harm his popularity in the Council. He could also be incredibly indiscreet and I once overheard him tell one of the ladies at the summer meeting how he had personally put Pat Smith's salary up to a certain figure and quoted her wage.

He always had the best interests of the game and its image at heart and he was justly rewarded with a knighthood after piloting the FA through its darkest days of the eighties. It is my opinion that he allowed his reputation in the game to be dimmed by his personal foibles towards the end of his time, but others, particularly his former UEFA colleagues, may feel his standing as a true English gentleman remains entirely unaffected.

One area where he was implacable was when he set his sights on a particular appointment. He was very keen to recruit his Midlands neighbour David Davies as the Director of Public Affairs to replace Mike Wilmore, who had been recruited by our Commercial Director Trevor Phillips. Mike had done a reasonable job with little resources, although he was unable to protect me when I appeared in court on behalf of Brentford's Gary Blissett. We also had David Teasdale working for Graham Taylor on press relations which had not been terribly effective.

Earlier we had Glen Kirton handling press relations on a part-time basis, with reasonable success, and David Bloomfield as press officer also did a good job. But we needed to professionalise our response to the press and beef up our resources.

The problem I had with David Davies' appointment, so keenly advocated by Sir Bert, was that it completely destroyed the entire pay structure of the management of the FA. With Bert so enthusiastic to have him on board, David was able to call the shots. He made it clear he did not intend to move to the London area, so not only the salary but also the expenses would be higher than most and this caused resentment among other members of my management team. Like home-grown footballers who often felt undervalued, those with considerable years of service to the FA who had personally incurred the high costs of living and working in the capital expressed displeasure, not at the person, but because principles were being compromised.

It was not as if David Davies were the only choice for the job. I had alternative professionals who might have come in. I liked Ray Stubbs, but he wanted to stay in television. Graham Miller of ITN, who had similar qualifications to David Davies, would have joined us. I felt strongly enough to take my complaint to Sir David Hill-Wood, who was on the Appointments Committee. He said that he understood my concerns, but his only reaction was to invite Davies out to lunch which did little to solve the problem. The third member of the committee was Chris Willcox from the Gloucestershire FA who was never going to stand up to Sir Bert. So I lost the argument.

Despite my initial concerns over these principles, I was never worried about David's abilities and professionalism and he did an excellent job as Public Affairs Director. He was anxious to ensure that the FA were pro-active in media affairs and also that the FA should be on the front foot rather than, as was so often the case, on the defence.

Through his work with television, which was much broader based than just sport, he had good political contacts which proved to be invaluable. From a personal point of view he did not actually provide very much personal guidance for me in my dealings before the television cameras. I was frequently criticised for being dour and unsmiling, but his only advice to me was: 'When you are in front of the television cameras, don't lean forward, sit back.'

After our difficult start, we eventually worked reasonably well together, but it was never quite as it should have been after my initial protestations about his appointment which he would have known about from his neighbour Bert. My position was similar to a football manager who wants his own people around him. David Davies quite patently was not one of mine. I regarded the management of the FA as my team, my right hand people.

There were never any violent disagreements but, understandably, we never became close. I always thought of him as a very ambitious man, but whether he was looking for my job I never knew. When I left, he quickly took it on a temporary basis and he did not seem to dislike the opportunity which my enforced resignation afforded him. But he needed to overcome the reservations of a number of the rank and file Councillors who thought him just a little bit too smarmy and insufficiently committed to the smaller competitions.

David telephoned me as I was on my way home the night I departed. He said he was very sorry about it all and did not think that there was anything he could have done to avoid it. A couple of months later he wrote to me thanking me for everything I had done for him. I do not think it was insincere, but the scars I was bearing from my leaving made it a difficult letter to accept.

There are some strong people lurking around the dark corners of the corridors of power, not always those holding the titles or positions you would expect from such men.

Ken Bates, the controversial Chelsea supremo, was and is never short of a word or three. He has always been outspoken about anything close to his heart, but that outspokenness masks a shrewdness and cunning which are seldom out-thought. You take him on at your peril, as many journalists have discovered to their cost. I also witnessed his sensitivity – he cried when a much loved pet died.

He maintained his position as a Council member notwithstanding that Chelsea were fined £150,000 for paying unauthorised inducements to players. He announced that he would not appeal against the decision of the Football League Commission, because any appeal would not be conducted fairly. He followed this up by adding that he wanted to bring out into the open how iniquitous the Football League was. He wanted big changes, he said, and was prepared to fight for them. He refused to resign from the Management Committee after what he felt was a travesty of a vicious and vindictive penalty.

I pointed out to him from the Football Association that it was not awfully good for a figure like him to be criticising the League Management Committee in this way, but he said that he was merely responding to press hounding and that he would recommend changes to the constitution of the Football League.

He was never one to pull punches, particularly insofar as the FA staff were concerned. In 1993 he said Charles Hughes was a an exponent of kick and rush football while later, when discussing the National Stadium, he accused me and my colleagues of having a cosy relationship with the English Sports Council. This was far from the case as we had been fiercely fighting some of the Sports Council's more bureaucratic requirements.

He complained about the Council members going to Italy in 1990 for the World Cup semi-final. He protested to Sir John Quinton, then the Chairman of the FA Premier League, when the FA wrote to the League inviting an equity shareholding in the new National Stadium, even though his colleague on the stadium committee, Dave Richards, was in favour of taking a stake.

Sir John told me that Bates was unhappy with Peter Leaver expanding his staff. This rang true because he was always against what he saw as empire building. Nic Coward, our Company Secretary, was said to be reeling under Bates' onslaught when Bates complained to Quinton about the equity invitation. Nic never did reel; he found it amusing and became a real asset to the FA after joining Lancaster Gate from Freshfields, the FA's prestigious legal advisors.

Bates often used his notes in the Chelsea programme to express his opinions and, more often than not, to vent his spleen. Many from all sections of the game suffered his venomous remarks and the FA were a regular target. He said in his programme notes that Euro 96 had been a financial disaster for the FA, but when we made a presentation to explain the figures he did not bother staying to listen to the story of how the tournament had been an outstanding success for the member nations.

Another of his hobby horses was 'unnecessary' international matches, although how any England coach can prepare for competition without playing a few friendly matches is beyond me. With fewer and fewer English players appearing for Chelsea, he turned his attentions to UEFA and FIFA.

Never was his direct style more in evidence than when he said: 'Matthew Harding thinks he can do a Franny Lee. Well, he can go fuck himself because I am tougher than Peter Swales.'

Memorably, Bates wrote to the Managing Director of Wembley Stadium in 1998 and said that we all had to 'stop pissing about.' In the end he received the backing of most because people realised that he was simply cutting through the red tape. His style was epitomised at an early meeting to discuss the National Stadium. All the relevant staff members and advisors were present, but when Michael Cunnah attempted to start with an up to date report, Bates insisted on everybody but the Council members being thrown out of the room. As Chief Executive I took exception to being treated like, in one of Bates' own terms, an office boy, and it was only when he rang the next day to explain he was really getting at Keith Wiseman's style of proceeding that the matter was smoothed over. He had his way as Keith nominated him as Chairman of the Committee!

Irving Scholar, formerly the Chairman of Spurs, was a member of the FA Council as a representative of a particular group of clubs in the South and East. I had a big bust-up with him once when he demanded to see the television contracts. He said that as a member of the Council and a Director of the company he was entitled to see them, but I pointed out that as a director of Spurs there was a conflict of interest. He eventually received copies, but only some time later after a protracted argument.

This row illustrated a point which many people in football were slow to recognise, the conflicts of interest. It came up in the National Stadium debate when Arsenal were interested in purchasing Wembley and David Dein was prevented from attending Executive Committee discussions because of his dual interests.

I think Arsenal were serious about moving from Highbury, where they were unable to redevelop, and they were encouraged by Wembley director Jarvis Astaire who disliked the FA and wanted to sell to Lancaster Gate only over his dead body. He had this emotional attachment to Wembley, regarding it as his baby. Even at the last minute he tried to introduce an American bidder into the equation when the deal had been settled with the FA and the Sports Council.

I had quite an argument in the Finance Committee at the 1998 summer meeting. It was only a routine gathering to elect the chairman and vice chairman for the following year and was scheduled to last ten minutes in the programme of meetings for that morning. However, the members wanted to hear from the staff what progress was being made with the National Stadium. The Chairman Sir David Hill-Wood was quite upset when I suggested that David Dein should leave the room while it was discussed. It was an astonishing reaction as David had already volunteered to absent himself whenever the National Stadium was discussed. Fortunately the other members of the committee supported me and David retired. Then Noel White complained about my buying space in the national press to thank the fans who had supported England in France. He thought a comment from Glenn Hoddle would have been sufficient, whereas I had insisted upon a more fulsome tribute on behalf of the whole FA. Maybe seeds were sewn then that were to be reaped at a later date.

The National Stadium was an intriguing issue. Originally the Premier League, via Rick Parry, wanted to invest money in the new National Stadium as a commercial exercise. Sir John Hall was chairman of the Millennium Commission and thought that there was some money to be obtained from there. In the event the Government decided it should be the Sports Council that would help bring about the new stadium and the FA, the Premier League and the Football League entered into talks with them.

We then invited tenders from interested parties and received five applications from Bradford, Manchester, Birmingham, Sheffield and Wembley. There was certainly no better site than Wembley in the South east.

Birmingham was ruled out because it was thought that they would have planning problems from the Solihull Council on their site at the NEC and there was also the problem with the motorway system which tended to clog up when there were big events in the Midlands. The Bradford and Sheffield proposals did not go very far and it left us with a shortlist of Manchester and Wembley.

Football in a rare united voice insisted on Wembley rather than Manchester. Wembley has the infrastructure and the rail system. It also has years of experience in shifting the number of people around despite the complaints about the traffic. It also had the magic of the Wembley name, which was highly marketable worldwide and whether we like it or not, it is in the high-earning South East, making it a better commercial proposition.

The FA were contracted to Wembley up to the year 2002 and the negotiations to persuade Wembley to sell their stadium proved to be very difficult. The Sports Council announced a grant of £120 million for a new stadium but unfortunately £103 million of that was needed to buy out Wembley.

The Sports Council were very slow-moving and at one meeting 34 people attended! It was even worse than the FA and maybe we should have put them all in a room together and let them fight it out.

We tried to persuade the Government to help us to do the entire project ourselves, but Heritage Minister Chris Smith was not awfully interested and instructed Sports Minister Tony Banks to tell us to stick with the Sports Council, who seemed to want a veto over the FA's ticket prices and television contracts.

They had this requirement that there must be public access. What does that mean? I can only suppose that it means affordable ticket prices and people should see the games on television, but it smacked of unnecessary interference in how we ran our business.

The situation desperately needed a character like Ken Bates to bulldoze it through and he responded by setting up meetings with Wembley on his own. He just ploughed ahead, trying to get the thing sorted in his role as chairman of the National Stadium Shadow Board.

Keith Wiseman thought that he was the right man to put a bomb under the Sports Council and I believe that Ken did a good job in getting that through. It certainly progressed a great deal more quickly than had it meandered through the usual channels.

It was extremely difficult to work with the Sports Council, as they displayed when they produced a 52 page framework agreement for the lottery money. As if this was not enough, they then issued a nine page clarification of their original 52-page document as they tried to protect the public money they were contributing to the project. The FA's bureaucracy had found a rival!

One of the Sports Council's great concerns was over Manchester, knowing that they had to build a new stadium for the Commonwealth Games. They kept asking us why we did not take our events to the North West, to which we replied that they already had a good football stadium in Manchester called Old Trafford, and in any event, if we were putting money into Wembley, we would want to make it work and take most of our events there. We were more than prepared to take one international match a year to the provinces in order to allow fans in other parts of the country to watch England more easily, but the new venture had to be commercially viable.

The number of interlocking contracts needed to knock down the old stadium and build a new one was huge and without the much-maligned Ken Bates, they would probably still be wading through the red tape.

Doug Ellis of Aston Villa was a man who was difficult to dislike. He was so transparent that I could always tell what he was thinking and he was easily upset, as he showed when he was not invited to the press conference to announce the appointment of Technical Director Howard Wilkinson. But Doug was a superb businessman with his heart and his wallet in Aston Villa and he has done a remarkable job for the club. It is just that when it comes to debating national issues, he brings a narrow viewpoint.

He can also, like Bates, be somewhat outspoken, and when Terry Venables resigned from the England job, he said on television that football managers are like women, saying 'no' when they meant 'yes'. How he got away with that one, I will never know. No one took him up on it apart from two lines in one newspaper, and that was it. Can you imagine what would have happened if I or Glenn Hoddle had said the same thing? We would have been hounded from pillar to post, and rightly so.

Looking for something to keep the Council members occupied, I once organised a penalty competition at York during a summer meeting. Twenty or so took part shooting in with Yours Truly in goal. It took me a long while to live it down after Doug won the shoot-out, scoring four out of five past me. He was wearing his best patent leather shoes and toe-poked the first two into the corner of the net before I was ready. The others were convinced that it was a fix. I scoured the city that afternoon to come up with a certificate which was presented to him at dinner that evening. He was as pleased as Punch.

Trevor Phillips was another fascinating character; he was brought in from the Football League to professionalise the commercial activities which were so important to funding the grass roots.

Trevor delivered the first package of sponsors in 1994, having first re-negotiated the ground advertising rights back from Wembley so that we could see to the needs of our sponsors. He managed to get Wembley to agree to split the fees and then set about winning the co-operation of the international players taking over the players' pool from Jon Smith of First Artist Management.

He tried to persuade his former League colleagues to join the FA in commercial activities in 1995, but the intervention of the Premier League led to the League signing their own television contract which upset a lot of their leading clubs. Trevor found it difficult to take the Executive Committee along in this because Keith Wiseman, then of the Premier League, and Gordon McKeag of the Football League, were privy to his discussions on tactics in the Executive Committee.

Trevor's downside was that he upset people by his plain speaking. He did not want to be perceived as an FA person and this often came across as lack of loyalty to his colleagues in management who thought we should be working as a team. He would denigrate the FA publicly at any opportunity which we thought was unprofessional. Moreover he was not averse to criticising his own colleagues to the Chairman of the Commercial Committee, Jack Wiseman.

He eventually landed himself with a very hairy situation over ticketing arrangements for Euro 96. Tickets were coming onto the market without the knowledge of Pat Smith and Glen Kirton, who were organising the tournament, and the police were called in to investigate. It transpired that Synchro Systems, the contractors for the supply of tickets, had been allowing the tickets to go out to hospitality companies on the say-so of Trevor Phillips, who had been trying to maximise the sales.

With the right hand not knowing what the left was doing, the police very publicly raided premises including the prestigious Cafe Royal in the heart of London, believing that the tickets being sold were dishonestly handled. It caused massive embarrassment for some very respectable and high profile people and for the Football Association when Synchro Systems said that they had been authorised by Trevor Phillips to release the tickets.

Trevor Phillips had not told his colleagues that he had set this train of events in progress and because of the embarrassment he had caused at Lancaster Gate, he had to go.

Phillip Carling came in from his job as marketing manager at Arsenal to succeed Trevor. His first task was to re-negotiate the four year contracts expiring in 1998 which he did successfully, uplifting the income to above £50 million, but in so doing he managed to upset the Premier League by taking the arrangements with England players to the next stage. There was always the danger that the activities of their players, particularly those wearing their England shirts, could be used to ambush the sponsors of the FA, so Phil decided to buy out their image rights as England players for a sum in excess of £2 million a year. The Premier League complained, because in their eyes they were their players and they didn't think it right that we should be paying this amount of money direct to the players' pool.

In reality, what the Premier League should have been doing was re-negotiating their full-time contracts with the players if they wanted to control this aspect. They would then be able to claim the money back from the FA to offset the wages. But I could never see the players agreeing to this.

What I was trying to do throughout my time with the FA was insert a bit of steel into the organisation. By its very nature it is a large, complex organisation with authority vested in different areas and as such was very easily deflected. On any major issue you could have someone disaffected standing up and complaining and the tendency of the top table was to respond by taking the matter back and looking at it again.

I tried hard to dispel the notion that the FA were a soft touch. The Centres of Excellence changes which Charles Hughes, the Director of Coaching, recommended in the Blueprint in 1991 were not implemented for another three years. We were unable to get the players in at a younger age – as they do in the other countries in Western Europe – and employ more time coaching them because of internal arguments within the game, notably with the English Schools FA. The delay and procrastination needed to end; we needed to be firmer in the principles we espoused.

The idea of the Football Association instigating a £1 million court case over the establishment of the Premier League would not have been countenanced previously, but I managed to get everyone to agree to it. Pat Smith and I rang all the Council members and told them it was crucial for the FA not to be diverted from the policy on which they had agreed, and they were all happy with what we were doing.

The appointment of a Technical Director was another example of the FA moving forward and being modernised. Before Howard Wilkinson's arrival in 1997, the FA Coaching scheme under Charles Hughes suffered because of his unpopularity in the professional game. They regarded him as a remote and distant figure who never came down from his ivory tower at Lancaster Gate to watch games. He, for his part, thought that much of the professional game was riddled by cheating. And so a gap opened up between the FA coaching department and the League clubs.

The gulf was exacerbated by the increasing pressures on managers. In previous times all the managers would want to take time off at the end of the season to go to Lilleshall and discuss coaching with the likes of Walter Winterbottom, Allen Wade and Malcolm Allison. Latterly they were not interested. The publication of Charles' book *The Winning Formula*, including his use of statistics designed to prove that more goals were scored from moves of five passes or fewer, reinforced his reputation for route one football.

There were many contradictions about Charles Hughes. If you analyse the recommendations he brought forward and laid them alongside those of Howard Wilkinson seven years later, you would find very few differences in principle. But the sad fact was that he was not acceptable to the clubs, and he did not communicate well. He believed in direct play, pressing and getting forward at the first opportunity; there wasn't much wrong with that as a tactic, but his reliance on statistics led to his views being over-simplified.

Charles was naive in the extreme if he did not realise that his comment would not be used to attack the then England manager Graham Taylor when he said towards the end of Taylor's reign: 'Positive thinking and single-mindedness of purpose are the hallmarks of international management. Changing both the method and the players compounds the problem.'

I did my best for him, and in a bid to improve his standing amongst the media, I arranged for all the leading football writers to listen to him for a couple of hours. He made a big impression, but it did not have a lasting effect.

Had Bobby Robson stayed after the 1990 World Cup, Charles Hughes' career at the FA may have taken a different path. Bobby could see Charles' faults, but could also see the good points in the man and the two enjoyed healthy arguments about the game they both loved even though they were so opposite in so many ways.

When Bobby left, I recommended that Charles be appointed Director, having been Bob's assistant. But he never got to grips with the modern game or, more accurately, the people in it. Gordon Taylor of the PFA was his biggest critic. He complained vehemently that Charles ignored the professionals in favour of schoolteachers. Charles disputed this, but when we went out of the World Cup in 1993, Gordon produced his own blueprint for coaching called *a Kick in the Right Direction* which contained some very strong criticisms of Charles and his teachings.

I spent a lot of time with the current Liverpool manager Gérard Houllier in 1994 during the USA World Cup and I asked both him and Jozef Venglos, now at Celtic and one-time Aston Villa manager, what was the biggest problem in English football. Both said quite independently that it was the gulf between the clubs and the FA coaches. There was no doubt we were two separate armies (three, if the England team were included).

Houllier and I were based in San Francisco and, with the stadium at Stanford University 20 miles away, we used to travel together every day in a transit van. Gérard invariably went to sleep until the San Francisco mists cleared, but towards the end of our time there I told him he had to forgo his sleep because I wanted to sit in the back with him and go through how they developed their football in France. He brought out his briefcase and went through the entire profile from the age the clubs could sign their youngsters, the relationship between the clubs and how they financed their Clairefontaine training centre in Paris.

Based on that conversation I wrote a report which included a job specification for a Technical Director with three main aims: to integrate the development and community schemes with the excellence programme; to integrate the clubs and the FA; and to integrate the International department and the Coaching department at Lancaster Gate, which were increasingly separate armies going down different roads.

The report was duly accepted and, inevitably, we set up a small committee to recruit a Technical Director, consisting of Jimmy Armfield, who had become our international coach head-hunter, the well-versed Jimmy Hill, myself and Rick Parry. Eager to obtain the best views possible, we talked to Roy Hodgson, who had great experience of working abroad, about the concept, and to former Scotland manager Andy Roxburgh, upsetting Lennart Johansson in the process because he thought we were trying to steal UEFA's Technical Director. To be truthful, we would have taken him like a shot given the chance, but I doubt whether he wanted to move to England at that time. Hodgson was also happy in charge of the Swiss team, but he gave us some interesting tips.

I invited Gérard Houllier over to England both as a candidate for the job and to discuss the parameters further to our conversation on the roads in California. He is such a nice man, he finds it difficult to say no to anybody. For a while we thought we might lure him, as he is such an Anglophile and loves it here. But he wasn't going to leave France two years before the World Cup when he was so heavily involved. He eventually talked to both Sheffield Wednesday and Celtic before going to Anfield in 1998.

We also spoke to Crewe Alexandra's Dario Gradi who had built himself such a reputation for nurturing young talent, but he was not keen to work in committee rooms. He preferred to be out on the training ground in his tracksuit.

Another top coach who interested us was David Pleat but we were refused permission by the Sheffield Wednesday Chairman and FA Executive Committee member Dave Richards. Pleat is a deep thinker about the game, well respected by his fellow professionals and by the public through his work on radio and television. Richards' excuse was that they could not do without him, that he was so valuable to them and that he was just settling in. Then they sacked him a few games into the new season. Funny game, football.

Howard Wilkinson came for an interview but did not seem as though he really wanted it at that time as he was settled at Leeds. He was also wary of the FA structure and he was much less convincing at that time than when we discussed the job with him two years later.

We had to put the search on the back burner because Terry Venables left the England coaching job and we spent the first half of 1996 making the appointment of Glenn Hoddle. We came back to Technical Director at the end of the year, appointing Howard on 1 January 1997. He remarked when he took over as the caretaker manager for the friendly against France in 1999 that he was glad that I had persuaded him not to take the Manchester City job back then, but to join the FA instead.

He is doing an excellent job. His *Charter for Quality*, the setting up of the academies and his general progress have been excellent. He was the first and only choice when we came back.

We had to change the format of the FA Cup draw in order to satisfy our sponsors. I thought it was a good idea to have personalities involved in a live event, as I was never convinced that the Cup draw itself made for good television anyway, and to my mind the drama was simply in anticipating who your team was going to pull out of the bag.

Everyone speaks fondly of the old days of the Monday lunchtime draw on radio when Bryon Butler would walk solemnly into the Council Chamber at Lancaster Gate and announce in hushed tones that the next voice you would hear would be the secretary of the Association, Ted Croker. But the audience statistics never in reality reflected the affection with which people nostalgically look back on the radio draw.

The first celebrities to perform were Denis Law and Terry Venables and they gave the new format a flying start, although they did ham it up a bit, rather like a cabaret act taking us from one extreme to another, from two old men, not exactly sitting in deck chairs, to these two lively characters.

One of the last I was involved in was with old Liverpool and Scotland room mates Graeme Souness and Kenny Dalglish, who tried to convince me that there was a ball missing when the last tie was being drawn. I saw my whole FA future flash before my eyes in front of millions of viewers. As it turned out, it would have been a short flash as my FA future was not to be very long anyway.

The Spurs French star David Ginola was very charming with the studio audience. That day the audience was not the usual organised group, perhaps because this was a short draw late in the season. I had brought in one of my many football teams and, as with almost any group of supporters, there were a fair number of Geordies present who were delighted to meet Ginola.

The easiest draws were, perhaps somewhat surprisingly, with George Best and Rodney Marsh at Sky who performed the draw a number of times in the early part of the season. They were very professional to work with and it makes a great difference to have someone alongside who is not going to make a mess of something which is very important to a lot of people. While Best and Marsh were the easiest to work with, the most enjoyable pairing from a personal point of view was that of Nat Lofthouse and Sir Tom Finney. These two old professionals are lovely, warm characters who came across superbly to the viewers.

Sadly, that could not be said for the then unreformed Arsenal captain Tony Adams. Somebody should have realised that Sunday afternoon was not the best time to catch him for an event like this. He arrived without a tie and caused one or two anxious moments by putting everyone on edge. Poor Garry Richardson was doing the presenting and when we had a run-through, Adams inquired if he was going to ask him the size of his penis. Fortunately, we came through the live broadcast without any undue upsets, but it was a difficult afternoon for everyone. I am very pleased that Tony has been able to tackle his problems so successfully since then for, without the drink, like George Best, he is a really nice person and an honest professional.

Martin Peters, one of the 1966 World Cup heroes, gave me the jitters when he left two balls hidden in the folds of the famous velvet bag. Fortunately I retrieved the error before Geoff Hurst commenced the draw.

I was always concerned about the possibility of a cock-up in the live FA Cup draw – before my time at the FA, Middlesbrough were ostensibly drawn twice on one memorable occasion – but my anxiety to avoid mistakes was even greater at the FA Cup Final, which was shown throughout the world.

Disaster almost occurred in 1995 when our heir to the throne Prince Charles, not noted for his interest in football, tried to give the FA Cup to losing captain Steve Bruce of Manchester United instead of the victorious Everton captain Dave Watson. Bruce, who had been substituted by Manchester United, led his team up first as the losers and the Prince of Wales immediately reached out for the trophy to give to the losing captain, despite the blue and white ribbons and the instructions on the procedure given to him beforehand. For a moment we wrestled with the famous trophy as I held firmly onto the top of the Cup to stop him giving it to Bruce before he realised what I was about. I suppose that the booklets we sent to the Palace are not read by the Prince and, perhaps, the information not passed on by those who did.

Last up the stairs was successful Everton manager Joe Royle and when the Prince congratulated him Joe could not resist telling him that he was a member of his family but the Prince, not having the vaguest clue who he was, totally ignored the comment Joe passed. I could not help but remark that it was another one which had been totally wasted.

Before I joined the FA there was another close shave. Again Manchester United and Everton were involved, but this time it was United who won in 1985 despite having Kevin Moran sent off by referee Peter Willis – the first dismissal in 104 Finals. An extra-time goal by the young Irishman Norman Whiteside settled the game and this time it was Manchester United who came up the steps last, including substitute Mike Duxbury but minus the disgraced Moran.

The Royal Box had emptied when my guest, Fred Eyre, the noted raconteur, author and failed footballer, spotted that the Heinz Baked Beans carton containing Moran's medal had been left on the ledge. Anyone could have taken the precious medal and Fred gleefully took it downstairs to the appropriate authority. He could not hide his disappointment as he thought the medals should have been carried up on purple velvet.

I left Lancaster Gate in the same way I had entered ten years earlier – fired with enthusiasm! I had professionalised the organisation in the most vital areas of commerce, finance, the technical development of players and public relations.

The FA, with the PFA, had led important initiatives to reduce the unsavoury examples of racism which had permeated the game. We had introduced higher levels of medical education and care of young players, particularly with the testing of all YTS players for heart defects. And significant progress had been made to develop girls' and women's football since the FA took over from the Women's Football Association in 1993.

But the biggest upheaval in the game's history had been the advent of the FA Premier League.

CHAPTER FIVE

Crock of Gold

The Football Association Premier League finally and officially came into being on 23 September 1991 when an historic document was signed by the Football Association, the then Division One clubs and the Football League.

Even then there were obstacles strewn in the way as Gordon McKeag said that the document needed to be ratified by the full Council. But fortunately the FA's Deputy Chief Executive Pat Smith, who was attending on my behalf as I was away at a UEFA meeting in Montreux, was able to verify that we already had authority to conclude negotiations.

David Dein and Rick Parry promptly cracked opened a bottle of champagne in White's Hotel, saying: 'It's a momentous day.' But Bill Fox, the then President of the Football League, gloomily responded: 'No it isn't, it's another bloody cock-up.'

Those few brief words just about summed up the strife that had bedevilled the discussions for over a year with football split in two over the proposed changes by court action, lawyers, in-fighting and insults.

I was described as both a 'Hitler' and a 'Rapist' and there were many old friendships that would never be the same again.

But, for the future of football in England, the formation of the FA Premier League was absolutely essential and its subsequent success speaks for itself.

To trace the origins of the Premier League, historians would have to go back to the terrible disaster at Hillsborough, the Lord Justice Taylor Report which followed it and, strangely, the issue over Swindon Town and illegal payments.

While attention was distracted by the 1990 World Cup in Italy, the Management Committee of the Football League held a commission which relegated Swindon, newly promoted to Division One, down to Division Three. The club had pleaded guilty to over 30 charges and there was a widespread feeling in the higher echelons of the League that they had cheated their way to the top by offering secret inducements to players.

When the appeal came up in July there was no one from the Football League available to sit on the Board of Appeal which consisted of three FA people. The Board decided to restore Swindon to Division Two.

The affair descended into farce right down to a brown envelope containing £150 in cash given to the club secretary Dave King to keep him quiet.

He promptly passed it on to club director and staunch FA man Lionel Smart who, in turn, gave it to me. There was little I could do with it other than pass the parcel on to the Secretary of the Football League David Dent. I am still waiting for the brown envelope to come back and one day I will ask whether the stories of the improved League staff party were true.

But while that episode was amusing, the rest was not and had great repercussions. Gordon McKeag was voted off the Executive Committee at the summer meeting that year and lost the vice chairmanship of the prestigious Challenge Cup Committee for a period.

At the same time that leading officials were falling out over the Swindon business, there was another controversy raging over the size of the 20-club First Division. Far from wanting to reduce it further to a manageable 18, the Football League wanted to increase it back to 22 clubs.

The Management Committee meeting held in June were not in favour of the increase, but by the time of the Extraordinary General Meeting in August, enough lobbying had been done by Ken Bates and Ron Noades, and the committee suddenly dropped their opposition with only Arsenal, Spurs and Manchester United voting against. The clubs claimed that they needed the fixtures to fund the recommendations of the Taylor Report, but I saw this as a retrograde step.

I believed it was no coincidence that England had reached the World Cup semi-finals at a time when there were fewer clubs in Division One.

PFA Chief Executive Gordon Taylor agreed with me that it was wrong to go back to 22 clubs but, sadly, he failed to argue the case strongly enough. I believe now that had we battled it together, we would have won the day. Gordon, when he makes a stand on something, usually has a significant effect on the debate, but in this instance it was muted and therefore lost.

Ken Bates threatened to boycott the FA Cup if we did not sanction the increase. Bill Fox, in his role as the President of the League, threatened disaffiliation from the FA if we blocked it. This serious threat he was to repeat later over the Premier League.

This 22 club First Division was a real issue, as was the resentment over the Swindon case which was keenly felt by Bill Fox and his colleagues. Fox was in Italy at the World Cup with us when the news of Swindon's reinstatement came through and he went ballistic on hearing that Swindon had, in effect, stayed where they were.

Bill Fox had supported my efforts to bring in a streamlined Board of Directors at Lancaster Gate, but he and his colleagues were not prepared to wait forever for change. Stimulated by disputes over Swindon, the size of Division One, payment by the FA for free Saturdays prior to international matches and the distribution of money received from television, Arthur Sandford, Trevor Phillips (then at the League) and Bill Fox came up with the idea to form a joint Board comprising equal numbers of FA and League representatives. They said if we could not agree, we should go to arbitration under Minister for Sport, Robert Atkins. That suggestion went down like a lead balloon at Lancaster Gate.

The League also planned a competition to replace the FA Cup but, unfortunately for them, their secret was discovered at birth before they had time to develop it.

It was Vaudeville farce rather than high drama as Aston Villa Chairman Doug Ellis had scribbled the details on the back of an envelope, along with the question of how much notice the clubs needed to give in order that they could leave the FA Cup.

Doug was no James Bond and, unfortunately for him and his co-conspirators, he left the envelope behind in, of all places, our reception at Lancaster Gate. Not only that, but it was picked up by a journalist who handed it to me. He asked if I knew whose writing it was and I said it looked suspiciously like that of Doug Ellis and, indeed, this was confirmed for on the other side of the envelope was his name and address!

The League entitled their joint Board proposal 'One game, One team, One voice'. We thought it all a little naive and, far from one voice, they were trying to blur the roles between us. The FA and the League were distinct organisations with their own individual roles.

Robert Atkins, who knew little about the game or its administrative workings, asked how he could deal with two governing bodies. I reminded him that there was only one ruling body and that the League, as strong as it was, was simply one organisation under the FA's large umbrella.

I thought the League's plan was a hastily hatched curate's egg. When they launched it, Arthur Sandford made some comments on the FA disciplinary system, saying that the modern trend to litigation must be resisted. He quickly forgot this when the League sued the FA six months later.

Bates upset the Council members again when he called the armed services a rag-bag collection while complaining about all the different areas of representation on the FA Council. This did not go down well amongst the older members who valued their connection with the forces. I told him that his comments had caused great offence and he said that it was my fault for releasing a letter to Arthur Sandford to the press!

I gathered together some senior members of the FA staff, Pat Smith, Mark Day and Charles Hughes, to draw up our own blueprint for the future of the game. We produced our wish list, wanting more free Saturdays for the international team and also the absolute right to deduct points as we had done with Arsenal and Manchester United, in the event of serious indiscipline by players. Needless to say, we also wanted Division One to come back down to 20 clubs and the system of developing young players was in urgent need of reform.

As the row rumbled on, Robert Atkins threatened that the reduction in pools betting duty would not be extended beyond 1995, saying that he would let it run out and not allow it to carry on for the full ten years to help clubs comply with the Taylor report unless we sorted things out. It seemed that this Member of Parliament for Ribble had been successfully lobbied first by the Football League and we were paying the price for being a bit slow. But he was not a football man and we hadn't come across him before.

Out of all of this controversy the Premier League surfaced. It came to light when Noel White of Liverpool and David Dein of Arsenal visited Bert Millichip on 6 December 1990. They were uneasy about the power sharing proposals which the Football League had put forward to the FA and they were worried about the effects of the Lord Justice Taylor Report which obliged clubs to invest massively in their grounds. They could not see a way for the major clubs to generate the revenue required under the existing Football League structure.

Exactly a week later I announced the *Blueprint for the Future of Football*. This was designed to cover every aspect of the game, not just the power-sharing proposals previously put forward. I said that unless we planned properly for the future, the benefits of the existing post-World Cup boom would be short-lived. One of the major failings of the game was its lack of strategic planning. The pace of change was constantly increasing, yet our game was bereft of an overall view which the blueprint would provide. I was proposing to the FA that such a blueprint be drawn up as soon as possible.

I announced that the blueprint would include the following key elements:

- A national plan for stadia to comply with the Taylor Report.
- A separate limited company to exploit the commercial properties of the FA for the benefit of the grass roots.
- A Junior England Club.
- A full scale review of the development programme with regard to the best young players.
- The expansion of community activity.

The snowball had begun its descent downhill and three days later, Bert Millichip, as Chairman of the Football Association and Bill Fox, the President of the Football League, were called in to see Robert Atkins as a matter of some urgency. The Minister had tended to side with the Football League in their claim for joint power sharing and so Sir Bert was forced to agree to the League going round the country meeting the Counties to explain their claim for a joint board.

At the Executive Committee meeting that day it was quickly decided that the FA blueprint must go ahead, whatever the cost.

I saw Noel White and David Dein on the same day and we rapidly reached the conclusion that we needed some outside help on the project to set up a new League. Obviously I saw the new Premier League as being central to the blueprint and so I recruited Rick Parry whom I had known from his previous consultancy work for the Football League Management Committee. I saw Rick as a good listener with a wry sense of humour, sometimes quite cutting, and he had done a good job when he headed up the Manchester Olympic bid. I thought he would bring financial expertise to the discussions, he would be at arm's length and would not be seen as the FA doing everything themselves. Rick Parry had the ability to bring objectivity to the situation.

The biggest concern at this stage for Noel and David was the Football League's three year notice rule and whether it was legally enforceable. I was able to tell them that the regulation had certainly been sanctioned by the FA.

There was a great difficulty in disentangling the clubs from the Football League. They had pension schemes, television contracts and a tremendous number of commitments to contend with, not least the League's arrangements with the PFA.

David and Noel met Rick Parry for the first time and any initial reservations were quickly dispelled as Rick began to organise meetings of a few top clubs to discuss the establishment of the Premier League.

The clubs contacted were keen and soon Everton, Arsenal, Manchester United, Spurs and Liverpool demonstrated their eagerness to take up the cause.

The rationale for the Premier League was:

- Fewer games for the top clubs and players.
- Better preparation for the England players.
- Stronger commercial activities.
- Better arrangements for developing young players.
- Compulsory qualifications for managers.
- The end of the power struggle between the FA and the League.

The Football League voting system was geared towards keeping the status quo. The Management Committee make-up reflected the voting structure, represented self-interest and did not provide independent leadership.

Both Rick Parry and I thought that we could improve on the Football League because there were so many vested interests and a serious lack of independent direction. As an example I had written to Arthur Sandford, Chief Executive of the League, early in 1990 pressing for improvements to the system of developing talented young players. There was no common policy in the game. However, the League set up their own working party and there was no progress whatsoever in probably the most important aspect of the game's future. Moreover, the League were ambivalent towards the National School. It was obvious that you could not have Manchester United trying to operate at the same pace as Halifax Town as neither would be happy.

At the same time that the Premier League talks were being held secretly, the Football League were going round the counties in February and March. At the meeting I attended in Sheffield I asked Arthur Sandford whether he had prepared regulations giving authority to his representatives, because they were demanding a joint Board with five from the Football Association and five from the Football League. The authority from within the League needed to be transferred to those five people. All he could say in response was that the general approach had been discussed in regional meetings, so it was clear he did not have the authority from the big clubs for power to be vested in their five representatives.

We were meeting the Executive Committee in session without Bill Fox, the President of the League, and resisting their claims without divulging that we had the Premier League as part of the blueprint. The big clubs wanted us to take the lead over the three-year rule, but to do that I needed to have the clubs under the FA's umbrella.

We produced an interim report on the Premier League in March which was submitted to the five clubs. The idea was to overrule regulation ten, the three year rule, and phase the top division down to 18 clubs as soon as possible. We also recommended that all clubs in the Premier League should have a seat on the FA Council.

We did not believe that the clubs in the Football League would be disadvantaged financially. We reckoned that the money they lost – around £3 million a year – would be made up quite easily. This proved accurate because the League were later able to negotiate their own contracts with television. All was falling nicely into place and we paid a visit to Bert Millichip towards the end of March to give him a full briefing. He agreed to an announcement about the Premier League. Bert said he would be happy if at least half the First Division clubs were interested.

I went to watch Norwich City play Manchester United on 30 March at Carrow Road. Chairman Robert Chase was enthusiastic, as was

Manchester City's Peter Swales whom I also saw the same weekend.

Doug Ellis added Aston Villa's name to the growing list. Last time they talked about a Premier League, he said, they wanted to do it on club criteria and not playing performance. Not surprisingly the Midlands club were near the bottom of the table at that time!

It was not solely the clubs who needed to be brought up to speed. I informed Littlewoods Pools and they were comfortable with the developments. I also tried to tell the Minister for Sport, but he was not particularly interested and said he was going off on holiday. Kenneth Clarke had told him to stay out of football politics. Probably not a moment too soon.

We finally made it public with an announcement to the press on 5 April 1991. Some of the football writers were sceptical as to whether the clubs would want to move to the FA Premier League.

We overcame another potential hurdle when Richard Faulkner of the Football Trust said that there were no problems with Premier League clubs enjoying Trust grants although, he added, they would have to clear it with the Treasury who had relaxed the pool betting duty.

We favoured adopting the German system where the League is an integral part of the FA. It did not come about for a number of reasons. We were not able to give the Premier League the number of seats on the Council that we had envisaged as the Council would not concede much influence.

In any event, many club chairmen, like Ian Stott of Oldham argued against their becoming an integral part of the FA.

Inevitably, one of the main issues was the size of the Premier League. The blueprint had clearly laid down 18 as the optimum number but, unfortunately, at the only meeting Bert Millichip attended with the First Division clubs in May 1991, he kicked the door wide open when he said that the size was up to the clubs themselves. This destroyed our negotiating position. We could have insisted on 18 clubs if that is what we wanted. They say size isn't everything. It might have been in this case. The smaller the better.

We put the Premier League proposals to a special Council meeting which had been called to discuss the Football League proposals for power sharing. We changed the agenda and put the Premier League first. That went through quite easily because we had briefed the County members at a private meeting the night before. The Football League proposals sank without trace.

Bill Fox and Maxwell Holmes of Leeds, along with Ian Stott, voted against the Premier League out of loyalty to their Management Committee colleagues. Trevor Phillips accused us of stealing their plans and said they had kicked a sleeping dog when they published their power-sharing proposals. Now it was barking, he asked, would it sit down or jump up and bite them in the face?

Phillips' position was that the Football League could be restructured to operate the Premier League themselves. He also questioned the FA's ability to dispense justice whilst managing a League.

We met David Dent and Arthur Sandford. The League Management Committee had asked Arthur to do a full report and he asked whether the Premier League was provisional or definite. I assured him it was definite. David found it difficult to accept, saying that some of our own Councillors whom he had approached knew nothing about it.

Gordon Taylor wanted to ensure that we had promotion and relegation of two up and two down as the major clubs had initially wanted just one. He expressed his concern over a number of issues. He naturally wanted to preserve the PFA's television money and he very much wanted the PFA to be involved in the running of the new League. The pension and insurance schemes needed to be safegaurded and Gordon was at pains to protect the finances of the Football League. We felt that we could probably meet him quite easily on all these points.

Arthur Sandford complained about lack of consultation and threatened claims for damages against clubs which left without giving the three years' notice.

With so much infighting it was inevitable that the legal profession would become an integral and expensive part of the affair and we soon became involved in some fairly heavy deliberations.

I doubted whether the Football League would win a case against us, but they could cause an enormous number of costly problems.

The League constantly challenged the figure of £112 million a year we had estimated would be generated by new commercial arrangements. They kept wanting to talk to us, but it was merely a stalling tactic.

In May Arthur Sandford presented his Management Committee with a 15-page report and concluded by saying that by taking the top clubs and players we had made the agreement between the Football Association and Football League nugatory ('of little value, trifling, not valid', according to the dictionary). He was very much the lawyer.

They were trying to argue at one point that a League was not a competition and that while the FA could run competitions, the League did not fall into this category. I found his argument extremely hard to follow.

The League had three options: (a) accept the position, (b) disaffiliate from the FA or (c) restructure to accommodate the top clubs. Sandford recommended that they do their own restructuring and took counsel's opinion as to whether they should commence legal action.

On 20 May Robert Chase, one of their members of the Management Committee but also one of the proponents of the Premier League, told me that he had seen counsel's opinion and in his opinion it was very woolly. I went to see Crystal Palace Chairman Ron Noades and tried to get him onside, but he made it quite clear he was going to play us off one against the other, and whichever deal suited him and his club best would determine which he would go for. Very interesting and very Ron.

I also met up with Gordon Taylor on the day Argentina played USSR in the Rous Cup. He was desperately keen for the PFA to be involved in some capacity to help run the Premier League which seemed strange to us because we were meeting all the points he was making. We eventually settled their role. We agreed the TV money, let them keep the pension schemes and pledged to look after the Football League clubs. It was also agreed that the chief officers of the FA, the Premier League, the Football League and the PFA would comprise a new committee which would discuss all aspects of the game.

Bill Fox went to Australia with the FA international team and still the rumbles came from Down Under of possible litigation. Bill was a nice man, very straightforward and honest, and when he was asked what was going on, he said bluntly : 'The big clubs want all the money – that's what's up.' He summed up all his feelings in one succinct comment.

Wimbledon's Sam Hammam came up with an interesting idea when he said that clubs who were on TV should pay the others because they had enhanced value for their commercial activities, ground and shirt advertising and, indeed, their players by virtue of being given exposure. Needless to say not many of the Premier League clubs agreed with him.

The England manager Graham Taylor dropped a small stone into the pool when he remarked caustically that people thought he had a lot to do with the FA blueprint but, in fact, that there was none of his thinking in it. He added grudgingly that the extra free Saturdays would be useful, but a lot of what was in the blueprint was based on greed. That did not help a lot.

We had an Executive Meeting on 11 June when we published a summary of the blueprint. It led to Ted Powell from the Executive saying that it did not do enough for the counties, although Geoff Thompson assured him that the final document would.

Terry Annable voiced the opinion that nine Council representatives from the Premier League (it had gone down from 18) was too many. Some of the League representatives, Reg Burr of Millwall, Michael Sinclair of York and Leslie Kew of Bristol City, wanted us to take Division Two along as well. So did Ron Noades, but he was not prepared to give them any voting rights in the new League. Instead he said he would give them 10% of the TV money, thereby giving the Premier League a bigger TV contract with more games to offer. He did not gain an awful lot of support and I certainly did not fancy diluting the Premier League concept.

This idea never actually went away. Noades himself brought it up again six months into the first year of the Premier League at the end of 1992.

Dr Ben Brown, the Oxford University representative on the FA, said that if there was a public wrangle, it was because the Football League were attempting to exceed their brief by trying to take the game over with its power sharing proposals.

The position of television was, of course, critical to the Premier League plans. The BBC were willing to share; they did not want everything but they wanted recorded highlights and the FA Cup and internationals.

Greg Dyke at ITV was very much opposed to Sky because he wanted ITV to have exclusivity as they had in 1988. He reckoned the last deal had been significant because of its exclusivity. We were only talking approximate figures at that stage because we were still a year ahead of the launch of the new League.

Every trick and stroke was being pulled to delay, deter or destroy the new League and when we arrived at one Executive Committee meeting, Bill Fox threatened to have the Football Conference allied to the Football League so that there would be football anarchy, cutting off promotion and relegation, disaffiliating from the FA and continuing with just themselves and the Conference.

We went to see our lawyers, confident that we could resist all challenges if we changed our rules slightly. It was our opinion that if the Football League had requested arbitration under FA rules, that would have been their best course of action but, for some reason, they neglected that route.

The League were using a public relations company called Paragon who produced statistics claiming that 68% of supporters were against the Premier League. Their slogan was *consensus, not conflict* – the problem was that they couldn't achieve consensus amongst themselves in the League and this fragmentation had begun to jeopardise the game's progress.

In June lawyers Herbert Smith & Co., acting for the League, asked for acknowledgement that the FA had no power to operate a League; no power to alter the contract between the League and its members; and that the FA would discontinue the Premier League and would not talk about resignations from the Football League, other than under the three-year rule. The lawyers quoted Lord Denning who, on a previous occasion, had said that the Football Association was nothing more than a legislative code. I thought this was very selective.

They claimed that we would be responsible for millions of pounds of losses if we did not agree. They were whistling in the wind.

Suddenly we had a plethora of blueprints with the latest offering coming from Gordon Taylor at the request of Robert Atkins. Gordon came up with a Football Federation Executive Board with an independent chairman and three representatives from each of the Football League, the FA and the PFA. Atkins described it as a refreshing set of proposals which deserved serious consideration. I told Gordon that I was surprised that he had come out with this as we had already promised him his television money, that his existing schemes would continue, that there would be no financial loss to the Football League and that the PFA would be given adequate representation in the new set up.

I responded with a rather bitter letter to Atkins, telling him he would listen to anyone who came whingeing to him.

We decided that with the threat of legislation we would pre-empt the League and go to court ourselves to resolve the uncertainty, allowing us in effect to do what we wanted to do. Arthur Sandford was still talking about his proposals, giving autonomy to each division, while the First Division clubs threatened to go it alone if the FA failed in court. This was seen in some quarters as the clubs turning against the FA, but they were just showing their determination to leave the Football League.

At the end of July we received the ruling we wanted from the court. Mr Justice Rose stated on 31 July that the FA had the powers under its constitution to set up the Premier League and that, if it were to be challenged by judicial review, the challenge would fail. His declaration gave us exactly what we wanted.

It was a tremendous relief to get this settled in our favour. In retrospect there is always the feeling you are going to win but, presumably, this applied to the other side. No one could have put hand on heart and said they were truly sure. I had pinned so much on this over the course of the previous seven months that it was just a massive relief that we had won the case.

There were still many hurdles to overcome. The PFA had a very powerful weapon at their disposal for they could threaten a strike if they wanted to stop the Premier League, or they could take action against compensation fees at the end of players' contracts. We took legal advice on the question of a strike and it was felt that they had no rights under the Trade Union Regulations merely to stop the Premier League, but there was nothing to stop them taking action over compensation fees which had little basis in law.

There was also an interesting scenario on the commercial side of the Premier League. Alex Fynn of Saatchi and Saatchi was advising us and a great deal of what he recommended was very good. He suggested that all the commercial properties of the FA and Premier League be put in one basket with a central marketing policy which would enable us to reach our £112 million target.

Glen Kirton had previously handled the commercial activities and he was unhappy at Fynn being on board, even though Glen was heavily committed with his duties as press officer and secretary to the international team. He thought Fynn had not established his credentials and that we should be putting our commercial portfolio out to competitive tender rather than going to the first name we thought of. He also doubted whether we would attract eight sponsors in a package for the FA Cup and was unconvinced of the need for expert negotiators to negotiate. He recognised experts were needed for advice, but he thought negotiations for commercial properties should be handled by the FA themselves.

In the event the debate was academic because the Premier League refused to put their sponsorships in one basket with the FA. This demonstrated that, despite our success in court, not everything was plain sailing either within or without. Eventually the FA and Premier

League moved further apart, much to the consternation of many of the Council members. We were not able to cement the relationship we envisaged because some of the members did not want to give the Premier League too many seats on the Council. It started off with 18, then went down to nine and then down to no increase at all. The existing ten League places were subject of an argument as to whether it should be a 7–3 or a 6–4 split between the Premier League and the Football League. I wanted the Premier League to have a majority, but in the end, disillusioned by the growing resentment at the new League's ambitions, the Council decided it must be 5–5.

The Premier League made it clear that they were not going to come 100% in-house and report to the FA as a committee. We wanted to put a director on their board but they refused and had a board comprising of only two people, the chairman Sir John Quinton, who was appointed by the clubs in preference to the Duke of Westminster, and Rick Parry. Our lawyers told the Executive Committee that any FA person becoming a director of the Premier League would be placed in a conflict of interest, but many Councillors remained unhappy at the Premier League's rebuff. It was proving impossible to please everybody.

We eventually solved the problem thanks to a suggestion from Mark Day that we take a special share in the Premier League which would give us special rights over such things as the number of clubs promoted and relegated, the right of veto over the name of the FA Premier League and the right of veto against any future breakaway. Under their Articles of Association they would have to stay within the FA rules.

The upshot was that we drifted further apart. Rick Parry, sensing this, applied to Sir Bert Millichip for the Euro 96 Director's job. When negotiations for television came to a head, Rick Parry completed his deal with Sky and the BBC in May 1992 while we at the FA did our own deal with Sky and the BBC.

We were quite happy with the £72 million deal over five years which at that time was a massive uplift. I don't think we would have done better if we had stayed with the Premier League. Trevor Phillips, having been such a major opponent of the Premier League while he was working with the Football League, was soon to be on the other side of the fence at the FA and he felt that we should have made bigger efforts to keep ITV involved, but we were following instead of leading.

Trevor remained apt to speak his own mind regardless of the company or the consequences. I recall going to a Conservative Party Conference when the FA and Premier League invited a number of Conservative MPs to dinner. We were stressing the unity between the two bodies and how well we were getting on until Trevor threw the cat amongst the pigeons by disputing it, saying that we were competing for the same sponsor's dollar. This did not go down at all well with Sir John Quinton and Rick Parry, whose face was an absolute picture. They complained bitterly afterwards and I had to suggest to Trevor that we keep our feelings in-house, rather than air them in front of people we were trying to lobby.

The potential for commercial activities was brought home to me when Mark McCormack approached me. He was very keen to get his IMG company involved in April 1991 and his estimates tallied with ours. It did not come off at the time, but eventually they did a deal for the FA properties with Trevor Phillips.

In the midst of all the acrimony over the Premier League, there was a dispute between the two arms of the Football League when Trevor Phillips sold the rights to the Arsenal – Manchester United match live for an additional £400,000. Bill Fox persuaded the Management Committee that it was worth £619,000 which was the value of each live match under the contract. The League ended up locking the League trophy away in Lytham St Annes, refusing to allow it to go down to Highbury in anticipation of Arsenal winning the Championship. Sponsors Barclays weren't too pleased that their trophy was locked up in the safe where it was hardly likely to get them a great deal of press coverage! In the event Liverpool lost at Nottingham Forest and it was not an issue, but it demonstrated that all was not well in the opposing camp.

There were some frantic negotiations going on both before and after the judgement in the High Court. The Divisions in the league were splitting into separate negotiating teams. John Dennis of Barnsley, a lovely character (albeit slow to admit ladies into his boardroom!), was put in charge of Division Two and he took a realistic line early on, as did the majority of the clubs who recognised that there was going to be a Premier League, come what may. It was only the Management Committee who resisted the inevitable as long as they could.

The successful judgement did not remove the problems. The League could still appeal or pursue their own writ against the FA. Negotiations went on fairly frenetically throughout August, leading up to an EGM which had been deferred until 23 September. It was a highly charged time in the game and on the eve of the opening day of the season, Friday 16 August, the Football League were refusing to apply for official sanction without the inclusion of rule 10 in their rules. We had disallowed rule 10 so that clubs were not obliged to give three years' notice, but they said their clubs had not agreed, and if they applied for sanction it would have to be with the old rule included.

The argument continued right up to 7 pm on that Friday evening. The League were saying that the Football Association were not able to attach conditions to sanction. We said that clubs could apply for sanction and that it would not jeopardise any appeal. If they won on appeal the rule could come back in.

We also had an offer from Arthur Sandford for us to take over the administration of the Football League as well as the Premier League. We held tentative talks on the subject but a lot of people at the League disliked it and that was when Andy Williamson said: 'It's like a rapist asking his victim to marry him.'

There were still considerable pockets of resistance and Bob Murray of Sunderland said that the League should fight and not allow promotion to the Premier League from the Football League, nor allow the Premier League clubs to play in the Football League Cup. Andy Williamson supported Bob on that, but Trevor Phillips said it was financial madness, so once again we had two opinions coming out of the League. It was the *Observer* which said: 'Last time Tranmere were in Division Two, Hitler's bombers were preparing to unleash the same sort of devastation Graham Kelly seems to be intent on inflicting on the Football League.' That was when I was a rapist one weekend and compared to Hitler the next.

Bill Fox always thought that Gordon Taylor was going to rescue him from the Premier League, having saved the League from break-up in 1988 by making considerable concessions and playing a part in the negotiations between the various divisions after the superleague threat. Right to the end of the arguments on the Premier League, Bill thought that Gordon would ride in on his white charger. But sadly for him it was not the case this time when, after a lot of hard work, we were able to get Gordon to signal his reluctant agreement to the final arrangements.

There was a great line from David Lacey in the *Guardian* amid all this confusion when he said: 'With the prospect of 22 club chairmen running the Premier League, it is not difficult to imagine Graham Kelly ending up like the British envoy in the last reel of *Lawrence of Arabia* who is surrounded by quarrelling sheikhs and wishes aloud that he had stayed in Tunbridge Wells.'

We even had the Scottish League objecting to us using the word 'Premier' because of their own Premier League. The observant Lacey was not far off, for we were still arguing about how much money we should pay to the Football League and how many clubs should go up and down. Phil Carter, leading the First Division clubs, wanted to stay at 22 until he could be sure that the new money was coming in. We could not agree to that and told them that we needed a date when it was to come down to 20.

It was all eventually settled on 23 September 1991 when we had a document signed by the FA, Division One and the Football League, and David Dein and Rick Parry opened their bottle of champagne in White's.

Ron Noades reckoned he could have done a better deal in some respects but he went home before the vote was taken. It was 50 votes to 9 in favour of the agreement between the three parties.

With the contract in our pocket we went North to discuss things with David Dent and Michael Foster at the Football League to try and get things on an even keel as we were going to have to work together. Division One were flexing their muscles after the court ruling in favour of the Premier League. David Kohler of Luton did not realise that the FA had certain powers over them while Len Cearns of West Ham objected to it being called the *FA* Premier League. A lot of clubs were unhappy with only having five places on the Council while David Dein wanted a 22 man board and a joint venture partnership with the FA. They asked Rick Parry to carry on until August 1992.

Despite the signed agreement, the full detailed agreement was not signed until many months later. It was one hell of a long road. One of the most contentious points was how quickly we could come down to 20 clubs. Rick Parry and I were determined it should be 1994 but Gordon McKeag was equally adamant and wanted it deferred until 1996. We finished with the classic British compromise, settling on 1995.

The agreement eventually provided for the FA to pay the Football League £2million a year, providing the FA had sufficient new income to cover it. The Premier League would also carry on paying the 3% gate levy and they would allow the Football League to keep the copyright on the pools fixtures until 1996.

The four-year-old golf prodigy. leveleys Professional Edwin Marsh instructs me how to grip the cut-down club.

Setting out on a round with mother Emmie.

Goalkeeper for Anchorsholme Under-14s at a gala refereed by England international Jimmy Armfield.

Stanley Matthews, a hero of mine, demonstrating his superb balance and control in Blackpool FC colours.

World Cup Final 1974,
Holland v West Germany.
English referee Jack Taylor
cautions Dutch captain
Johann Cruyff for backchat.

My enrolment as an honorary member
of the Charlton Athletic Supporters Club
(Bromley branch).

urnley's outspoken
hairman, Bob Lord.

Rising passions before the European Cup Final 1985, Liverpool v Juventus, at the Heysel Stadium.

The aftermath of the Heysel Stadium tragedy. Thirty-eight fans died on one of the mo shameful days for British sport.

nfield is transformed into a sea of flowers after the Hillsborough tragedy, 1989. It
ad been a mere two months since I'd taken on the role of Chief Executive at the FA.

rime Minister Margaret Thatcher visits Hillsborough, with Press spokesman Bernard
igham on the right of picture.

Alan Sugar and Terry Venables during the early days at Spurs before they fell out.

Terry Venables after one of his many legal battles with Alan Sugar.

George Graham before being sacked by Arsenal for accepting 'unsolicited gifts'.

The seat of power.
The Council chamber at
FA headquarters
Lancaster Gate.

Members of the FA
management and their
partners support the
Football Writers'
Association Annual ladies
night at the Savoy.

Listening intently with
FIFA's Joao Havelange
(left) and David Collins
om the Welsh FA *(right)*
as Sepp Blatter answers
the press.

You never lose it! Lunch hour in Hyde Park. Mates Bob and Pete are left gasping ...

With my wife Romayne and David and Margaret Will *(right)*.

Hampered by lack of talent at ball games, I turned to distance running.

I don festive garb for the FA Christmas card. Ho, ho, ho.

However, no sooner had the Premier League started in 1992 than it was thrown into turmoil by a dispute with eight clubs, some of whom were disenchanted with the TV contract which Rick Parry had struck with Sky and the BBC. The rebels negotiated in private with a company called Dorna to provide ground advertising. These secret negotiations cut across the concept of commercial co-operation and effectively provided the consortium of clubs with a block veto.

Arsenal, Liverpool, Everton, Manchester United, Leeds United, Nottingham Forest, Aston Villa and QPR were against the sponsorship deal with Bass which came up at that time because of their commitments to Dorna. Sheffield Wednesday and Spurs both declined to go with Dorna and it was all becoming so fraught that I was forced to fly back urgently from Northern Spain, where England were playing a friendly, the morning after arriving because the FA were concerned about what had happened. Many of the 14 clubs, including Palace, Wimbledon, Spurs, Chelsea, Middlesbrough and Southampton, had walked out of the Premier League meeting on 7 September.

I commented that it was unlikely that the FA would sanction a second division of the Premier League which Ron Noades was advocating, and that the wrangling must stop because we had to have early talks on a title sponsor.

Rick Parry had gone ahead with the sponsorship talks with Bass without consulting the FA and when I expressed my disappointment about it, he said that the FA's behaviour was extraordinary, showing the world in the process just how far we were apart at this stage.

Ken Bates once again used his programme notes and sounded off against the Dorna clubs. He alleged that they were arrogant, cheating and trying to gain an unfair advantage over their more honourable competitors. He referred to them as 'smart arsed, get rich quick spivs' in welcoming Norwich, one of the 'clean 14', to Stamford Bridge.

This upset Arsenal's Peter Hill-Wood, who complained. It was sorted out by Parry whose main strength was to get these warring clubs with their own agendas to work together. It was largely to his credit that after these early teething problems they went from strength to strength. They even agreed that there would be no secret negotiations in future and brought in new rules whereby they owed each other a fiduciary duty. Parry said that to get those rules through he would go softly, softly on any central commercial negotiations which could adversely affect the bigger clubs. After a very hairy start, he got them working together very well. Dorna carried on for a while, extending from their original eight clubs, and Bass' Carling sponsorship was accepted a year later.

We tried to get Mike Foster to come on board at the FA to help in running the Premier League at a very early stage when we wanted to play a bigger role in its administration. I would have valued Mike's contribution very highly. He had come to the Football League as a young lad in the early 1970s, applying for a job on the magazine, the *Football League Review*, and although he did not have the qualifications for that job he was very keen on football, a hard worker, a strong character and someone I had no hesitation in taking on in a different role. I would have very much liked him to join the FA in 1992, but he preferred the offer Rick Parry made him to become a staff member with the Premier League. He saw more opportunity in being Secretary of the Premier League in a small administrative organisation rather than joining a big set-up.

I was concerned at Rick Parry taking his office to Manchester. He seemed unwilling to move his family down to London and be full-time in the Premier League office in Lancaster Gate and in fact never moved, eventually going back North to work as Chief Executive with Liverpool in 1997. I was disappointed when Rick left the Premier League. The clubs failed to reward him well enough for the new television contract worth £643 million.

In 1997, just two months before the important pre-World Cup tournament in France, Newcastle proposed at the Premier League meeting that England should withdraw, another example of clubs complaining about so-called meaningless friendlies and wanting to deny the England coach preparation time with his team.

The Premier League also wanted the FA to pay the salaries of the international players while we had them on duty. This would not only have cost the FA £2.5 million a year and destroyed our programme with the grassroots, but it was also against FIFA regulations which stipulate that clubs should pay.

A lot of the clubs complained about the Mexico game we played on Easter Saturday at Wembley in 1997. In actual fact, when compiling the fixtures for the World Cup we had kept that date clear at the request of the Premier League, but because of matches involving the other Home International countries they had to cancel their programme of fixtures. Sometimes, it seems, you just cannot win.

CHAPTER SIX

Sweet as Sugar

One of my major concerns is the club versus country dilemma which is deeply rooted in the game.

Chairmen, some of them with little knowledge or experience in the running and structure of the game, are becoming increasingly influential as they are armed with the power of making decisions whose effects can ripple right down from international football to the grassroots.

There have been instances in the recent past where history may have been altered, had the critical decision-making been left to the chairmen of the Premier League, and the future of England's participation in events such as the World Youth Championships and, indeed, in full international friendlies will be in doubt if the Premier League eventually take full control.

One of the early controversies in the Premier League involved the FA's wish to take a strong team to Australia for the World Youth Championship in 1993. We had previously sought assurances from Terry Venables the previous year, when he had withdrawn Andrew Turner from an international match and played him for Spurs instead. We discussed the situation with Rick Parry because it was clearly difficult to take first-team players to the other side of the world during a critical part of the year, and we eventually reached a compromise whereby the use of first team players would be limited to one per club.

England were due to play Korea, Turkey and the USA on 7, 9 and

11 March and Terry wanted to keep his forward Nick Barmby for the FA Cup quarter-final against Manchester City on the day of the first England game against Korea and then send him out after that game.

I thought it was quite an important principle because I had always been led to believe how critical international development was, but Terry was saying that Barmby would gain much more by being in the Spurs first team. I thought it a more compelling argument that he would be playing against the very best young players in the world in tournament conditions overseas.

David Burnside, the manager of the youth team, duly sent out notifications on 24 February, asking that Nick Barmby report to the Holiday Inn, Maidenhead on the following Saturday. If he was playing in a match that day, then he would be allowed to join up later in the evening ready for the departure of the squad the next day.

I personally wrote to Terry Venables next day when it became apparent that there was some doubt about the release of Barmby. I pointed out that we were obliged by FIFA to put out our best team to represent England and I threatened that we would be forced to take legal action against Spurs if they failed to comply with our request. We had the passports of everybody in the party except the Spurs player and, to force the issue, we said we would send somebody to White Hart Lane to collect it, only for the club secretary, Peter Barnes, to write back saying that the player's passport was with director Jonathan Crystal, so it would not be available for collection at 2.30 pm as requested.

This was becoming ridiculous and we were then forced to ask our lawyers to fax another letter to Spurs, because we could not understand why they were saying that they were not interfering with the arrangements of the players on the one hand and yet the player's passport was not at the club as we would have expected, but with Mr Crystal. They gave no indication of where Mr Crystal was.

We were quite firm and promised that we would take legal action the next day if it became necessary.

Crystal wrote back to say he had the passport with him and that it was ready for collection. In the event, just as we were about to submit the necessary affidavits to the court, Spurs announced that Barmby would be going to Australia after all.

Terry Venables said that it was not appropriate to discuss the matter any further in the light of the sad death of Bobby Moore the previous day. Presumably he was as cut up as he was to be subsequently at the sudden death of his great friend Bobby Keetch, the former Fulham centre half.

The row did have one useful, personal side effect. There was a banner headline in one of the tabloids quoting Brian Clough as saying Graham Kelly and Peter Swales were idiots. I was able to dine out on that piece of paper for many months afterwards, saying how much it had upset me but that at least he had got it half right!

Still the problem of club versus country had not been resolved and the same thing happened for the 1999 World Youth tournament in Nigeria. England sent a sub standard team and lost all three of their group games without scoring a single goal. It did little for the stature of English football abroad and yet a full strength side would have competed for the title, gaining invaluable experience against the likes of Brazil and Spain on the way.

It doesn't help, of course, that these tournaments are invariably held when leading Western European countries are reaching the climax of their season.

Another seemingly ongoing problem within the FA Premier League is over the worth of the Intertoto Cup, a summer tournament held by UEFA for the benefit of the continental pools and given added importance with three teams being given a passage into the UEFA Cup. The Premier League clubs had voted 14–6, the narrowest of margins, to participate in the Intertoto in the summer of 1995 but it became a major problem for English football when UEFA advanced the date of the draw to early April.

Premier League clubs discovered, contrary to what had originally been thought, that it was then too late to change their minds and England had to find three teams to fill the places they had requested.

No volunteers were forthcoming as the end of the season approached and Keith Wiseman was left to try and explain the problems to UEFA via the Club Competitions Committee of which he was a member. But to no avail, as his pleas fell on deaf ears.

English football was not the flavour of the month at that period and, at the time of the European Cup Final, the top brass of UEFA, including Lennart Johansson, Egidius Braun and Gerd Aigner were furious with Bert Millichip because England were perceived to be letting UEFA down over the competition. Keith and Bert came back to advise the Premier League of the dangers and prompted a crisis meeting of the Premier League where Wimbledon, Sheffield Wednesday and Spurs volunteered to save English football's bacon but only on condition that the Premier League as a whole underwrote their costs. With much relief this was hastily agreed.

But that was far from the end of the matter and when the tournament took place both Spurs and Wimbledon sent out weak teams, performed abysmally and further enraged UEFA because they were seen to have damaged the credibility of the competition and angered the pools promoters. Wednesday escaped censure, but UEFA banned both Spurs and Wimbledon from Europe for one year on the basis of a short written summary of the case which Gerd Aigner had prepared for the disciplinary committee.

This provoked another crisis meeting involving myself, Pat Smith, Mike Foster, Ned Hammam, Sam's brother and a director of Wimbledon, and Alan Sugar. We had to move quickly to lodge an appeal against the decision, arranging to travel to a hearing of the Appeal Board at the Movenpick Hotel at Geneva Airport.

The clubs had got together and travelled over from London with Rick Parry, Alan Sugar, Daniel Sugar, Ned Hammam and their lawyers, but I arrived separately and promptly bumped into Rene Eberle, the secretary of the Appeal Board. He invited me to join him and his fellow board members, including chairman Leon Straessle, for dinner.

We were on the first course when the English delegation walked in, raising their eyebrows when they saw who I was dining with. Straessle gave me a ticking-off for not telling the clubs that they had to field their strongest teams and then broached the subject of a deal with an agreed statement whereby the two clubs would be fined a nominal amount and the ban would be lifted. Clearly they did not relish the prospect of a lengthy hearing the following morning.

We finished the meal in good humour, and when we broke up I went and joined my colleagues from England and told them we had a fairly easy day ahead providing they agreed to pay the fine. Alan Sugar was a bit jumpy about it, having had experience of discipline at the hands of the English FA, but they eventually agreed and the hearing took only five minutes with Spurs fined 150,000 Swiss francs and Wimbledon 100,000.

The problems, such as they were, between the FA and UEFA stemmed from two factors. Firstly, that UEFA had a particularly inflexible way of approaching problems. Once they had made up their minds it was very difficult to shift them. Secondly, I always felt that there was an element of the great divide between our island and the rest of Europe and they attributed the islander mentality to us. Like successive British Governments who never embraced the European ideal, we were seen as a nation of Euro sceptics.

There was another confrontation over the winner of our League Cup going into the UEFA Cup. It came to a head in Oporto in September 1995 when the French announced they were considering a League Cup competition. UEFA said any country which had more than 34 matches per season in its top division would not be allowed to enter its League Cup winners in the UEFA Cup. Although this was a direct response to a new situation developing in France, in reality UEFA knew full well that it was an attack on England who resolutely stuck to 20 teams in the Premier League.

I made a speech at the conference of European Football Associations in Oporto, drawing attention to the fact that the Football League Cup was a long established part of the English calendar and contributed considerably to the coffers of the poorer clubs in the lower divisions. My comments were noted, but no one undertook to take them on board as became immediately clear when they issued their edict that in three years' time the League Cup winners would only be admitted into Europe if the Premier League were reduced to 18 clubs.

This was mounting an offensive against the wrong target, as to take action against the League Cup winners was hardly likely to worry the Premier League. The UEFA Cup place would simply be transferred from the League Cup winners to another Premier League club based on their finishing position in the League table.

We sent a great many letters to UEFA headquarters, but it was only when David Sheepshanks complained to the European Commission in Brussels that UEFA even began to recognise the problem. Johansson admitted as much to me later when he said that he had not appreciated they were on completely the wrong tack. The penny started to drop after the Ipswich Chairman's complaints to a higher authority and in November 1997 Aigner met Sheepshanks and me at White's Hotel in London to argue the point.

'There's too much football in England,' was Aigner's opening salvo.

By this time my commitment to a smaller Premier League had waned and I replied that this was not the case. There was only too much football for two or three clubs and their players and if he was to talk to the chairmen and fans of the less illustrious clubs like Coventry City and Leicester City, he would find out pretty quickly that they did not want to see their fixtures reduced.

Aigner then claimed that the Premier League clubs didn't want the League Cup. Again we endeavoured to explain that there were one or two clubs ambivalent about it, but that there had never been a decision by the FA Premier League to weaken the Coca-Cola Cup.

Part of his obvious antipathy towards our problem was that he had taken exception to the letter I had written to Brussels when asked for observations about the Football League's case. I told him I had simply set out the facts and that I had been arguing the point since the conference in Oporto two years earlier.

He eventually came round to our way of thinking and promised to suggest to the UEFA Executive Committee that they should grant a moratorium for three years for the League Cup winners. Sheepshanks said that this would be helpful because hopefully the Football League would get together with the Premier League to co-operate more closely on television contracts in future and this would give them time to organise their affairs.

I was then called, at short notice, to another meeting in Geneva and I travelled over and met Marcus Studer, Aigner's deputy, and Fritz Ahlstrom along with Sheepshanks and David Dent. A deal had been ironed out, the three year delay had been agreed and all that remained was for the League and UEFA formally to sign a sheet of paper embodying the main principles and obliging the Football League to withdraw their complaint to the European Commission.

Relations with UEFA had definitely taken a turn for the better, albeit temporarily. It was one year to the day since they had sent their fax from Lisbon ordering us to withdraw from the World Cup 2006 campaign and I reminded them of this over coffee, sitting at the very table where Alan Sugar had held his ultimately unnecessary council of war on the eve of the Intertoto decision two years earlier.

Wimbledon, who had been involved in the Intertoto fiasco, threw us another curved ball when they announced in the 1996–97 season that they were planning to move lock, stock and two smoking barrels to Dublin. They were having problems finding a new ground in the Borough of Merton and they claimed that their best chance of financial survival for the future was to move to Dublin whilst remaining in the FA Premier League under the jurisdiction of the FA. The Football Association of Ireland were considerably upset, as they did not want Wimbledon competing for the fan base in Dublin with their own clubs.

I could quite see the attraction of the Dons playing in Dublin considering the number of supporters of major Premier League clubs across the water. Sam Hammam announced that they needed gates of at least 25,000 to survive and they weren't going to do that without a permanent home.

The Premier League clubs heard Wimbledon's arguments and did not raise any objections, leaving the matter to the Board. This was at Peter Leaver's first meeting in April 1997 and he didn't realise the hot potato he was being handed.

Hammam said that there were plenty of other examples where clubs played in a 'foreign' league, citing Derry, Berwick, Cardiff, Swansea, Wrexham and Monaco. Wimbledon had spent £700,000 in seven years seeking planning permission and had been turned down on five sites.

They felt that they could easily build a new ground close to Dublin Airport. The difficulty was that the case did not easily fall within any FIFA or UEFA rules. Certainly the consent of the Premier League would be required for them to move their ground, but the only recent precedent in international football law was the insistence by FIFA that the Welsh clubs returned to the Welsh League and this had been overturned at law.

The FA were in a difficult position. On the one hand we had a member club fighting for financial survival, whereas on the other hand a friendly local national association was making it clear to us that Wimbledon would be an unwelcome visitor.

Some of the cases which Hammam had quoted were exceptions to the general rule. These exceptions had very deep roots in the history and politics of the clubs concerned. What he was talking about was something entirely new.

When I departed it was still far from being resolved. The FA set out all of the very real practical considerations which Wimbledon would have to overcome, such as security questions, and said that we doubted very much that we would put ourselves in conflict with the FAI. It would help Wimbledon's case considerably if they could obtain support of the FA in Dublin.

UEFA, after asking for observations and offering to hold a meeting if all parties agreed, backed off and decided they had no standing in the matter. They would not be making a ruling.

That was interesting because it points up the difference between UEFA and FIFA. Traditionally FIFA were the governing body. The majority of the national associations of the world were initially members of FIFA, who now have over 200 members. UEFA came on the scene in 1954 merely to organise the European Cup competitions. UEFA took over the Inter Cities Fairs Cup, renaming it the UEFA Cup after a few years. But, gradually, UEFA has expanded its influence.

They have constantly sought to obtain powers from FIFA to handle more matters which are domestic to its own area. FIFA, not unnaturally, resisted. UEFA, for example, thought that they could better handle transfers of players within the continent, but FIFA refused. The result has been that national associations have in more recent years had to pick their way through the statutes of UEFA and FIFA very carefully indeed to see which body had authority over any particular issue and UEFA have increased the direct control they have over associations.

But both were left floundering when they were hit with the now historic Bosman affair. I hate the case. I do not hate him. I just hate the case.

The Belgians did in the 1990s what Newcastle United had done in the 1960s. The Belgians were intransigent, they hung on to Jean-Marc Bosman's registration without paying him and refused to let him move in the same way that Newcastle United, against the advice of the Football League, cost the sport the old retain and transfer system and the maximum wage when they kept George Eastham out of the game in 1960. History so often repeats itself.

Much to the concern of powerful chairmen, like Sir John Hall, with money invested in transfer fees, UEFA completely failed to get to grips with the problem soon enough.

Virtually everything they did in the case was too little, too late. It could have been argued that Bosman, an ordinary, honest player, had the ability to leave his Belgian club and transfer to another club in Europe under UEFA compensation procedures. But the Belgians prevaricated and UEFA did not step in, with the result that in December 1995 the European Court of Justice disallowed rules which provided for a transfer fee when a European Community player on the expiry of his contract moved from one country to another. Rules which restricted clubs to only a limited number of foreign players were also outlawed.

Long after the ruling UEFA held meetings to discuss how to reach an agreement with the European Commission to preserve transfer fees at the end of players' contracts. Given the clarity of the Bosman judgement and the fact that there is no provision for exemptions in the

Treaty of Rome, I cannot see how the commission could be expected to agree to any compromise.

It can be argued that if transfer fees at the end of contracts disappeared, the effect on the game would not necessarily be all that startling. The net expenditure by Premier League clubs to Football League clubs remained fairly static over the initial years of the Premier League. Fees within the Premier League rose, but not those to the Football League. Expenditure overseas increased. It could be argued that transfer fees have everything to do with market forces, for example the massive injection of television cash into the game, and relatively little to do with compensation for development, the argument that UEFA were advancing with the European Commission.

The effect on the smaller clubs was not quite as dramatic as was feared at the time. It merely perpetuated a situation where it was more difficult to sell a player to the Premier League. It was already tough.

There was also a need to amend the domestic transfer system for players at the end of their contracts and it was agreed with Gordon Taylor and the PFA that fees would continue for players up to the age of 24, but after that there would be no compensation fee.

I do not believe that the effects are quite as cataclysmic as some countries across Europe were proclaiming. In relatively few cases countries maintained compensation for players right up to the age of 30.

But, of course, the ruling led to higher salaries for players as the clubs no longer had to pay a transfer fee. Linked to the astronomical sums now coming in from television, the Bosman case has widened the gulf between the rich and the poor clubs.

Speaking of transfer fees, I find Nicolas Anelka's behaviour over his transfer from Arsenal disgraceful. Why is it that so many foreign players regard their contracts as one-way only and if it does not suit them, they appear determined to angle to get away? Arsene Wenger and David Dein have done the best they could in the circumstances, given the player's difficult attitude. The only role for the FA would be to take Arsenal's side and support them in a claim to FIFA if the club wanted to take action on the grounds of an improper approach to one of their contracted players by a foreign club. How far they would go I'm not sure, given that Arsenal received a massive fee for a player who had cost them next to nothing. FIFA need to introduce firmer rules and stricter monitoring of agents.

UEFA was not the only European body to cause the FA problems. When FIFA ruled that only approved footballs could be used in international matches, some manufacturers complained to the European Commission. The Brussels mandarins sent four inspectors on a dawn swoop to Lancaster Gate.

Faced with these unannounced and unwelcome visitors, I ushered them out onto the rain-soaked pavement. Nic Coward was horrified. 'Let them back in while I consult the lawyers,' he pleaded. 'You could be fined or even jailed for obstruction of justice.'

I relented and the investigators spent two entire days reducing our entire filing system to a shambles in pursuit of a case that had nothing whatsoever to do with the FA.

From much of the foregoing it will be clear that my hopes of ending the power struggle with the advent of the Premier League were dashed at a very early stage. The FA were not strong enough on the number of clubs and not flexible enough in embracing the Premier League concept. Sensing weakness, the top clubs were never going to submerge themselves in the FA structure once they had their freedom granted in the High Court.

The Premier League itself has been spectacularly successful, but I was unable to come up with a structural formula which would overcome the suspicions on all sides. Mistrust and ambition prevailed.

CHAPTER SEVEN

Holes in my Soles

Any dreams I had of becoming a professional footballer ended one bleak winter day on the East Lancs Road when I was pushed out of the Blackpool team bus and sent to make my own way to play for Blackpool Mechanics.

The dreams were just that. It was never a realistic prospect and I never managed to go beyond a handful of games for the Blackpool third team while I was working for Barclays Bank. But it was still a hard way for an impressionable 18-year-old to be told that he was not up to the mark.

I could catch the ball, had a bit of talent and was passionately in love with the game, but I was never daft enough to put my head in where it hurt and everyone knows that you need to be barmy to be a good goalkeeper.

However, I plugged away until the occasion when I was travelling to Liverpool with the 'A' and 'B' teams. It was in the days before substitutes, and being a bank clerk, I realised that, counting me, there were three goalkeepers for two places. The puzzle was solved when, half way down the East Lancs Road, the coach stopped and the fellow in charge asked me if I would like to play for Blackpool Mechanics, who were playing at St. Helens in the Lancashire Combination.

'Do I have a choice?' I asked.

'No, you don't,' he replied and pointed me in the direction of the ground. The coach drove off to Liverpool and I watched my football career disappear down the East Lancs Road.

At least Blackpool Mechanics won 1–0 and I kept a clean sheet. St Helens had a player called Derek Hennin playing for them, one of a fearsome group of Bolton Wanderers defenders winding down their careers on the unsuspecting forwards of the Lancashire Combination. Before the game he sized up one of our players with the immortal question: 'Which way does tha want t' land, lad?'

I never heard from Blackpool again, but I had already got the message loud and clear. They did not want amateurs taking up the places in their teams. I remember Emlyn Hughes saying to me after one heavy defeat in 1965: 'You will always be a banker,' or something that sounded very similar. He, of course, went on from Blackpool to captain Liverpool and England. I did not. When David Mellor called me the Captain Mainwaring of football, he scarcely realised how near the truth he was.

If there were any doubts about my true roots, they were revealed on 23 December 1995 when my wife-to-be Romayne organised a surprise 50th birthday party for me and many of my friends. It was held at Grizzly's transport caff on the A1. They opened up specially for us on that Saturday morning to serve everyone with a great British fry-up.

It was Romayne's response to my almost daily wish to stop for egg and chips on my way past, travelling from Lancaster Gate to my home just outside Peterborough, and merely a reflection of my early days in Blackpool where money was tight enough for a boy brought up in a council house to put cardboard cut outs into my shoes to make them last that bit longer. However, they were not so good for someone who wanted to kick a football in wind or rain – and we had plenty of that in the winter. I used to play on Saturday for the school in the morning and the Blackpool Boys' Club in the afternoon. I used to turn up with wet boots and socks feeling most uncomfortable.

But football, in fact, was not my first sport. That was golf. Indeed, I was regarded as something of a child prodigy.

My father Tommy was a tram driver in Blackpool, taking the guests through the illuminations to see the famous Blackpool lights or along the Golden Mile in the summer months. On my mother Emmie's side, the family managed the Cleveleys Hydro Hotel. The pre-war brochure stated: 'Holiday life can offer no happier, healthier pleasures than those of Cleveleys Hydro. Down on the sea's fragrant brim, five miles north of Blackpool.'

I am not quite sure that the EEC inspectors of beaches would nowadays call the North West coast the fragrant rim and by the time I came along in 1945, the hotel, having been requisitioned for a military hospital in the Second World War, was closed down. All that was left was an 18-hole golf course and some disused tennis courts. This meant that I was taught golf at the age of three, with my picture in the national papers at the age of four. Not many children took up golf in those days.

It was a great life for a kid because it also meant that I had the run of the grounds and could invite all of my friends around to play football, making me quite popular not on account of having a ball, which was usually the case, but because I had the pitch. It tended to be the older lads who came around to play and I remember one particular name, Peter Rice, who became quite a local hero when he went to the 1958 World Cup in Sweden as a supporter.

Not surprisingly the first ever game of football I watched was at Bloomfield Road where I saw Blackpool reserves and Liverpool reserves. I remember it for a fearsome collision which took place between two Liverpool defenders, leaving them with their bloodstained shirts and me with an indelible imprint on my mind.

There was also the wonderful Matthews Cup Final in 1953 when Blackpool beat Bolton Wanderers 4–3 in a spectacular match which finally gave Stan Matthews his cherished Cup winners' medal. I did not actually see the winning moments myself. Although we did not own a television set, I went to a mate's to watch and at 1–3 down we decided we had had enough and went out to play on our bikes, which was something of an inauspicious start to my involvement with the national sport.

I have, of course, watched the match many times subsequently and have a video given to me for my birthday some years ago. If you watch the entire 90 minutes it is an awful game. It is advertised as one of the best Finals ever and for pure drama I am sure it was, but the standard of play, the sloppy passing, the poor defending and some not very good goalkeeping makes you appreciate the quality of football today.

The first Cup Final I attended was when my mum took me to watch Manchester United play Bolton Wanderers in 1958. We travelled down to London by train on the Friday night and slept on Euston Station before going to the game where I stood behind the goal into which Nat Lofthouse, the Bolton centre forward, charged Manchester United's Harry Gregg. If I was not brave enough to be a goalkeeper, neither was I fast enough to be an outfield player. I was deceptive, slower than I looked – although in later years my vision and perception surely compensated!

Blackpool signed quite a few South Africans in those days. There was Bill Perry, of course, who scored the winning goal in the 1953 Cup Final, but also Peter Hauser and Brian Peterson who made the grade, while they also boasted one of the first Chinese players, Cheung Chi-Doy, who stayed with the club for two years, playing just two games and scoring one goal. His one home match at Bloomfield Road was marred by poor visibility. A dense fog (or smoke from the railway behind the west stand) descended and he did not get a look-in (literally).

Nowadays I tend not to boast where my allegiances lie, but when I was a kid in Blackpool my team had four players in the England team. The notorious England team that played Hungary at Wembley in 1953 included Harry Johnston, Stan Matthews, Ernie Taylor and Stan Mortensen. England may have lost 6–3, but Blackpool had some of the best players in the country in their side.

Billy Wright was also in that England side and, many years later, provided me with one of my most poignant moments, coming out of Wembley after an international match. He was with his wife Joy, and while I was asked for my autograph, they were both ignored. He had 105 caps for England and she enjoyed a glittering stage career as one of the Beverley Sisters, so it was acutely embarrassing that the power of television, rather than any achievements, had made my face instantly recognisable rather than theirs. Not that television is a disadvantage. It may sound stupid, but there is no doubt that people treat you more kindly.

Blackpool had a gang of supporters in the early 50s known as the 'Atomic Boys'. Their mascot was a live duck which they painted orange and called Puskas after the Hungarian captain. I was far too young to be a member but can you imagine the furore if that happened these days! If I said that some of today's mascots dressed as animals irritate me immensely, I would merely be confirming the widely-held view that I am a boring old fart.

I used to think that Blackpool was the centre of the football universe. Everything seemed to happen there and, not many people know this, the first live televised league match was from Blackpool. It was the second half of the game against Bolton Wanderers transmitted live by ITV in 1960 and it was so awful that they did not do another live game for more than 20 years. It would have been even worse in colour, but at least in black and white it was instantly forgettable.

During the school holidays I used to go to Bloomfield Road each day and every picture which appeared in every magazine or newspaper I had signed by the Blackpool players who were usually prepared to put up with our regular requests. There were two exceptions. One was Stan Matthews, who seemed to have a special exit all of his own. He was a will o' the wisp on and off the field. He would suddenly materialise next to his car in the car park and be off before we could catch him. We never found out how he did it! The other was Scottish international goalkeeper George Farm, who was very sour and surly towards his adoring young fans.

To have any chance of George's signature, you had to make sure it was not a picture of him in the 1953 Final, for, although he had his winners' medal, he did not play very well. Sometimes he would sign it *Geo. Farm* with his own fountain pen which we thought was very flash. He also had this distinctive way of catching the ball with one hand underneath the ball and the other on top. Very strange, but then, aren't most goalkeepers?

I once saw George Farm score a goal. It was in the days before substitutes were permitted and, after injuring his arm, our goalkeeper was unable to continue in goal. He came out to play centre forward and scored with his head in a 6–2 win over our local rivals Preston North End in October 1955. I was pressed up against the perimeter wall behind the Kop goal when the ball went in.

My first ever organised game of football was at age seven for Norbreck Primary School when I played in goal in my best (and only) shoes on a muddy pitch because the regular goalkeeper failed to show. I received the expected clip around the ear when I reached home for the state of my footwear. I think I then played in every position before eventually becoming a centre half at the age of 11 for the town schoolboy team. No one from that team went on to make the grade.

There was only one secondary school, Baines Grammar School at Poulton-le-Fylde, which had football in the curriculum, and fortunately I did well enough in my 11-plus exams to win a place. I never even bothered putting down a second or third choice, because there was no way I was going to a school like Arnold and being forced to play rugby like Jimmy Armfield, although I suppose it did him no harm.

I used to walk the five miles along the beach – at least it was that far according to the brochure – to watch Blackpool train. They had a trainer called Wilson who had a contraption called Wilson's sling which catapulted the ball 80 yards in a looping trajectory to the waiting player who had to control this guided missile which appeared on the breeze out of the leaden skies. This was how they honed their players' ball skills, but the sad thing was that they did not possess any players who could deliver the ball 80 yards accurately so the move could never be translated into match play!

Imagine those great heavy, water-soaked leather balls hurtling at you. I wonder what the modern footballer would make of it. It certainly would not have done David Ginola's hair style a lot of good.

I first started watching football in the old South Stand at Bloomfield Road where the family had season tickets. It was considered a prime vantage point right behind the goal and fairly close to the action. A marvellous place to savour the atmosphere of watching football.

While our hotel closed, the nearby Norbreck Hydro Hotel stayed open and many of the professional teams used to come to stay. Wolves, one of the great teams of the time, were regular visitors and I recall the England international Eddie Clamp signing our books 'Yours in sport'. We always thought that 'Best Wishes' or a similar inscription was much more valuable than just the name, although if a boy asked for one, he was considered a bit wet.

I once had the privilege of sitting next to Nat Lofthouse, the Lion of Vienna, in the dug-out at Blackpool, although how I achieved that honoured position is a total blank. The occasion must have overcome me and blotted out everything else.

When the teams came to stay at the Norbreck Hydro I would make a point of having a haircut at the barber's shop in the hotel so that I could hang round the players. I finished up with the shortest hair in the school. When Tommy Taylor of Manchester United came in one day I was next in the queue, but I happily let him go ahead of me and sat there listening to the conversation, although I waited in vain for him to be asked if he wanted anything for the weekend!

United were regular visitors and one of the most widely seen pictures of the pre-Munich Busby Babes was a team sheet of them in the white kit they wore in the 1957 Cup Final against Aston Villa. That was taken on the golf course at Norbreck.

Blackburn Rovers trained at the Norbreck before the 1960 Cup Final against Wolves in the Derek Dougan days when the unconventional Irishman asked for a transfer on the morning of the

Final. Dave Whelan, the left back, broke his leg in the game but went on to become a multi millionaire with a chain of sportswear shops before taking over Wigan Athletic.

Apart from the wide open spaces of my 'private' football pitch at the hotel, we also had a big garage door at Cleveleys where we lived in a flat. I used to play 'wallie' in the yard for ages, kicking the ball against the wall, and when a friend came around it was a perfect goal and ideal for penalties. The only problem was that the wind was so strong, you had no chance of running round your weaker foot. If you tried, the ball would be halfway across the Irish sea, so it forced Blackpool youngsters to become two-footed.

Many of the celebrities who appeared on the Piers or at the Winter Gardens would come and play golf at the course and I vividly remember Hylda Baker, all 4 feet 11 inches of her, arriving in a huge white Cadillac half a street long. She let me caddie for her and was quite generous. Another regular celebrity on the course was the multi-talented Roy Castle. He wasn't born in the locality, but lived in the area for many years.

My own golf game suffered, because if you were a kid playing in those days you were on your own. Even though I was a bit of a loner, I found myself drawn at the age of 7 or 8 to the other kids playing football and as soon as I became keen, golf took a back seat. I did not play again until my teens when I went down to single handicap figures. Since those days I enjoyed only the occasional round while I was in football.

When I was at the League we would have a regular four during the summer meeting comprising Deputy Secretary George Readle, Sir Matt Busby, 'Jolly' Jack Wiseman from Birmingham City and me. Invariably we would be at a coastal resort for the summer meeting, so it made for a pleasant diversion once the meetings were over. Jack Wiseman could hit a very sweet golf ball and was quite a decent middle handicap golfer. Matt, on the other hand, had a problem with consistency where he would hit one good shot followed by four or five when he would wander off into the bushes, wondering why he bothered playing the game. The only time I ever saw him exasperated was on the golf course. 'Oh Jeez,' he would mutter. 'Carry on boys, I'll play another ball.'

We had a game at La Baule during Le Tournoi in 1997. The England players were like little kids anxiously waiting for the rain to ease up so that Glenn Hoddle would let them out to play. I partnered David Seaman against Alan Shearer and Stuart Pearce. The grit and determination of our opponents prevailed, though Pearce's swing won few marks for style!

I think that being exposed to the world of entertainment and the theatre at such an early age has stuck with me for ever. When I was young I had a friend whose mother was secretary to the legendary Reginald Dixon, the Blackpool Tower organist. We were often given tickets for a radio programme called *Blackpool Night*. We used to go along to the old Co-op building for the recording where the warm-up man was also the producer of the programme, a fellow called James Casey who was in BBC light entertainment in the North West and the son of Jimmy James, the renowned comedian. He was the best warm-up man I have ever seen before or since. His patter was hilarious. I still love to go and see the shows with entertainers like Ken Dodd and Roy Hudd who have a feel for the old theatre. The old Music Hall jokes will never die.

I also like some of the contemporary comedy. I have a great admiration for comics like Jasper Carrott who can talk for half an hour about nothing, just observing the peculiarities of life, and Bob Monkhouse's tremendous timing and ad libbing.

I came across Carrott in various grounds when he was a director of Birmingham City. He was always witty and amusing whenever Romayne and I met him in one of the boardrooms, and never more so than when he was telling us about the crocodiles which disturbed his holiday in the Florida Everglades.

My football career developed as I played for the Town Under-15 side under the tutelage of our own sports master Ellis Tomlinson. 'Toss', as he was nicknamed, was a fearsome chap to us, even though he was in his sixties. He wore a windcheater and long navy blue shorts and you would see his gnarled legs bearing down on you with solid steel tipped football boots. You didn't want to get in the way of him.

Mr Tomlinson terrified the kids and was quite caustic if you rubbed him up the wrong way. He told one of my team mates that he was about as much use as a chocolate teapot and the unfortunate individual became known for the remainder of his school life as Teapot.

John Hurst went on from the Town Under-15 team to play for Everton for many years as a strong and consistent defender who laid off the ball quickly and simply to Alan Ball, Colin Harvey or Howard Kendall; the last I heard of him was as a youth coach to Joe Royle at Everton. Another, John Craven, who played for Blackpool and Coventry, sadly died a few years ago.

We could be equally as cruel as Mr Tomlinson but not quite as brave, as we enrolled a less fearsome teacher in the 'Teen and Twenty Disc Club' with Radio Luxembourg. He took a dim view when he received his little yellow member's badge through the post. The finger of suspicion pointed only one way and the entire class was given a detention.

Mr Tomlinson could not have been too bad because he used to invite the football team back to his home to watch the England internationals, something which would probably be frowned upon nowadays. He was a real football fan and a big Blackpool supporter. He used to stand at a part of the ground at the South End which he called 'Martin's Folly' after a horrendous misunderstanding between our English international goalkeeper Tony Waiters and left back Barrie Martin, who slipped the ball back to Waiters when the keeper was looking elsewhere. It was an awful own goal. Mr Tomlinson was strict and insisted that we wore our shirts inside our shorts. When we pointed out that Charlie Buchan, whose *Football Annual* we were given every Christmas, had worn his shirt outside, our teacher pointed out that he was dead! Maybe he thought that contributed towards his death.

He had this concept of the elastic minute which was fine if you were winning or if it was a nice day, but if it was pouring down with rain or you had to get away to do your paper round it was not so good. I would ask whether it was an elastic or a real minute, but he would always tell me I would have to wait and see. Rarely was I on time for my paper round on a Wednesday afternoon.

It was important to supplement the pocket money with the part-time work and I had a milk round as well as a paper round. I also worked in a fish and chip shop every summer.

It did not seem to affect my studies or my sport for I left school with three GCE A-levels in French, Latin and History and put my talents to work for a while breaking up toffee in a factory. The money was not great, but you could eat as much as you wanted. Once I had had my fill of toffee, I joined the bank.

I played for a youth team called Anchorsholme Rovers, coached by Jim Kelly, a Blackpool wing-half and no relation, and also, on occasions, by Jimmy Armfield. I suppose now that I have revealed that I watched Jim play for my favourite team and was then coached by him, I could be accused of cronyism by taking him on at the FA, but he was well worth their money. I cannot understand how he did not remember me as a young player – maybe it's his age!

When I was 14, I went on a foreign tour to Holland and Belgium, which was a great experience. I went around Blackpool with old fashioned punchboards to raise money for the trip.

It was around then that my dreams of making my living from the game began to grow when I was spotted by a scout from Accrington Stanley. You read stories of professional clubs sending a set of shirts or boots to the amateur side when they find a star player. My fee on this basis would have been a pair of laces.

I had a sad life! I went for a month to train with their first team in 1960 and was awed by a player named Mike Ferguson, who was released by Burnley and went on to play for Blackburn, Coventry, QPR and scouted for Terry Venables in 1996. The Leeds and Manchester United central defender Gordon McQueen's dad Willie was the goalkeeper.

Somewhere in the archives my name is in the records as a registered player, although I was only 14 years old and should not really have signed. I would probably have been drummed out of the school team, had they known. I never actually played for Accrington and they went out of business shortly afterwards – I promise, it had nothing to do with me.

When the light was too bad to play football at the Hydro or against the garage door, we used to play in the winter by lamplight right on the promenade against the sea wall with those popular plastic Frido balls. Heaven only knows how many of those we lost on the back of the gales blowing them into the Irish sea. There were no volunteers to fetch them back. I never learned to swim.

As one of the prominent local players, I was invited to go training at Bloomfield Road for a spell, but that mainly consisted of running the length of the pitch and walking the width on the track. Like a much more illustrious player of that age, Danny Blanchflower, I was not enamoured at the lack of ball work. One of my most memorable games of the period was an 'unofficial' match when our school beat Blackpool Grammar School who did not have football on their curriculum. We had lots of mates at the Grammar School who played for other teams and we persuaded our teacher to arrange an ad hoc game. It was probably totally illegal with no insurance, no groundsman, no nothing and probably if it had been reported to me at the Football Association I would have recommended serious disciplinary action and, taking into account my crime of signing for Accrington Stanley, I could have banned myself *sine die*. But it was one of the best games I ever played in as we won 5–4.

They could never understand in school how I was always playing football, yet when it came to cross country through muddy farmyards I suffered from asthma and was unable to run. Strange too, that so much later in my life, one of the few things outside football I do regularly is to run for charity. I train regularly, have taken part in the Great North Run four times and, in 1999, ran the London Marathon, no longer having the excuse that I was too busy to train properly for it. Even then I had to scrutinise the list of finishers in *The Times* for over a week before they reached my time, which was nearer six hours than three.

Looking back, I was something of a rebel for I started playing for a Sunday team called Highfurlong at a time before Sunday football was legalised in Blackpool. They refused to allow the council pitches to be used on Sunday, so to beat the ban we travelled out of the borough to play.

I used to spend hours playing 'keepie-uppie' with a lad called John Staves, who went on to be a useful League cricketer. Those hours in the backyard bouncing a football up and down paid rich dividends some years later when I astounded the Council on the last day of a conference at Bournemouth. We were desperately searching around for some way of entertaining the remaining Council members who had not departed for home on the Sunday when I took bets on how many times I could keep the ball up in the lounge of the Royal Bath Hotel.

The estimates ranged between 20 and 30, and one member came reasonably close, but no one managed to guess the 72 I achieved below the glittering chandeliers.

As we grew older we were spoilt for choice watching football from where we were based in Blackpool. It was nothing for us to pop off to Liverpool, Manchester, Bolton, Burnley and Blackburn, all top division teams in those days, and even Leeds was only an hour and a half away. I find it difficult to believe nowadays that at that stage I actually preferred watching to playing. Nowadays, of course, it is virtually impossible to decide on the day to go to a top match, but then, with the larger capacities, it was easier and it was only once, at Liverpool, that we suffered the indignity of being locked out.

Today Blackpool is very much a love affair from afar. Although I see them two or three times a season, mainly on their travels, I have never seen them win in ten years since leaving Blackpool. They have achieved the odd draw, but never a win. It was reaching the stage where they were not at all keen to see me and when I walked through the door there would be uproar from the directors.

It was wonderful living in a holiday resort like that as a boy and a young man. There was entertainment in abundance with the many shows staged for the benefit of the tens of thousands of tourists who flocked into our town. There were shows at the Opera House, on the three piers, in the Winter Gardens – in fact there were five or six major theatres in those days. Morecambe and Wise were massively popular and achieved record takings. Most of the artists were paid in cash at the time and many of them used to come straight round to the bank to put it away. I recall Eric Morecambe coming into Barclays with his wages to pay them into his account. Pam Lawrenson, one of the tellers, made conversation and asked him how many children he had. Eric answered: 'Two.' Pam then asked: 'Is that a boy and a girl?'

'No,' replied Eric straight-faced. 'It's a girl and a boy.' He could not help himself. He was just the same off the stage as he was on it.

One particular posting with Barclays was to the Central Drive branch directly behind the Golden Mile. In the summer the three members of the staff worked flat out, taking in stacks of pound notes smelling of chip fat. In the winter, however, the pressure was considerably less and we were able to indulge our passion of shoveha'penny. There were only a handful of customers who came in between 9.30 and 3.30, so it gave lots of time to replay the Blackpool–Bolton Wanderers 1953 Cup Final, albeit on a sloping pitch (a desk) which required a special technique. But at least we didn't need to worry where the coins would come from.

I used to like the variety of entertainment and, of course, the sports facilities in Blackpool. There are a staggering nine golf courses, Stanley Park and lots of smaller cricket grounds. I enjoyed playing cricket until I became fed up with the captain sending me in to bat in the middle of a bowler's hat trick, although since leaving the FA, I have joined the Celebrity Bunbury's XI.

We had the Lancashire county cricket team in the town once a year until the club made the apparently grave error of giving Yorkshire's Geoff Boycott a testimonial. The Lancs committee took a dim view, took the county match away and gave it to Lytham instead.

The Leagues were very strong at the time in the area, and one of a number of top players we had playing for Blackpool at Stanley Park was the great West Indian Rohan Kanhai. He used to knock the ball out of the ground with that famous falling sweep. I saw him score 153 in no time at all.

It is an eye-opener today to see the kids with their computers and video games. If bad weather stopped our ball games we reverted to Subbuteo or Owzat, a cheap and simple game of dice which gave hours of pleasure to boys keen to replicate the Ashes series.

One of the great benefits of my job with the Football Association was that it allowed me to play at some magnificent venues entirely out of keeping with my limited ability. Places like Wembley Stadium, Old Trafford, the City Ground Nottingham, the Maracana Stadium in Rio, and Stanford University, scene of the 1994 World Cup qualifying matches, joined Holker Street, Barrow and Preston North End's legendary Deepdale. I was awed with Barrow and Preston when I played there for my schoolboy team. But at Manchester United and Nottingham Forest I played for the FA staff team.

As the boss I was an automatic choice for the FA, even though I did not actually select the side. The *Guardian* once telephoned Brian Gee, who did pick the team, before we played our annual grudge match against the Football League, a game we never won, and asked if it were true that I was actually playing. The reporter asked what position I played and Brian dryly answered: 'Any position he wants.'

It got better. I used to be made captain around March time just in advance of the annual salary review when they were really pandering to me.

I left Olympic Champion Daley Thompson gasping for breath once when we played International Management Group. He maintains that he collided with a defender as I wheeled in triumph after putting away our equaliser, but I prefer to tell everyone that I outpaced the world's greatest all round athlete at our home ground, Barclays Sports Ground, Hanger Lane.

I cannot exactly claim to playing a match in the famed but faded Maracana. We went to Rio for the International Board meeting in 1996 and George Cumming of the Scottish Football Association and I took a ball onto the pitch and kicked about in front of what we imagined were 200,000 screaming Brazilians. In fact there was not another soul to be seen in the pouring rain.

I actually played a proper game in Rio at a different venue. Players these days complain about kicking off at odd times to satisfy the demands of television but our game kicked off at 6.30 am. A friend who used to play in our games in London when he was a student,

121

telephoned to say he had read in the paper that I was in town for the meeting and he wondered if I fancied a game of football as they always played Saturday morning. He offered to call for me – at 6 am. I thought I had problems but he had to drive from Belo Horizonte, 300 miles away. Despite the unusual time of day, it was a super game on a shale pitch which was fully booked throughout the day.

I scored my debut goal at Wembley at the age of 51, playing for the Football Trust against the Members of Parliament. I would like to be able to say it was a volley from outside the box, but it was a tap in from 18 inches. I was reminded recently that I actually took two touches as I was so nervous to make sure on that famous turf.

That was not the first time I played at Wembley. My actual debut came before I started on my rigorous fitness routine which eventually led me to distance running. The occasion was a shortened game before the Freight Rover Final. I was invited to pick the teams and made sure that there was only 21 and, as usual, had my boots with me.

To reflect the big event later, there was one team in Bolton Wanderers kit and the other in Bristol City kit. It was probably the biggest crowd I have ever played in front of, with about 20,000 in the ground when we kicked off.

But there were problems, not least of all the fact the shorts were about four sizes too small. I could hardly move. Another was that George Best was on the other team. He was wonderful, so laid-back, just kicking the ball around in the dressing room before the game – but not so unassuming on the pitch where I could not get near him.

I also faced another disciplinary threat, because standing next to me in the tunnel before the game was the former England international Stan Bowles. We exchanged the usual pleasantries and I asked him who he was playing for at that time. To my horror he replied that he wasn't, because he had been banned *sine die*. I thought to myself 'Oh no, here I am waiting to go out and play at Wembley with a player who is banned for life.'

Worse was to follow. I have checked the game out thoroughly on the video and can confirm what everyone suspected, that I played for 12 minutes of the 20-minute game and did not touch the ball once. I was substituted at exactly the moment two Freight Rover vans drove around the pitch as an advertising plug for the sponsors. Television presenter Mike Morris, who was commentating over the tannoy, suggested it was the ambulance sent to help me off.

Frank Worthington, Ray Cashley, Micky Burns, Gordon Taylor,

Brendon Batson, David Webb, Chris Garland and others can also testify that I did not make a single bad pass that day. Fred Eyre was also playing for the opposition and, apart from being a very amusing author, he had quite a good football head on him. Every time goalkeeper Peter Bonetti had the ball, Fred would drop back to the edge of the box and make himself available but, without fail, Bonetti threw the ball to Bobby Moore. Well, you would, wouldn't you?

I can also tell my grandchildren of the day I played with Glenn Hoddle in Rome on the eve of the crucial World Cup qualifying game in 1997. The staff had been threatening all week to have a game between the coaches and the physiotherapists. I had let it be known that I might just be free for half an hour that afternoon, or any afternoon the contest was arranged. I expected Hoddle to be disdainful of the entire proceedings but with a line-up of Ray Clemence, Hoddle, Kelly, John Gorman and Glen Roeder against the likes of Gary Lewin and Alan Smith, he took it surprisingly seriously.

We won 5–4 and I scored four. It has dawned on me since that the chances laid on for me were all tap-ins. Do you think that Hoddle and Gorman were playing for a new contract that day? They even signed the ball which I carried with me to the game next night and then all the way home afterwards.

We also had one or two good games with the press team which has played all over the world on their travels, with and against some of the best players ever to lace on boots, albeit long after their professional careers had ended. I played in Moldova when coach Peter Taylor missed a sitter in front of all his Under-21 team. Terry Butcher, a regular contributor to the media, was always good to have on your side in a sticky situation in Eastern Europe. His attitude to the game had not changed a jot since his magnificent days with Ipswich, Rangers and England.

Perhaps the funniest moment in one of these press games was in Tbilisi where we played on a public park. The groundsman was late and we kicked off without the advantage of nets on the goalposts. After about ten minutes he arrived, put the nets up at one end and then proceeded to march straight up the middle of the pitch with his net in one hand and his step ladders in the other, oblivious to the game going on around him. Someone commented that he had been sent on with his ladder to mark our tall striker Henry Winter from the *Daily Telegraph*.

I was just moving into position to complete a long flowing move when Henry rose in front of me and headed wide. He claimed afterwards that he never heard a shout, not even a 'no comment', from the Chief Executive. It was also the notable occasion when the gentlemanly Trevor Brooking somehow managed to involve himself in a punch-up and was duffed up by the opposition.

Another regular venue for me is Hyde Park where, with coats as goalposts, a team called Dinosaur Thursday play. The name may suggest a team of FA Councillors with nothing better to do on a Thursday afternoon but, in fact, most of the team are from the Natural History museum.

But one of the most special games for me was in 1993 when I was honoured with a match put on specifically for my benefit on my one and only trip to the Scilly Isles. They boast only two teams and play often enough to become quite familiar with each other. We were visiting Romayne's relatives when we played in torrential rain and ankle deep in mud.

The most memorable thing about an enjoyable game was the presence of the one spectator, John Young, who takes his own portable stand to every game. It is rather like a sentry box outside Buckingham Palace except that you could see his lower legs when he stood up and walked it away. It was the forerunner of the all-seater stadium.

My keenly-developed, if somewhat twisted, sense of humour often stood me in good stead, for my position at the FA led to all sorts of mockery. I even had my photograph taken by the renowned photographer David Bailey alongside an eagle, otherwise known as the Crystal Palace mascot, for the magazine *FourFourTwo*. I turned up at Bailey's studio just off the Grays Inn Road and he had no idea who I was. I explained that I was Graham Kelly, Chief Executive of the Football Association. This really impressed him, for he replied: 'Jolly good – what's that all about?'. The 'eagle' held its head under its arm.

I was also the subject of an award from the irreverent football magazine *When Saturday Comes*. I topped the category for the man who did the most damage to football in 1993. I never did discover if it was a real poll or a spoof. Mike Wilmore, who was looking after the FA's public relations at the time, said they had me over a barrel and that I couldn't win whether I attended the awards night or not.

I thought about it while lying on a holiday beach in Cyprus when I suddenly decided that I would go and confront them in the comedy club in Camden attended by around 500 people. I thought I could turn it around and take the mickey out of them. It was very late, in fact just before midnight, when the alternative comedy acts finished and I was the final recipient for the awards, presumably for setting up the Premier League. I went on stage dressed in a dinner jacket and pulled out a sheaf of papers and proceeded to give a Dickie Attenborough-type speech of appreciation for everyone who had helped me in my career. It was fun and went down a storm. I was the only one to turn up. Others like Harry Harris of the *Daily Mirror*, Jimmy Hill and Alan Sugar, not surprisingly, failed to show to collect their 'awards'.

I had learned very early on in my football career the value of humour. The first ever speech I gave was to the Southern League Annual Dinner in 1973. If any members of the audience are reading I will apologise to them right now for my speech about the burning issues of the day which was entirely inappropriate to an end of season dinner and went down like the proverbial lead balloon, so much so that the comedian Jim Bowen, who was following me, tore my pitiful effort to shreds, telling the audience that I was to public speaking what Lionel Blair was to Rugby League. From that day to this, I have never stood up before an audience without some form of sensible preparation together with a joke or two. Thankfully this now stands me in good stead when my agent David Davies (not that one) books me to speak at conferences and dinners.

I also failed with my debut in the world of pop videos. I presume I failed, because I am still awaiting the royalty statements from 'On Top of the World', the official England team song for the World Cup in France when I was briefly featured on the drums with Ian McCulloch from Echo and the Bunny Men with the Spice Girls in the chorus. To my son's eternal regret I was not in the studio at the same time as the girls.

In the video I also shut the garage door on the musicians as if I hated them. I think that was about right as it didn't sell too well by all accounts, with the fans preferring the old *Three Lions* song from Skinner and Baddiel.

I quite enjoy radio and television, and when I left the FA I embarked on a number of appearances, a newspaper column for the *Independent* and was even seriously groped by Gary Lineker and Rory McGrath as 'Guess the Sportsman' on the BBC's *They Think It's All Over*. The balls in the velvet bag ensured that Lineker was spot-on.

Just as any footballer will testify to the banter of the dressing room, so I believed in the value of humour in defusing the tensest moments of the ardent debates that characterised the multi-million pound industry that is today's football.

CHAPTER EIGHT

In League with the Devil

I came across some larger than life characters when I worked for the Football League – Alan Hardaker, Bob Lord and Sam Bolton to name but three – but few were larger or more controversial than the Czech-born multi-millionaire publisher Robert Maxwell.

Captain Bob, as he was known, played a fascinating role in the story of the Football League in the 1980s. In 1982 Oxford United approached him and he bailed the club out with a fairly modest level of investment from his resources. When he decided he could not make money out of Oxford, he wanted to merge them with Reading and the idea of Thames Valley Royals was born. Maxwell, never one to shilly-shally, threatened that it would be the end of football at Oxford without the merger.

Both clubs were in the Third Division of the Football League, so the Management Committee, led by a former Labour Party colleague of Maxwell's, Jack Dunnett, did not harbour any strong objections. However, Roger Smee, the new chairman of Reading, did. The fans of the two clubs, as fans always will under these circumstances, made their objections strongly felt. Roger Smee had a lot of trouble ridding Reading of Maxwell. Even though the owner of the Mirror Group of Newspapers only had 19% of the shares, he blocked everything Smee tried to do.

When, for all his bullying and strong arm tactics, the merger never happened, the avaricious Maxwell began to turn his attentions to bigger fish.

In 1984 he saved Derby County by buying the Baseball Ground. The Management Committee still raised no objections as he put his son Kevin in charge at Oxford. He also famously tried to buy Manchester United but did not succeed, although his *Daily Mirror* made life difficult for Michael Knighton who almost did.

Then on 20 November 1987 the crunch finally came for the Football League when Maxwell and Elton John agreed a deal whereby Maxwell's company BPPC would buy 94% of the Watford shares from the singer songwriter for £2 million. The deal would see the Chief Executive of BPPC, John Holloran, take the chair at Watford and Elton would become Life President after his 11 years as Chairman, during which time the club had gone from Division Four to Division One, reached the FA Cup Final, finished second behind Liverpool and played in Europe.

At this time Maxwell was Chairman of Derby County, so the Football League Management Committee had to examine the issue closely. Since Ron Noades had been involved with both Wimbledon and Crystal Palace at the start of the decade, there had been a League rule preventing one person being involved in the management or administration of more than one club. Maxwell, in typical style, laid down the gauntlet. He said that if the Football League did not welcome the deal, he would pull out. The Management Committee called his bluff, refused to approve the deal and expressed the hope that he would walk away from it. Some hope.

Maxwell quoted the Moores family with holdings in both Liverpool and Everton as reasons why he should be allowed to continue to build his power base in Division One. He said that, as far as he was personally concerned, he was fully committed to Derby County and that Oxford and Watford would be independent. Whether Mark Lawrenson, a former manager of Oxford, would testify to the independence of anything belonging to Captain Bob is debatable. He had been in charge at Oxford when Dean Saunders was sold above his head to Derby County, a very disturbing development which should have awakened everyone to the potential problems. Lawrenson's protests resulted in his dismissal.

Maxwell claimed that he was trying to sell the Reading shares he still held and denied any breach of rules. He was being heavily backed by Elton John who asked Maxwell to stay and, given this support, Maxwell commenced a verbal assault on the rulers of the game, coining the phrase 'the Mismanagement Committee' and adding that the game was dominated by incompetent, selfish, bumbling amateurs, who had failed on every issue including television, pools and hooligans. Presumably he wanted to change all that and become an incompetent, selfish, bumbling professional!

The League, obstinately sticking to their ground in the face of such insults, said that they would change the rules if Maxwell persisted and Phil Carter of Everton, the President at the time, said that if Maxwell was so dissatisfied, he should stand for the committee himself.

But there was to be no let-up. Maxwell's *Daily Mirror* libelled David Dein of Arsenal in connection with his business and was forced to apologise the next day.

There was a suggestion that we should report Maxwell to the FA over his comments, but I thought that pointless and said that we should fight our own battles. In the meantime, our solicitors Herbert Smith and Company were doing some research into the control of BPPC where they thought the answers might lie, and I authorised them to seek counsel's opinion. David Oliver QC thought there was a possibility that Maxwell could be proved to control BPCC, and thus both Derby and Watford, through a Liechtenstein foundation. On the basis of counsel's opinion we had the chance of an injunction on the grounds that League rules were being broken.

I then had to consult the members of the Management Committee to see if they approved of this course of action. The majority of them agreed, with Ken Bates being one of the few dissenters. He claimed that he had been working behind the scenes to try and resolve the matter and that we would finish with egg on our face if we pursued the matter into the courts. He disliked things being thrust upon him by telephone, he said, and, in any case, we would not win. It was out of character for Ken to object to things being done quickly and decisively.

David Dein could not be contacted so I went ahead and asked the solicitor to obtain the injunction. Maxwell was predictably furious, saying that Carter was two-faced and threatened to hold all the Committee personally liable. It transpired that Dein was trying to broker a deal with Maxwell who turned up at his house the following morning on 5 December. He breezed past David's wife Barbara, saying: 'Can you put the kettle on, dearie.' The tea must have done the trick because they reached an agreement.

Phil Carter, who was also present, agreed that the League would withdraw the legal proceedings and in turn Maxwell agreed that 'in the best interests of football' he and his family would dispose of their interests in Oxford United to a suitable purchaser who would guarantee the future of the club.

I had to convey the results of the meeting to other members of the Management Committee. Most of them made it clear that under no circumstances would they have countenanced a deal with Maxwell and would not be likely to sanction the withdrawal of the litigation.

With the Management Committee in disarray, the initiative gained in court was quickly lost, because no instructions could be given to the solicitors to carry on the action. Maxwell, sensing victory, gave the League 48 hours to ratify the agreement between him, Carter and Dein.

Carter wanted a meeting with the rest of the Management Committee who refused to endorse a deal done behind their backs, particularly Bill Fox who was not going to meet on a Sunday again. They ignored Maxwell's 48-hour deadline and the judge confirmed that the approval of the Football League was needed for the deal to be completed.

Phil Carter thought that the deal they had done was preferable to legal action. He felt that the Maxwell family would sell their shares in Oxford and Reading and would agree not to influence the affairs of Watford.

Maxwell, presumably using information supplied to him by his sports desks at Holborn, cited PSV Eindhoven in Holland and Juventus in Italy as two clubs which were run benevolently by corporations in the way he envisaged for Watford.

But, for once, Maxwell was unable to have his own way and because of the unsettling effect at Oxford United and Derby County, Elton John eventually persuaded Maxwell to withdraw from their deal.

The Management Committee immediately strengthened the rules against multi-ownership and the positions of David Dein and Phil Carter were seriously questioned. The subsequent BSkyB dispute in 1988 was the final nail in their Management Committee coffin.

There was plenty of fall-out and another one with his nose out of joint, Ken Bates, criticised me to a meeting of First Division clubs, saying that I was wrong to conduct important business by telephone. I don't know how he conducts all his business. Perhaps through his programme notes!

I did not have any more contact with Maxwell until I joined the FA eighteen months later. His *Daily Mirror* was raising funds at the time on behalf of the Hillsborough victims. He rang me at Lancaster Gate.

'We haven't spoken since your appointment,' he said. 'Many congratulations. I am sure that you are the right man. You will do an excellent job.' He continued, 'I would like to talk to you about the presentation of the million pound cheque from the magnificent readers of the *Daily Mirror*.'

'Yes,' I said.

Encouraged, he went on: 'I would like to present it on the Wembley pitch at half time during the Cup Final.'

I responded very carefully. 'I am sorry, Bob, but you and the *Daily Mirror* cannot hijack the Cup Final in that way.'

His cool exterior quickly crumbled and he snapped: 'That is a fucking impertinence' and slammed the phone down. I never heard from him again.

I had gone from being a superb administrator to an impertinent twit in less than a minute. Fortunately in football administration, you quickly develop a thick skin.

My decision to quit the safe world of banking and head for the unknown world of the beautiful game came in 1968 after four years with Barclays. I answered an advert for the post of junior clerk with the Football League at Lytham St. Annes. I was happy enough working as a cashier but did not see my long term career in the bank. I did not fancy studying economics and law to ensure a steady climb up the ladder.

I was given the job at the Football League thanks largely to secretary Alan Hardaker, who seemed to want someone with a bit of life about him. I proudly told him at the interview that I had driven to London in my Morris Minor to see the European Cup Final at Wembley where Manchester United beat Benfica. It had the reverse effect for he said: 'Oh no, not another bloody Manchester United supporter.'

Even so, he gave me the job and I started as assistant to accountant Norman Thomas in July 1968 at £1,050 a year, a lot more than I was earning at the bank and for doing a job which involved my hobby. I have to admit that the work was about as close to football as my previous employment at the bank and the job was a little tedious in the early years, to say the least, as I entered players' wages from the pension returns. In those days before computers this was done manually. There were probably 3,000 or so players registered in those days and the returns, on a large, grey form, came in intermittently throughout the year.

I suffered in silence for two years before I found myself in a far more interesting environment as I assisted in carrying out book inspections at the League clubs. We were to do eight semi-random inspections a year. We gave very little notice, but there was no point turning up unannounced as, with football clubs, it was quite likely that no one would be there.

It was highly topical as Port Vale and Peterborough United had both been disciplined by the League for irregular payments. My old hero Stan Matthews had inadvertently got himself caught up in it at Port Vale, and Peterborough were demoted a division. The punishments were largely for payments which were not in the players' contracts or authorised by the League.

When we turned up at Derby County, Brian Clough was there to make a fuss of us, as he would, making sure the coal fire in the boardroom where we were to work was well stoked. Not by himself, of course, as he called in 'Ruby' in a very loud voice. Ruby had to shovel the coal on the fire.

His concern for our welfare did not help him as Derby were fined £10,000. They had applied for permission to pay their captain, the gritty Scottish international Dave Mackay, for writing a programme article. They had been refused but they paid it to his company anyway. This, plus a few more irregularities, saw them disciplined and, more seriously, they were also banned from the European Fairs' Cup, the predecessor to the UEFA Cup.

Manchester United were another club we caught out for paying their players too much in bonuses for the World Club Championship against Estudiantes. After the kicking they took over in South America, I personally felt they deserved every penny, but they had also exceeded the lodging allowances for young players and they were fined and banned from playing in European friendly matches for two years.

The clubs were a cunning bunch. They would always ensure that they took Norman and me out for lunch on the premise that the more time we spent dining, the less time we had to go through the books. It was a fairly obvious ploy and one that did them no good at all. But we enjoyed our lunches.

We also went to Ipswich and met dear old John Cobbold, one of the first directors I had met and one of football's great characters. He possessed a white Rover and when we came out of Portman Road his driver was lounging inside the car, would you believe, watching television. John said: 'Shift your arse, * * * *face' and told him to get himself out of the back and into the front to take us back to our hotel but first, having enjoyed one or two glasses of white wine, he watered the training pitch before jumping in his car to join us. Quite obviously he had nothing to hide and his books were fine too!

I loved my new duties. Here I was, a football fan, going round the country behind the scenes to see how they did things – or rather how, in some instances, they didn't do things.

Although I had not wanted to study economics at the bank, I quickly realised I would be filling in players' pension returns for the next 40 years if I did not do something about my prospects. I decided to take a correspondence course to become qualified as a chartered secretary and studied via Rapid Results College to get the FCIS qualification. That was instrumental in helping me gain the appointment as Assistant Secretary in 1973.

Alan Hardaker, our autocratic master, wanted to wind down. He was always at the eye of every storm and felt that he had no one he could really confide in. Thus he tended to take his problems home with him. His closest confidant appeared to be Ernest Francis from Solihull who published the programme insert called the *Football League Review* or *League Football* as it became known later. Francis seemed to act as Alan's commercial guru, making the early sponsorship deals which led to the Ford Sporting League and the Texaco and Watney Cups. The obvious choice of confidant should have been Alan's assistant, Eric Howarth, a nephew of Alan's predecessor Fred Howarth. Fred had refused to accept the inevitable when Alan was recruited to succeed him by the Management Committee in 1951 and the ambitious Hardaker was condemned to the filing cabinets for six years before Fred grudgingly threw the keys on the table and said: 'You had better have these. For some reason the Management Committee don't want me to stay any longer.'

Alan saw Eric as a crony of the Management Committee and wanted a more vigorous approach. He duly advertised for a Deputy Secretary. There were three people in the ring: George Readle, who had been the referees' officer of the Football League, having come from the Association of Football League Referees and Linesmen; Jim Kenyon, secretary of the Lancashire FA, who was fairly close to League Vice-President Bob Lord, who was also the President of the Lancs FA; and me.

After two series of interviews, one with a sub committee of Len

Shipman of Leicester City, Sam Bolton of Leeds United and Bob Lord and one full interview in London with the entire Management Committee, they appointed George as Deputy Secretary and me as Assistant Secretary.

Len Shipman, the President of the League, always said he wanted to be 'master of the situation'. He was one of the old school, a gruff haulier who made lots of friends in the game. He endeared himself to them with some wonderful malapropisms; the Anglo-Scottish Cup became the Anglo-*English* Cup while one club was warmly congratulated by the President on their 75th Centenary!

Alan Hardaker was quite a character. He saw himself as the guardian of the true values of the League. He had a considerable ego and did not want any other major players on the stage competing with him. He liked Tom Finney more than Stanley Matthews and abhorred the growing personality cult epitomised by the likes of Brian Clough and Malcolm Allison. But he himself had a massive office.

I was called in once for transgressing office rules in a fairly minor way and I was so pleased to escape relatively unscathed that I took the wrong way out and in classic comedy style narrowly avoided ending up in the loo.

One of the earliest issues I faced was the problem of clubs calling off fixtures because of illness. A few injuries often turned into a viral epidemic necessitating the closure of the ground and an application to postpone matches.

Alan Hardaker instructed me to make a stand. The unlucky recipients of the new harder line were Exeter City who, in 1974, were down to only nine fit players including two goalkeepers, and called off a match at Scunthorpe United against my recommendation. They were fined £5,000, deducted two points and ordered to pay costs of £1,000.

Hardaker bitterly opposed the clubs who wanted to reform the Management Committee by introducing regional representation. He thought the best men should sit, notwithstanding where they came from. He lost the argument because the clubs were becoming disillusioned with the lack of communication which they construed as autocracy. In reality, he had the *nous* to be able to twist the committee around his little finger.

One of his first duties as Secretary was to pursue the legal action in 1960 against Littlewoods which established the clubs' right to a royalty on the pools coupons.

He was a very shrewd administrator and it would have been fascinating to see how he would have handled the moguls of later eras, particularly someone like Bob Maxwell. I am sure he would have given as good as he got, because he was a hell of a fighter.

Hardaker was the guiding force behind the Football League for 20 years. He had a terrible temper first thing in the morning; he could be in a foul mood usually because of what was in the papers or perhaps something in the morning mail had upset him. He would dash off a stinging reply to whatever had upset him, but fortunately later in the day he would have had a chance to light up his first pipe, have a chat with Ernest Francis or Jimmy Armfield, someone he wanted to recruit, and then his sense of humour would come to the fore and I could persuade him to omit some of the more blistering paragraphs.

His robust sense of humour was his main redeeming feature and meant that you could just about live with him on a day-to-day basis.

He also knew how to look after himself. He had a nice sideline when he chaired the panel which decided where the ball was for Littlewoods and Vernons' 'Spot the Ball' competition. When he died in 1980 the pools companies asked me to take over from him. It was worth £65 for a Saturday morning visit to Liverpool, quite good money at the time, but I did not want my first act to be taking a job with Littlewoods. I needed my independence at that stage of my career.

Hardaker led the discussions in 1972 when the FA and League were considering televising live the crucial England qualifying European Championship game against West Germany, but when the meeting with the television executives was arranged, he was snubbed and Sir Andrew Stephen, Chairman of the FA, sold the rights which Hardaker reckoned were worth £100,000 for £60,000. Hardaker said: 'Regrettably, there appears to be a state of war between the FA and the Football League.' What's new?!

Alan Hardaker did not dislike all other football administrators, however. He had great respect for Sir Stanley Rous, the Secretary of the FA who had gone on to be President of the FA, and he thought that Rous' successor Denis Follows was an even better administrator.

Alan Hardaker persuaded ITV to get involved in football back in the 60s, when previously there had just been the BBC. The problem was that when they came together, they negotiated as a cartel and refused to do so individually. We were to feel the effects of that for many years until genuine competition came with the advent of satellite and forced up the price of football.

There was no one quite like Hardaker for getting into scrapes and then getting out of them again. He launched a partnership with Ladbrokes to 'Spot the Ball'. It flopped miserably because Ladbrokes were more interested in getting hold of the pools companies' collectors, but eventually it led to the setting up of the Football Trust after Hardaker made an agreement with Cecil Moores of Littlewoods and Denis Howell, the Minister for Sport.

He took an immediate dislike to Ted Croker, the Secretary of the Football Association, which did not seem to be based on anything other than the fact that in one of the newspaper features on Ted Croker's appointment, the new FA Secretary said that his shirts cost him £8 and Hardaker thought that was incredibly extravagant.

He did not get everything right as he displayed at one Management Committee meeting when the discussion turned to Sunderland FC and, as it was a delicate matter, they asked Sunderland director Sid Collings to leave the room. Hardaker promptly forgot about him and it was a couple of hours later that they remembered and someone was sent to find dear old Sid who was leaning against the corridor wall smoking a cigarette rather like Private Walker of *Dad's Army*. 'Quite all right,' he said, 'No problem.' There were not too many like him, however!

Hardaker became involved in yet another scrape with Jimmy Hill because Hill was the only club director who opposed the so-called 'Snatch of the Day' in 1978 when the BBC's established *Match of the Day* lost out to ITV. Jimmy said that it was akin to football hooliganism, the way the Management Committee had done a deal with London Weekend Television to screen the football highlights programme. Hardaker and the League commenced defamation proceedings which meandered on for ages until Hardaker died, leaving only Jack Dunnett who wanted to carry it on. The case was eventually settled out of court.

Another threatened legal battle was evoked by Brian Clough who wanted to sue Hardaker for calling him an idiot. But, not surprisingly, that was another one which failed to last the distance.

Hardaker's introduction of a specially designed ball was not as successful as the sponsored competitions he inaugurated. First, he gave the contract to Stuart Surridge & Co., one of the smaller manufacturers of balls, when the clubs preferred Mitre or Adidas. Second, the unusual design, a red flash on the white ball, gave the appearance of a wobble in the air. Its debut at the League Cup Final in

1979 between Nottingham Forest and Southampton made little impression on Saints manager Lawrie McMenemy.

One of Hardaker's most interesting relationships was with Burnley's vociferous chairman Bob Lord, who had been one of the League's biggest critics in the 60s. Burnley had been fined £1,000 in 1961 for fielding a weak team, a lot of money back then. But they became firm friends when Lord joined the Management Committee in 1967. Bob used to preface everything with the phrase 'In my 'umble estimation, Mr President' and then proceed to give us his less than humble views on everything under the sun. He could not be underestimated as an administrator, as he really knew the game well, particularly the refereeing side.

He used to conduct the interviews for the referees' promotion to the Football League. Unwittingly one day he asked an unsuspecting referee: 'What would you do if a manager stopped you and blocked you in the passage?'

Some of the potential referees were petrified of the man and did not give of their best when being interviewed. Robbie Hart of Darlington, a good referee who later made the Premier League, was one of these and eventually we managed to have him promoted without an interview. He could handle players, he could handle the toughest of matches, but he could not handle an interview with Bob Lord. He was terrified. Twice he arrived a bag of nerves and twice he failed the interview. By the time the third year came along, his marks were still excellent, so we put him on the list anyway without an interview. Bob Lord was part of that decision.

Lord was undoubtedly one of the most controversial characters of the 1950s, 60s and 70s. He epitomised the old breed of football club director, a local businessman made good. He was an outspoken butcher, always questioning. He was a staunch Methodist who even threatened to resign from the Management Committee over the decision to allow Sunday football during the power crisis in January 1974. Shortly after the Munich air disaster in 1958, he outraged the football world by calling Manchester United a team of Teddy Boys after a particularly stormy match. He also managed to upset a significant proportion of the population by referring to the television moguls as 'a bunch of Jews', and this at a Variety Club function! His chances of beating the diplomatic Lord Westwood for the position of President of the Football League plummeted after that remark.

He also angered his League colleagues when, contrary to the party line, he successfully argued at the FA against a move to allow directors to be paid. Jimmy Hill and Brian Winston of Orient were outraged, but Lord maintained they should be in the game for love, not money. Not that he himself was slow in putting in his expense claims to the FA, the League, the Lancashire FA and Burnley FC !

He was predictably sceptical when Jimmy Hill was advocating the seminar of 1980. 'Gone are the days when directors went round watching other matches,' said Lord. 'Now they want to blow their own trumpet after two or three years. It takes longer than that to learn the rudiments. I don't expect much to come of the seminar. Even if you do get a majority supporting a certain line, the chances are that they will turn turtle before the AGM when a three-quarter majority would be needed.'

But for all his bluster he was a wonderful character. He referred to Sir Matt Busby with the emphasis on the 'Sir' as if somehow he didn't feel that the honour was merited, yet the two became firm friends later in their lives.

He also had a problem placing aspirates, so Dr John O' Hara, chairman of the FA Medical Committee, became Dr Ho Ara.

Lord had a big bust-up with Ernie Clay of Fulham in the boardroom at Burnley at half-time in a match between Burnley and Fulham in 1980. Apparently he accused Clay of being a liar. This was just what Clay wanted and he complained of Lord's behaviour. When Clay sounded off in the press, Lord said Clay had impugned the referee as they left their seats at half time, implying that he (the referee) was on a hiding to nothing playing in front of Lord, the Chairman of the Referees' Committee of the Football League.

Eventually it came to a hearing before Lord Westwood, Jack Dunnett and John Deacon of Portsmouth. They threw out Clay's complaint, saying that it was designed to cause maximum embarrassment to Lord, who had been involved in a case previously where Fulham had been disciplined for making unauthorised payments to players including the accommodation costs of George Best.

Sir Harold Thompson, the chairman of the FA, was also involved in that earlier case. Clay called Thompson and Lord 'screws'; no one knew what he was talking about, as neither, as far as I knew, had ever been prison officers.

It was one of the more amusing episodes in the Football League's history. These people really hated each other. The FA and the League fined Fulham £15,000, which was a not insignificant sum in those days. Fulham appealed on procedural grounds and the penalty was reduced. The club argued bias which was difficult to refute in the circumstances, just as it was when Don Revie successfully challenged the FA's ten-year ban on him.

Bob Lord liked power and he was desperate to become President of the League. He would probably have been a good one, but when he was ready to stand in 1972, he suffered an ear problem which needed an operation and so withdrew his challenge to Len Shipman.

He used to complain bitterly about the catering at the Great Western Hotel in Paddington where we held many of our meetings; he would call the food rubbish and claim he had tasted better fish and chips. So we persuaded the hotel to bring him fish and chips in paper one Sunday evening, only for the joke to backfire on us as we sat and watched him put on the salt and vinegar and eat them with great relish.

He eventually contested the Presidency in 1974 when his rival was Lord Westwood of Newcastle, a distinguished gentleman with an eye patch, an excellent raconteur and an industrialist. He was not a long-time football administrator and was happy to rely heavily on Hardaker. Lord fell out with Hardaker again when the ballot forms were returned, as Westwood received 41 votes and Lord only seven. He suspected Hardaker of campaigning against him. I doubt whether he had, although he undoubtedly enjoyed working under Westwood who was such a good foil for him. Perhaps the League Chairmen merely decided they preferred a more refined approach.

Bob Lord sulked for a while about the result until Lord Westwood sent for him one day at a summer meeting. He proved himself to be as blunt and outspoken as his rival, saying: 'You think *I* was born with a silver spoon in my mouth – *you* were born with a bloody shovel in yours!'

From that day on, the Burnley Butcher and the Lord established a good working relationship. I had a high regard for Westwood. When I took over in 1979 he was still President, and he carried on in the same way, not changing his *modus operandi*, acting just as he did with Hardaker and expecting me to carry on advising him as Alan had done. That was one of the highest tributes I could receive from him.

In 1977 Hardaker reached the retirement age of 65 but decided to carry on for a while with the agreement of the Management Committee. Then he had second thoughts about George Readle taking over from him and became uneasy when Manchester City produced a picture of George in the programme with the caption: 'The next secretary of the Football League'.

George even started putting his name on the letter headings so Hardaker went to the Management Committee and they decided not to appoint Readle. The cards fell well for me as I was given the job in 1979.

Alan Hardaker may have been stepping down in 1979, but you would never have noticed. In fact, it was more like a promotion as he became Director General, saying: 'No one consults a consultant. I am not being a consultant. I am keeping my office and I am taking a new title.'

Poor George remained as Deputy Secretary even though the Management Committee had decided originally that the Secretary's job was his. They had minuted it, but never actually gave him the job when it came to the crunch. To his credit he did not bear any grudges against me and I felt sorry at the way he had been treated. He was a fine administrator and served me loyally for the last six years of his working life. He was 59 at the time and due to retire in 1985 but sadly he died suddenly a year earlier.

Most of the Football League dramas invariably occurred, as I remember vividly, at the summer meeting, usually held at some peaceful coastal town. This time it was in Bournemouth and it was on the roof balcony of the Palace Court Hotel in 1979 when Hardaker told me: 'The job is yours, make your own mistakes. I won't interfere.'

He went off on a couple of long trips, arriving back at the end of the year. After a comparatively short time he began getting fidgety about not running the show, complaining to Bob Lord, still Vice-President, that he was not being kept in the picture. Lord tipped me off that Alan was upset and, just as I was thinking about how I should handle it, Alan died on 4 March 1980. The problem was solved – but scarcely in the way I would have wanted.

He always reckoned that he would not be short of commercial offers when he finished, but as he never really retired I do not know what his thoughts were based on.

He left the League Cup as his epitaph, part of his *Pattern for Football* report. He had the vision to want to reduce the size of the divisions so that there were more meaningful matches. He wanted five divisions of 20 and to compensate for the loss of matches, he decided to introduce the League Cup.

But the clubs, as ever, wanted the penny and the cake, and rather than reduce the size of the divisions, they kept them the same and added the League Cup. Then a lot of the bigger clubs refused to enter in the 1960s with Everton one of the chief objectors, until it became compulsory. Everton were a continual thorn in Hardaker's side. In 1973 they objected bitterly to the television companies being allowed an extra five minutes of recorded highlights. Rather different to present times, when the clubs fall over themselves to be on live television!

There was another wonderful old character, Sam Bolton, who was a Vice-President alongside Bob Lord and a director of Leeds United. He was a real tartar. I recall when the Commission on Industrial Relations (CIR) investigated football in 1973 because the PFA had not been consulted for years, distinguished lecturer-in-law, Sir John Wood, came to see the Management Committee on the CIR's behalf.

Sam Bolton was all for walking out, saying: 'I'm not being talked to by the bloody interfering government.' He thought it was all a government plot.

No one escaped his tongue. He was a keen milk drinker and he would always complain about the price in hotels and restaurants, sending out the porter to the supermarket to buy a bottle.

He would regularly come on the phone to Alan Hardaker at League headquarters on behalf of Don Revie who would be pleading for a postponement or a fixture change and Alan would say: 'Tell him to bugger off.' The League Secretary didn't like Revie and told the FA they must be off their heads when they appointed him as manager of England.

Hardaker had a loudspeaker phone which was quite revolutionary at the time, enabling us to stand about and listen to the juicier conversations, which meant most of those with Sam. Alan would predict that he would be on the line at any moment, and sure enough he came through, saying: 'About these fixtures, Alan...'

Alan would respond: 'Are you ringing up as a director of Leeds United or as a member of the Management Committee?'

Sam would pause for a few seconds and say: 'As a member of the Management Committee.'

'Then bugger off,' the gleeful Hardaker would retort, having trapped him. 'It's nothing to do with you.'

A far gentler soul was Clifford Grossmark who, when the League's Associate Members, the Third and Fourth Division clubs, were given direct representation on the Management Committee for the first time in 1974, was the first to take the job. Previously they might have been represented indirectly by directors who were allowed to stay on the Committee if their clubs were relegated. The Gillingham chairman, a retired doctor, used to send food parcels to his old patients. He was a bit of a nervous sort and I remember him standing up before the Associate Members who could be bolshy, downtrodden and not afraid to tell everyone where to get off.

He addressed them: 'The picture is like this, gentlemen. We have got to take three steps.' He would then outline the route that I had carefully explained to him before the meeting but then added: 'That is what Graham Kelly told me to say – but personally I think it is a load of old rubbish.' They, of course, agreed with him, being the reactionary bunch they were, and we were back to square one.

Running most of the way through the 1970s was the so-called 'Freedom of Movement' debate which came directly out of the CIR report of Sir John Wood in 1974. We set up a new negotiating committee the next year, with the players represented by Cliff Lloyd, the secretary of the PFA; Gordon Taylor, who was playing an ever-increasing role; Terry Venables, a strident voice; Derek Dougan, the Chairman of the PFA and Bristol Rovers striker Bruce Bannister. On the Football League side there was myself, Alan Hardaker, Dick Wragg of Sheffield United and Sir Matt Busby.

Matt was included among the negotiators because of his long experience in the game as player, distinguished manager and director. However, he was far too gentle, kind and reasonable to be involved in arguments on behalf of the club Chairmen.

Sir John Wood, knighted for his expertise in industrial relations, was a respected independent chairman of the negotiating committee. He subsequently ruffled a few feathers as chairman of the transfer tribunal (Football League Appeals Committee), primarily because he would often side with Gordon Taylor when a player's move was jeopardised by his original club demanding an unrealistically high compensation fee from the signing club. But John was an ordinary guy, a Huddersfield Town supporter who eschewed a seat in the Leeds Road directors' box, and the criticism of some reactionary club chairmen never silenced his pointed questions and humour. In 25 years he never took a penny over his rail fare or petrol money from Sheffield.

It took ages for the changes to be approved. Alan Hardaker and Cliff Lloyd originally agreed a multiplier system whereby the fee for a player changing clubs at the end of his contract was determined by a complicated equation which took account of his age, old salary and new salary, but it was thrown out because it was far too inflexible. It could not cope with a move such as a Halifax player going to Manchester United. It was impossible to base the compensation on what Halifax were prepared to offer him for a new contract compared with the wages Manchester United would pay. It was out of all proportion. A system could not be moulded to fit every circumstance.

A change was eventually accepted in 1978 despite a lot of opposition from the Midlands, which was hardly surprising as Sir Jack Scamp, the trade unionist, was then Chairman of Coventry City. Another Midlander, Birmingham City's Jack Wiseman was delighted that first of all he was the last nationally-elected member of the Management Committee before the elections went regionalised in 1974–75, and in the first elections under the regional rules Doug Ellis of Aston Villa tried to oppose him. It went to a national vote and Jack won again.

The Football League Appeals Committee was set up to rule on compensation fees if the two clubs could not agree when a player moved at the end of his contract. It comprised of representatives from the Football League, PFA, The Secretaries and Managers' Association and the independent chairman Sir John Wood. I became the League's representative after a while and we used to deliberate long and hard.

The two managers might have been quite close in their negotiations, but by the time they arrived before us they tended to have hardened and it was difficult to find the appropriate level between the two figures to fix a fee. We reckoned that if both managers slammed the door on the way out, then we had got it about right.

The selling club always came and told us how vital the player had been to their plans and how much they would have liked to have kept him. Alan Harper was one such case when he moved from Liverpool to Everton and we were told that he was a vital part of Bob Paisley's plans and the Reds could not bear the thought of losing him. We asked, had they made him an offer? Was it long term? Was it a lot of money? The answer to all three questions was no, they had not got round to it. We asked where Mr Paisley was, only to be told that he was busy with something else. Needless to say, the decision of the committee was closer to Everton's valuation.

It was too obvious to take the middle figure between the two. We tried to base it on all the facts. If it was a young player with potential, we would do what they do to a greater extent now and base the fee on future appearances.

Sir Matt Busby's difficulty in arguing with the PFA was not his only experience of unease. Granada's *World in Action* alleged in an exposé that Louis Edwards, father of current Manchester United chairman Martin Edwards, had accumulated his shares in United irregularly and that the club had broken rules on payments to schoolboys. Matt had to lay himself at the mercy of the Management Committee, saying he had always done his best for the game. The authorities never followed through with their enquiries on that one.

Despite the introduction of three-up and three-down promotion/relegation in 1973, the biggest problem facing football at the start of the 1980s was falling attendances in the League and, consequently, clubs entering a period of financial difficulties despite rising ticket prices. Sports like snooker were gaining ground on television while football was perceived to be losing its attraction. Hooligans were ever-present and England had not qualified for the World Cup Finals in 1978.

Jimmy Hill at Coventry City and Bristol City's Stephen Kew were advocating a seminar, a general meeting of all 92 clubs with no formal agenda but only points of discussion prepared in advance by the seminar committee. It was intended to bring a new way of thinking with the sort of 'Think Tank' philosophy that many big businesses used with their senior executives. The Management Committee were against the idea, with Jack Dunnett strongly opposed, but he attended and took copious notes.

The meeting was held at the St. John's Hotel in Solihull. I regarded Jimmy Hill with some suspicion, because I had a fairly jaundiced impression of his activities so far. He was hardly flavour of the month at the League headquarters, owing to his long-standing uneasiness with Alan Hardaker.

But Hardaker had gone by 1980 and Jimmy led off the meeting on the structure of the League, trying to get a debate going about the size of the Divisions. Very astutely he moved on quickly because he was getting little consensus. He moved onto the points system, dismissing points for goals on the grounds they could be used to manipulate league standings, before reaching agreement on three points for a win, a roaring success used throughout the leagues since then. There were other recommendations that clubs should pay 50% of a transfer as an immediate down payment and the rest over not longer than a year; that the majority for rule changes be reduced from three quarters to two thirds; and in a far-reaching move, the clubs recommended that the so-called professional foul – the denial of a probable goalscoring opportunity – be regarded as serious foul play and therefore a sending-off offence.

It is interesting to reflect, all these years later, whether, had the cynical foul not been eradicated, Ryan Giggs would ever have reached the penalty area for his fabulous FA Cup semi-final replay goal against Arsenal in 1999. This is not a criticism of Arsenal, just the fact that the prevailing climate of the 1970s allowed defenders to be much more ruthless.

The meeting also suggested that apprentices should learn the laws of the game – it was crazy that players did not know the rules they earned their living under.

I have always had a high regard for Jimmy Hill since then. A lot of his ideas have been very sensible, although I did not agree with his idea of putting a white disc on the ground for the positioning of a free kick. I felt sure that the disc would be moved just as easily as the ball. But if you examine his record over the years, most of his proposals have been progressive and of great value to the game.

In 1981 Jack Dunnett of Notts County became President of the League by beating John Smith of Liverpool. The eight votes of the associate members went to Jack and made sure he won the ballot, despite the fact that the associate members had not voted unanimously for him. Jack Wiseman was let down by the Management Committee who had suggested he stand, only to allow him to fall at the first hurdle. A friendly but proud man, he was deeply hurt at the snub caused by his friends' failure to lobby on his behalf.

Dunnett received solid support from Group Four, the East Anglia and East Midlands clubs. He ran his regional meetings like clockwork and impressed Brian Clough immensely by occasionally inviting managers to attend meetings to let their voices be heard. No one else did. Meetings were held at the Haycock Hotel in Wansford at 11 am promptly and finished at 1pm – in perfect time for lunch.

He wrote the minutes himself, noted all complaints of the Management Committee and then diligently followed them up. He took his duties in the same way he did his parliamentary responsibilities. He said that he was going to come out of Notts County and be a full time President and that he planned to wind down his activities as a member of Parliament.

On his election he said that all of the Management Committee knew something was wrong. He said: 'We are not idiots. We are a beleaguered garrison.' He was an ebullient pragmatist with a sardonic line in humour. He carried a little white flannel around with him to mop his brow in times of stress, which were frequent. It was horrible.

Jack would make all his phone calls in the evening and I would sit at home waiting for him to call, knowing it was coming but not quite sure when. He tried to have me set up a London office but I didn't fancy the idea of being cut off from the rest of the staff who I recognised as important back-up. Even so he had us pounding the pavements of London looking for a base before I persuaded him to drop the idea.

Strangely, he never believed in giving a lead. He always wanted to follow the clubs, not leading from the front. He believed in serving, whether it was for football or the country. He had a charming wife and was devoted to his family. He represented Nottingham East between 1964 and 1983, always preferring the back bench to any ministerial position in the Labour Government. He tried to merge Brentford and QPR in 1967 and his friendship with Jim Gregory, controversial chairman at Queens Park Rangers, surfaced in the same year that he was elected President when he argued in favour of an artificial surface being laid at Loftus Road as an experiment. Club reaction was mixed, but QPR were allowed to go ahead until the First Division clubs became seriously concerned and artificial surfaces were phased out.

Jack was always anti-television, quite significant in view of the major part the television companies were to play over the years.

He was instrumental in the 'Snatch of the Day' in 1978–79 when Michael Grade had tried to get football exclusively onto ITV. The BBC commenced legal action, claiming that their agreement with ITV obliged them to act together (years later the two denied that they operated a cartel). The result of the row in 1979 was an unhappy compromise. BBC and ITV shared the League action with the popular *Match of the Day* moving to Sunday afternoon for two of the four years (1979–83). This disruption to scheduling contributed to the decline in audience statistics.

Jack Dunnett actually resigned from the Management Committee, having been sidelined once 'Snatch of the Day' was overtaken by events early in 1979.

A meeting of the Management Committee of the Football League to discuss the television situation began at 2 pm, and when Chris Needler from Hull arrived ten minutes late, he passed Jack Dunnett who was on his way out. He had quit because he thought that the deal took too little account of what would be the inflation rate over the next four years.

It was nothing but a clever political ploy for he knew he would get back on the committee. Nobody ever resigned on a matter of principle and, sure enough, he was voted back by his region fairly swiftly thereafter.

By the time the next contract came along in 1983, however, Jack was the President of the League with a strong hand to play. Dunnett went in strongly and managed to have television's £2.6 million offer rejected 52–0 by the clubs, a conclusive verdict indeed.

But the clubs had to change their mind sharpish after the brief emergence of *Telejector,* which flashed across the sky and disappeared like a meteor. Although I do not remember it ever being minuted, Dunnett told the clubs that the Management Committee recommended they accept this newcomer's offer to transmit matches only in pubs and clubs. In July the clubs accepted the original offer from BBC and ITV. Live League football was shown regularly for the first time.

By that time Canon had announced in May that they were going to be the first sponsors of the League and there was no way in the world that anyone could have a major sponsor without a TV contract. But the clubs had done enough to win the one important battle and they were allowed advertising on players' shirts for the first time.

In 1984 the League Management Committee put Sir Arthur South in charge of the television negotiations for the following contract. They were talking about increasing the number of live matches from 10 to 16 for the contract starting in 1985. It would have meant an increase to around £ 3.8 million a year, with inflation, added from 1985 to 1989. But the TV contract negotiations then became embroiled with the pools discussions with Jack Dunnett's connivance.

Dunnett did a deal with the Pool Promoters' Association for royalties on the pools coupons. Some of the leading critics, including Ernie Clay, thought the twelve year agreement far too long. Dunnett managed to get the clubs to agree to the deal, which increased the League's take to £1.2 million per year, by fuelling a controversy over the television contract.

Ostensibly he was the President, but he was doing nothing to counter criticisms of the television contract.

On 14 February 1985 Robert Maxwell, with little love in his heart, stood up at a meeting of clubs and told them that the £3.8 million was mad, bad and sad. The Chairmen agreed not to talk to the media about the discussions, but that soundbite duly appeared as a headline in the *Daily Mirror* the very next day.

Maxwell claimed we should be asking for 'at least 90 million'. Nobody asked whether he meant pounds or dollars. He was not the only voice raised in protest as other clubs wanted two years, not four, and did not want more than 10 live matches a season. As a result they added Irving Scholar, Ken Bates and Maxwell to the negotiating team. They in turn set up various working parties and pored over statistics for weeks. Bates managed, in his usual manner, to upset the TV negotiators by calling them 'office boys'. They then asked for tenders from both BBC and ITV and the two companies replied in identical terms.

John Deacon, Chairman of Portsmouth, suggested that the clubs walk away at the next clubs' meeting on 4 May. He said the clubs only needed an extra 300 spectators per match to cover their television money and the television people would begin to panic.

But it was not the television people who were panicking after the sad events at Heysel and Bradford later that month! Football hit rock bottom.

Robert Maxwell was trying to get himself appointed to a special government committee to solve the crisis in football and was talking to Number 10 – so he said! He could not elicit any interest from the Management Committee. Then he suggested that 'Phil Walker' replace Sir Arthur South as chairman of the television negotiators. We were baffled until we realised he meant Phil Carter.

When the clubs took no notice of him he just stormed off, and we never saw him again in football administration. Presumably the door to Number 10 was also shut in his face ... if it had ever opened!

Manchester City Chairman Peter Swales once referred to him as Sir Robert Maxwell and, of course, Captain Bob did not bother to correct him. That summed up the man as far as I was concerned, and those who had supported some of his preposterous moves in football must have blushed when revelations of his business dealings emerged after his sudden death.

The Office of Fair Trading, in the shape of Sir Gordon Borrie, was not interested in the two television companies colluding, despite the fact that we sent him a lot of evidence of their private meetings and an agreement not to make a unilateral bid for the World Cup in 1974. I asked how they could not be colluding when they were writing identical letters to the Football League.

Football was off the screens until the FA Cup came round in January 1986 and a deal was agreed until the end of that season. Not surprisingly, the first Super League story surfaced in October 1985.

Negotiations resumed for a further contract in March 1986. Shirt advertising doubled in size, TV paid £3 million a year for two years, there were 14 live matches, the overseas signal was given to the Football League, and the Littlewoods Cup semi-finals and Final were shown live.

After we had concluded that contract, the OFT rejected my complaint. They said there could be alternative explanations for the evidence I had submitted.

In the midst of all these discussions Jack Dunnett did not do himself or football any favours when he lost patience in the face of some persistent questioning from the *Daily Telegraph's* Christopher Davies at one press conference, admitting that he did not watch television himself but that his family, who did watch television, told him that the most popular programmes were those containing violence and therefore football should do well. The frightening thing about it was that he was quite serious.

There was a situation when Irving Scholar wrote to him, making certain comments on the negotiating committee's proposals. Dunnett responded that he doubted whether the proposals were going to be acceptable to the clubs, and that if the committee resigned, he would invite Scholar to join a new one. This was certainly strange behaviour for the President of the League to start recruiting a new committee before the old one had finished its work but, sadly, he had no qualms about undermining his colleagues in this way.

Dunnett defeated Phil Carter's challenge for the Presidency in 1984 by 35 votes to 17. But his time soon ran out. Phil Carter led the First Division Clubs when they pushed through a new structure after the Super League rumours of late 1985. Carter became President in 1986 and Dunnett became representative of the Third and Fourth Division Clubs. The writing had been on the wall for the effervescent former Labour MP throughout three years of haggling about voting rights and power in the League.

Sir Norman Chester had become involved again in 1983, 15 years after his first report, because the major clubs were complaining that they were not getting a big enough share of the League cake. The idea was to invite Sir Norman to do an update of his report in the 1960s. This was the second attempt to entice Chester back. The first time we took him along to a meeting at the FA but Sir Harold Thompson, with whom Norman Chester lost no love, came out with the time-honoured phrase: 'I think I have left my papers in my bedroom.' Norman Chester replied: 'I haven't come here to be buggered about' – and the chance was lost.

On the committee in 1983 he had banker Cyril Townsend, Sir John Smith of Liverpool, Jack Dunnett, Tony Boyce of Torquay United representing the Third and Fourth Divisions and Cliff Lloyd from the PFA. They recommended that the First Division be reduced to 20 clubs, despite opposition from Dunnett, while Chester himself wanted the League to go down to 64 clubs with the bottom clubs going into an intermediate league. That met with blanket refusal from the committee and the clubs who did not want to be party to reducing the League in such a dramatic way.

The Chester Committee set up a finance working party designed to impose financial criteria on clubs, but the clubs would not accept their recommendations either. Chester thought they should be looking ahead to a pattern of change established over the long term, rather than deal with problems piecemeal the way the clubs wanted to do.

The League had an argument with Norman Chester after his report was published in 1983. They wanted to invite him along to lunch to give him a present and thank him for all his work. He did not particularly want a present, but he did want to talk about his recommendations and complained bitterly when the Management Committee said they did not have time to speak to him because their agenda was too big. He attended but he didn't think that the League took him seriously, saying: 'There is no PM, no cabinet and no policy.' He was quite scathing about Jack Dunnett's lack of leadership.

All of this became relevant again two years later in 1985 when the Super League story surfaced. Brian Clough stated that the plotters were simply being greedy, while Jack Dunnett prevaricated. The First Division wanted 20 clubs, more television revenue and a reduction of the majority required for decisions from 75%, something which had been recommended but never implemented from the seminar earlier in the 1980s.

Jack Dunnett said that he wanted the second Chester Report implemented. This was an inadequate response to what the top clubs were demanding, possibly deliberate because, in his heart of hearts, Jack Dunnett did not want to meet their demands in any way.

The PFA became involved when Gordon Taylor joined the

negotiations between Divisions One and Two, who each set up their own committee. There was eventually agreement between the First and Second Divisions on a restructure of the Management Committee. They went for four members from the First Division; three from the Second and one from Divisions Three and Four together. What they failed to realise was that they were reducing their representation from 10 to eight members at the FA.

They also agreed to reduce the majority to two-thirds for changes of rules. They originally wanted the First Division to have two votes per club and the Second Division one vote. They wanted a new formula for the distribution of money with 50% going to the First Division; 25% to the Second and 25% to be split between Divisions Three and Four, and they asked the Management Committee to draft these rule changes. But Dunnett and I went to see Phil Carter of Everton, Ron Noades of Crystal Palace and Martin Edwards of Manchester United at a Heathrow hotel and we said that if they wanted changes they must propose them. We would not do the job for them.

The proposals we formulated for the EGM in March ignored a lot of the structural changes which they wanted to bring in. Instead we incorporated a link with the Alliance Premier League and, on the proposal of Ron Noades and Brentford's Martin Lange, introduced the play-offs.

The March EGM was quite bizarre. It had been agreed that there would be an adjournment but Arsenal and Manchester United attended to ensure fair play by Jack Dunnett. These three were the only ones present as it was formally agreed to defer until a new date in April.

The row dragged on and the following was eventually agreed:

The First Division would be reduced to 20 clubs over two years, 1986–88.

The First Division would have 20 clubs, with 24 in the other Divisions with play-offs.

A link would be established with the Alliance.

Division One allocated 50% of the TV and sponsorship money.

League gate levy was reduced from 4% to 3%.

The Management Committee was to be reorganised with four members from Division One, three from Division Two and one from the Third and Fourth Divisions; the three-quarter majority went down to two-thirds and the First Division clubs were given one and a half votes per club. It was a massive relief that these talks, having lasted six months, were concluded and that the League would continue in similar form.

But it was no more than a holding operation because the problems were going to surface yet again fairly soon afterwards.

Jack Dunnett took the consolation prize of Third and Fourth Division clubs' representative and set his sights elsewhere. I was pretty sure that Jack wanted to become Chairman of the FA. I could not see how anybody could volunteer themselves for all the days out and the afternoon tea trips at the summer meetings, as Jack did, if he did not want to advance his prospects at Lancaster Gate. Subsequently he moved from Notts County to the Portsmouth boardroom, but in a rare miscalculation failed in his bid to become Second Division Representative on the League Management Committee. A shrewd operator had taken one step too far.

A Management Committee was appointed in 1986 on the new divisional basis and it quickly became a case of a new broom sweeping too vigorously as, unfortunately, they swept the ball into their own net with one early decision. They decided to raise the salary of Lee Walker, then manager of the television department. But the letter that President Phil Carter sent to him contained a new figure *below* the salary he was already receiving. Lee was not awfully impressed with the benevolence of the new Committee and we had to point out to them that in their keenness to act, they had one or two things sadly awry. They also set up a Forward Planning Committee but their forward planning was so poor that they could not find dates to meet and only gathered twice! If you wrote such material for a television sketch, it would be rejected as too implausible.

It was around this time that I first came across Rick Parry when his company, Arthur Young, were invited to commission a report into the working of the League and the Management Committee. He attended a number of meetings and found that they were very subjective in the way they reached decisions, the agenda was not properly structured and, like most football people, they became entangled in anecdotal stories without deciding the issues properly.

He strongly felt that the Management Committee should appoint a Chief Executive and allow him to run the League on a day to day basis and the Committee should concern themselves with longer term planning. It was sound advice.

In the same year Ken Bates was struggling to find a sponsor for the

League after Canon left and was eventually bailed out when a new national newspaper, the middle-of-the-road *Today*, became involved. However, it lasted less than a year. The paper received little acknowledgement from the rest of the media and complained that they found Bates obstructive rather than helpful. Neither the sponsor nor the League made anything out of the deal.

One reason for *Today's* disaffection was the agreement Bates made for the sponsorship of the League's Centenary celebrations with Mercantile Credit. For a variety of reasons, the year was not successful. Some of the plans were too ambitious and the clubs were lukewarm. The Football League versus the Rest of the World match at Wembley was notable more for the magnificent performance of the recently retired Michel Platini than the £100,000 that had to be paid to secure Diego Maradona's appearance. Ironically, when Platini came out of the tunnel, he had just returned sun-tanned from a holiday and told me he couldn't understand the reaction of some of the fans who mistook his number ten shirt for that of the Argentinian. He was wrongly and roundly booed by supporters recalling the Falklands conflict – and (more importantly!) his 'hand of God' goal against England two years earlier.

Lee Walker's television department had remained busy and in 1987 Granada approached Phil Carter on behalf of British Satellite Broadcasting, in which they held shares. Trevor Phillips and I met BSB with Phillips recommending a joint venture over ten years which would give us control of our television destiny and also help with the marketing.

The main drawback as far as the big clubs were concerned was the prospect that BSB would not be operational for two years. They wanted BSB to sell on to the BBC and ITV until they were ready to broadcast because they didn't want to lose the exposure.

Once more they wanted their cake and to eat it. Obviously if BSB were buying something as expensive and important as this and had set up a partnership, they were averse to selling on the product, even though the BBC were prepared to come in and defray some of the costs.

BSB were offering us a share of subscription and advertising revenue and even part of the take from other sports like boxing.

All went well at the AGM in June but then on 24 June Jonathan Martin telephoned from the BBC to tell me that seven big clubs had met ITV and were talking about an ITV Super League with Greg Dyke. We held a meeting of the Management Committee and, when David

Dein and Phil Carter were pressed for details, they declined to say very much although Phil Carter admitted that the clubs were discussing a 'very interesting' proposal from ITV and would tell the Management Committee as soon as possible.

Dein, of course, knew all the facets of the BSB proposal when he talked to ITV but denied there was a conflict of interest, saying only that the proposal from ITV entailed exclusivity for the home matches of some of the clubs.

Gordon McKeag, a new member, declared his interest, saying that his club Newcastle United were one of the seven and therefore could not participate in a detailed discussion because of the talks with ITV, while the League's representative Trevor Phillips was excluded from joining the seven in their talks.

ITV offered the seven clubs £1 million per year each for the exclusive rights to televise from their ground for four years. They were guaranteed a minimum of one live game from each club and the right to televise a maximum of three live games with £50,000 per match extra as compensation for loss of income. Overseas rights were to remain with the clubs and ITV would have first option on European matches. They agreed to broadcast no more than 20 live games per season.

It was clear that they were attempting to sew up the market with the big clubs. I was very perturbed because I could see very well the merits of a partnership arrangement which BSB were proposing. Instead we were to destined take the short term offer of ITV's cash.

It was a particularly bitter time in the League Management Committee with both Carter and Dein being subjected to criticism for their conflict of interest.

Trevor Phillips accused David Dein of misusing the information, while Lee Walker rightly complained that he had not been told or consulted. Dein's reply was that he was concerned about the lack of exposure for two and a half years. Jack Dunnett sided with Phillips, saying that Dein should stand down from one side or the other. McKeag said that he attended the ITV meeting without knowledge of what it was going to be about and he felt that the negotiations should be carried on by the League. Ian Stott responded that there would be an unavoidable conflict of interest. David Bulstrode of QPR rightly added that TV had split the Football League yet again. And so it went on.

Trevor Phillips was told to get in touch with ITV to see what could be done. But the arguments continued in Plymouth at the summer meeting. Bulstrode was crucial to this because if he, as a First Division representative, had gone with Carter, Dein and McKeag it would have been a 4–4 draw, leaving Carter with the casting vote. The President rejected the notion of a conflict of interest so Fox, Stott, Bulstrode, Noades and Dunnett requested an adjournment and had a chat with me.

They told me that they were concerned that they could not discuss any major issues in front of the other three because of this conflict of interest. They were making the point that in their view anything of importance was in danger of being leaked or misused. They felt that David Dein had been guilty with the TV negotiations.

The Management Committee meeting in Plymouth went on from Thursday lunchtime through to Friday and it became so serious that we summoned our solicitor from Herbert Smith to join us. We also brought Gordon Taylor into the discussions as we thought he would be able to instil some commonsense into the situation.

I accompanied the five of them to meet Bert Millichip and Arthur McMullen at the FA. Ted Croker had been quoted as saying that, providing any new League complied with FA rules, it would not be right to veto it. We went to Bert and Mac and persuaded them to say that they would not sanction the new league.

The big clubs criticised Coventry City, Norwich and Chelsea for abolishing the compensation fund for clubs who appeared live on television.

There were a number of club meetings arranged for July to sort the whole thing out before the onset of the new season. I went to one at the Forte Hotel at Heathrow where Stuart Webb of Derby County summoned me into a small meeting as I arrived and told me that Guy Askham of Southampton, Bill Fox and Jack Dunnett had lawyers there seeking an injunction to prevent ITV signing a deal with the big clubs. They were also threatening to commence an action against Phil Carter and David Dein for breach of duty.

The Management Committee took over the litigation so that, in effect, they were trying to sue two of their own members, and an injunction was granted for seven days.

Next day the ten ITV clubs, their number having swollen with Sheffield Wednesday, Aston Villa, Newcastle United, Nottingham Forest and West Ham United linking up with the original big five, met at Old Trafford. Phil Carter went into the meeting and tried to speak for the 92 clubs, saying that it was only extremists who were advocating a Super League, but confirmed that the ten sought the increased interest that a Premier League would engender.

ITV then increased their offer from £32 million to £37 million and finally to £53 million over four years, easily beating BSB, backed by Reed, Virgin and Granada, who, at that stage, were offering £47 million. After all the years of the television cartel, we were finally into an auction.

The ITV deal was accepted and Jack Dunnett appointed chairman of the clubs' meeting in place of Phil Carter. When Ken Bates asked where Carter was, Dunnett said that he had a business appointment but Dein said that was wrong and that he had absented himself on legal advice.

Then it was Dein's turn to come under fire from Bates, Noades and Trevor Phillips. They were now arguing about the split of the money and how much should go to the First Division.

Phil Carter's solicitor complained when I said it would be inappropriate for him to chair the August EGM when the three year rule was introduced to prevent clubs from leaving.

With the season fast approaching events were moving quickly and on 2 August BBC and BSB withdrew their offer and six days later Division One agreed to take 75% while Gordon Taylor gave up half of the PFA's 10%.

The clubs started circulating a motion to dismiss Phil Carter and David Dein with John Poynton, Robert Maxwell, John Smith of Luton, Bill Fox, Patrick Cobbold, Ron Noades and Ian Stott amongst the first to sign it.

The Football Association completed their own deal with BSB and BBC for £30 million over five years for the FA Cup, internationals and the Charity Shield, a huge increase.

After all this controversy the Management Committee was reconstructed, bringing on Gordon Taylor for a time, although I do not know how effective it was because it did not last long. There were now three representatives from the First Division, three from the Second and one from the Associate Members.

Dein was unrepentant. He said BSB were not fully capitalised and that the satellite might not even be launched, that ten years was too long and, in any case, BSB and BBC could have taken the big five's away matches. The fact is that ITV never made any attempt to come to the front door, always preferring the back door. BSB were forced to submerge themselves in Rupert Murdoch's Sky.

It is amazing how often David Dein's name comes up in these conflicts of interest over the years. Like some of the old-timers before him, he knows his football and his footballers and possesses an acute commercial brain. But he did tend to find himself in the middle of some hairy controversies over the years.

I was invited by the Management Committee to receive a farewell present when I left the League in 1988. It took place at a dinner in Warwick and the committee were clearly split in two factions, with Dein and Carter in one corner and the rest elsewhere. They were voted off the Management Committee soon afterwards. It was certainly a different sort of farewell party, but I received only the one silver tea service. At least they did not seem split over that.

I had long been interested in going to the FA and spreading my wings. I was more than pleased with the job at the Football League but the prospect of being involved in international football on one hand and coaching and development on the other persuaded me to throw my hat in the ring when Ted Croker was coming up to retirement in 1988.

I had a problem when my application was not recognised by the firm handling the appointment. I went to an interview when they were clearly not interested in me and I had to speak to a couple of contacts from the FA, including the late Douglas Goodchild of Berks and Bucks, who made sure that my name went forward.

I had an interview with Bert Millichip and Arthur McMullen and afterwards received a telephone call from Goodchild while I was at the Freight Rover Final at Wembley, telling me that the interview had gone well and the FA were interested in me but, he added, that money might be a factor as they were only prepared to pay £60,000. Although it was more than I was earning at the Football League there was the serious consideration of the cost of moving south.

I went to London to see Bert Millichip again on the day of the 125th birthday celebrations. They were due to hold a dinner at the Royal Garden Hotel. Phil Carter was also there and was very helpful. I decided that the money was the critical factor with the cost of houses in the South and decided not to press what I regarded as less important matters like a company Jaguar or use of the flat at Lancaster Gate.

My deep thinking and subsequent tactics proved to be a bit of a waste of time as it transpired because, right at the outset, Bert told me that the car would be a Vauxhall Senator under terms of a new sponsorship agreement and that I could use the flat, but only for the first three months until I moved. They had taken umbrage at the fact Ted Croker had made it virtually his home throughout his time at the FA. My negotiating strategy went out of the window completely but I managed to raise them to £70,000 and agreed.

I started work for the FA on 5 September 1988. I was excited to make the step up. Obviously I was sorry to leave the League after 20 years. It was quite a wrench, but it was hardly as if I was going to be working with different people.

CHAPTER NINE

The Poisoned Chalice

There could never have been a more chilling or daunting welcome to a new position. Little did I know when I accepted the role of Chief Executive with the Football Association that within weeks I would be in the midst of the biggest tragedy ever to hit English sport, an event whose repercussions continued to reverberate through the game long after I had departed ten years later.

I officially took over on 14 February 1989 and I had only been present but a few weeks when 96 fans lost their lives in a crush at the Leppings Lane terrace at the Hillsborough ground about the time of the kick-off of the FA Cup semi-final between Liverpool and Nottingham Forest.

It was a scene from Hades rather than a football ground as metal crush barriers became twisted like coat hangers with the force of the human pressure exerted upon them, while advertising hoardings were used as makeshift stretchers to carry the dying to the waiting fleet of ambulances and the dead to the Sheffield Wednesday gymnasium which was used as a temporary mortuary.

A few of us privately wondered if we had seen the end of football as we knew it on 15 April 1989. Some thought this might not matter very much anyway.

The game had already been battered by hooliganism when in three totally unrelated events 191 people lost their lives at football matches and over 800 were injured in a span of slightly less than four years. A carelessly cast aside cigarette end on 11 May 1985, along with accumulated rubbish dating back almost twenty years according to a newspaper dateline, saw 56 souls lost and over 200 more burned at Bradford City's Valley Parade at a Third Division game against Lincoln City.

Then 18 days later, another 39 were killed on one of Britain's most shameful days in sport when drunken Liverpool fans rioted at the ancient and crumbling Heysel Stadium in the Belgian capital of Brussels, prior to the European Champions' Cup Final between Liverpool and Juventus.

Prime Minister Margaret Thatcher had left no doubts in the electorate's mind as to her attitude towards a sport she would rather not be associated with, while the business community not unexpectedly turned their backs on a sport which had scarcely lived up to its tag as the 'Beautiful Game'.

Fate meant I chose to go to Sheffield rather than the other semi-final between Everton and Norwich City at Villa Park, primarily because Bert Millichip wanted to go there and we tended to take alternate matches in the semi-finals.

I arrived at the ground at about 12.30 and was congratulated by Geoff Woodward, one of the Wednesday directors, upon securing England's return to European competition following the decision reached by UEFA. Forest fans were already arriving in the vicinity of the ground while it appeared that Liverpool supporters were late in arriving through problems on the M62.

I took my seat at 2.45 and was discussing with Bert McGee, the Chairman of Sheffield Wednesday, the Prime Minister's insistence on identity cards. He was pointing to the crowds and saying that this was what Margaret Thatcher could not understand, the fantastic atmosphere, the excitement of a big football match and the emotions of actually being there.

Six minutes into the game commenced the longest hour of my life. I first realised that something was wrong when my attention was drawn to fans at the Leppings Lane End scaling the security fence. I watched the drama unfold, uncertain at that stage exactly what was happening, as a police officer attempted to speak to a linesman on the near side, but the official brushed him to one side and carried on with play. Another policeman came onto the pitch from behind the goal to speak to the referee Ray Lewis, while Liverpool goalkeeper Bruce Grobbelaar was desperately and frantically trying to draw attention to what was happening only a few yards from him.

Ray Lewis immediately halted play and took the players to the dressing room. After a few minutes, with it becoming increasingly evident that something was seriously amiss, I went along behind the main stand where I was abused by the Liverpool supporters because they had not been allowed to occupy the preferred Kop End. I headed straight to the police control box in the corner of the ground, affording what should have been a perfect view of the terracing where the problems had occurred. Chief Superintendent David Duckenfield, the match commander, told me that a gate or gates had been forced, showing me a picture from a video camera which purported to represent this.

A little later, back under the main stand, supporters told me that a gate at the Leppings Lane End had been opened on the instructions of the police. This was a very different story to the one I had been told by the police only minutes earlier.

About 25 minutes after the referee had stopped play I called a meeting in the main boardroom, involving the three clubs involved, the hosts Sheffield Wednesday and the competing clubs Liverpool and Forest, the referee Ray Lewis and the police commander.

It was clear that the match was likely to be abandoned, but the police could not announce this for fear of exacerbating the situation and blocking access for the emergency vehicles.

There was a long period of uncertainty when people of all three clubs, the media and FA representatives were milling around, not knowing what to say, as the number of reported fatalities increased. I asked the police commander to stay in close touch with the referee and officials, but I do not think he spoke to them at all after that.

Brian Clough said at one stage that he was taking his players home and I had to go into the dressing room and tell them that, although there was only a slight chance of the game being resumed, they must not give any inkling that the game was going to be abandoned until the police said so.

All the time I was keeping in touch with Bert Millichip at Villa Park to keep him in the picture and discussing the implications.

It was awful not being able to do anything positive to help. The gut instinct was to get out there with the ambulance men, the St John's Brigade, the police and the supporters who were helping with the injured. Tears and total shock were the order of the day for most of them.

Feelings were understandably running very high amongst the

Liverpool fans. At one stage I had to move out of the tunnel where the BBC were trying to do an interview with me as the abuse was too loud.

Everyone was coping with the unfolding tragedy in their own way with the backroom staff at Sheffield Wednesday, many of them young boys and girls, shrugging aside the horror of the moment, involved in fetching and carrying and doing a magnificent job. Alan Smith, the Sheffield Wednesday and England physiotherapist, did a superhuman job tending to the injured.

After the announcement that the match had been abandoned I gave the first of many press conferences at about 4.30 pm and did live interviews with BBC radio and television. I was as honest as I could be and told them that there had been reports of 50 deaths and that I had heard two conflicting stories of how the crush had occurred.

The two teams left. It was particularly traumatic for the Liverpool party who knew that the dead were not only supporters of their club but possibly people they knew and, in some cases, maybe even family as they had given their tickets to loved ones to stand at the end where the unspeakable happened.

Both Nottingham Forest manager Brian Clough and Liverpool Chairman Sir John Smith promised before they left to co-operate with the FA on any replay plans. Clough said he would 'go anywhere any time'.

After the two clubs departed, an extremely distressed Bert McGee was persuaded to leave by his colleagues on the Wednesday Board.

In the middle of the evening I was called to a meeting of the remaining Wednesday directors. I told them that I thought it better to leave everything to club secretary Graham Mackrell and have everything channelled through him so that they could not be picked off one against the other. I stayed with the Wednesday secretary to deal with all the media demands.

It was clear where my duties lay at that time as I continued to try and piece together exactly what had happened to prepare for the more immediate demands of the media and for the long term inquiry which would begin on my return to London. I did the mid evening news interviews for BBC and Sky and went on *Match of the Day* live at the end of the evening.

Already the crux of the matter was the terracing. It was clear that in the aftermath of both Heysel and Hillsborough we would somehow have to move the fans' preference away from standing on these large terraces and I said this to Jimmy Hill on the programme.

The Minister for Sport, Colin Moynihan, arrived at the scene of the devastation just before 11 pm and went straight to the mortuary which I thought was very courageous of him. We then took him onto the Leppings Lane terraces and looked at the relevant areas.

Evidence had been building through the afternoon and evening. A lot of the fans had shown me their tickets with the counterfoil intact, indicating that there was obviously some sort of problem on the turnstiles.

I finally left the ground just before midnight, arriving home at around 2 am. The scenes of distress, anger, frustration and bewilderment would remain with me for a long, long time but I had no time to dwell upon them then because the media wanted to know whether the FA Cup would continue that season.

Sleep did not come easily but I was so exhausted that I drifted off into an uneasy couple of hours with the scenes of horror imprinted on my mind. The real impact did not hit me for years.

The media demands were, as expected, massive and I promised TV-AM that I would speak to them by telephone, but in the event I decided to appear in the studio. After the programme I went to Lancaster Gate to meet various members of the management team. I spoke with Glen Kirton, who had been at the game with me, and to Pat Smith to ascertain their feelings and when I went in front of the ITN cameras I said that I thought the Cup would carry on. But, in truth, I was not at all sure.

Personally I thought it would be a fitting memorial, to those who had perished while watching their team, to carry on.

I spoke to the office of the FA's President, the Duke of Kent, and was told that he was due back from a visit to the West Indies that day. I expressed the opinion that a visit by the Duke to Sheffield would be very appropriate and welcome. He agreed and went to the ground with Bert Millichip.

Difficult decisions were having to be made throughout the game. The Professional Footballers' Association's Annual Dinner had gone ahead on the Sunday, the day after the tragedy, with a much lower profile than usual and in an understandably subdued atmosphere. I cried off and Gordon Taylor obviously understood the reasons.

Bert Millichip agreed that we would make an immediate donation of £250,000 to the appeal fund. I also told Sir Bert that, if we were going to carry on with the FA Cup Final, I would be recommending that we increased the number of tickets for the fans of the finalists. He agreed 37,000 tickets for Liverpool or Nottingham Forest and 37,000 for Everton, a huge shift of emphasis from previous years to the real fans and away from those who attended lacking any allegiance for either team.

It was quite evident, even at that early stage of the developing aftermath, that football needed a reduction in betting duty to give us help in improving facilities to ensure that nothing like Hillsborough was allowed to happen again at one of our grounds.

I had more media interviews on the Monday morning and then went to the office where I consulted all the staff who were in and asked them whether they honestly thought that the Cup should carry on or not. Only Manolita Tedin, the tea lady, said no.

I caught a cab to the House of Commons to hear Douglas Hurd's statement. He talked about all-seater grounds and the setting-up of Lord Justice Taylor's inquiry.

I went to White's Hotel in the early evening and talked again with Bert Millichip, agreeing that we should carry on with the Cup. Ernest Brown, chairman of the Cup Committee, and the rest of the Executive Committee concurred and at 7.45 that evening we announced that the FA Cup would continue.

It was further decided that the replay would take place at Old Trafford, Manchester on 7 May with live television. We hoped that Liverpool would carry on and that whoever got through to the Final, it would be a fitting memorial. All the time the office were dealing with hundreds of calls, all with different opinions.

I examined my conscience as best as I could but I could not see that we should have done things differently.

To all intents and purposes the same match between the same teams had taken place successfully at the same ground twelve months earlier. The police had made it quite clear that they would not countenance Liverpool having the Kop End of the ground. The police ruled that the more southerly-based team, Nottingham Forest, would have the use of the Kop because of the geographical ease of access. Liverpool's experienced and highly-regarded Chief Executive Peter Robinson protested, but to no avail as we could see no real reason to alter the arrangements that had been successful in the previous season.

I appeared on the *Kilroy* programme on television. Afterwards I went across to speak to relatives of the supporters who had been killed and injured and a woman with a point to make slapped my face. She would not allow me to finish my explanation, she was so upset.

It was decided that all clubs should consult their local authority on terracing to make sure that the safety authorities were happy. The controversial fences were really a matter for the licensing authorities under the Safety of Sports Grounds Act.

I quite upset the Liverpool City Council's Working Committee on Hillsborough when I could not take time out to meet them and, in any case, it did not seem to be a good idea as there was an official inquiry about to start and I did not want to be diverted from that.

Liverpool issued a statement on Tuesday 18 April, saying that they were unhappy that the FA were rushing them into a decision, claiming it was putting the club under additional pressure at a time of grief and they deferred their decision for a week. Peter Robinson did not think that a replay would be possible on 7 May because of a lack of time and an idea was floated to play the game at Wembley on 20 May, which should have been Cup Final day, with the Final rescheduled for the Charity Shield date in August.

I understood that we were putting pressure on Liverpool, but we had to make decisions and couldn't afford to delay too long.

I did not think it was a feasible proposal to play the game at the start of the next season; it would sound the wrong note to begin with last season's Cup Final and prolong the mourning. The Football League were backing us all the way.

When I explained to John Smith that I did not want to see the Final go to the next season, he asked me to speak to Robinson who, in turn, invited me to speak at their board meeting the following day.

John Smith collected me from Speke Airport and we attended the Liverpool board meeting which was held at a secret venue in the city centre. The Liverpool manager Kenny Dalglish was very reluctant to play the game again and refused to countenance a decision at that time. Dalglish was proving to be as formidable in a time of disaster as he was as a player and he and his wife Marina had taken it upon themselves to act as counsellors not only to his players and their families but also to the bereaved. He took much of the burden upon himself and subsequently suffered from the pressures it had brought, claiming that it was part of the reason for quitting his job some time later.

My return flight departed without me as I waited for the Liverpool Board to make a decision, but they eventually decided that they could not make their minds up at that time. They expressed their gratitude at me attending.

I returned by train to London after speaking to a number of supporters at Lime Street, most of whom wanted Liverpool to carry on in the competition.

In the meantime Luton's David Evans had been shouting his mouth off. The Conservative MP member for Welwyn and Hatfield said that it was mismanagement by the FA which had caused the problem by putting the fans in the wrong end. I wondered who had rattled his cage and why he had not bothered to find out the real facts.

Another who put his foot in his mouth before being availed of all the information was the President of UEFA, Jacques Georges, who caused a stir when he said that once again football had fallen victim to the folly of certain spectators and referred to the aggressive mentality of Liverpool supporters. 'Beasts wanted to charge into the arena,' he said.

The FA challenged him immediately and said that his comments were untrue, disrespectful and insensitive. We sent Glen Kirton to Basle for a rather difficult meeting with him. Georges said that he was upset at us in effect calling him a liar, but he was not half as upset as the families in Liverpool had been by his comments. Glen patiently explained that we had not called him a liar; we had just said he was wrong to blame misconduct by the supporters. As justification for his remarks, he cited the allegations of the police as reported in the *Sun*.

Glen's reasoned arguments managed to persuade him to await the results of any inquiry before coming to any judgements or making any more comments. It was smoothed over, but to my mind not entirely satisfactorily as Georges should have been big enough to make a fulsome apology. Kirton took it as far as he could and UEFA gave 200,000 Swiss Francs to the appeal fund.

Liverpool immediately dismantled the fences at Anfield and drew up plans to seat their famous Kop. Their ground had turned into a vast memorial to the 96 dead with every inch, inside and out, covered with flowers and scarves and favours of clubs, not just from all round the country but from all over the world. At the same time we started contemplating making Wembley an all-seater stadium.

I spoke to David Phillips of the Association of Chief Police Officers who said that they needed eight days to put in place a comprehensive plan for the replayed semi-final on 7 May, but if the match was aborted after 26 April it would still cost the FA £75,000 in police costs to unscramble the arrangements already made. It seemed a large sum, but we were in no position to increase the pressure on Liverpool for a quick decision.

There had been a crowd surge at Hillsborough in 1981 in the semi-final between Wolves and Spurs but I didn't know about that until after the tragedy. I was told that it was caused by one set of supporters trying to move into another area. But I did not believe that this was relevant because the configuration of the ground had changed considerably in the intervening years. Some Sheffield locals had tried to stop semi-finals being held there and, indeed, there was a gap before we went back in 1988 for the first Forest–Liverpool semi-final.

In anticipation of the inquiry I was reviewing my own impressions of the day and I had seen no problems with disorder or alcohol or any particular problems when I arrived, admittedly quite early, at 12.30 pm.

I had come off the M1 at Junction 35 rather than 34 and joined the Liverpool traffic at a junction controlled by the police. I was not stopped by the police checking tickets in 1988, although I had been in 1987 on that same road.

At 2.40 pm Graham Mackrell told me that he thought that there were still 20,000 fans outside the ground but the police were against delaying the kick-off because of the operational problems it might give them at the end of the game. It is interesting to note at this stage that the kick-off had been delayed in 1988.

I spoke to Peter Robinson on 28 April. He was still uncertain about the replay and asked if there was any other option available to them. He said they probably would not play if the fans who had been at Hillsborough could not have seats this time, but I knew that this was not possible at Old Trafford. We spoke later that day and he expressed willingness to play but only if it was on a different ground. He did not want to play the game at Old Trafford. He was so firm on this point that he assumed that the FA would throw the club out of the competition.

But that was the last thing we wanted to do. We were not insensitive to the club's wishes and desperately wanted to do everything we could to smooth the path for them. With this in mind I spoke to Bernard Halford, the secretary at Manchester City, Wembley and Greater Manchester Police. Manchester City and Wembley were both confident that they could put on the match but I didn't think we could change horses at that late stage with such a delicate and sensitive game. There did not seem to be any problems with Manchester United who were most understanding, saying that those who did not want to attend would have their money refunded and could watch the match on live television.

I asked Liverpool if they would think again.

At Hillsborough Liverpool had fewer but better seats at the Leppings Lane end and in the North stand, while some of the Forest seats in the South stand were obstructed by pillars.

I attended the memorial service at Liverpool Cathedral on 29 April. Peter Robinson agreed to play the semi-final providing they could sell tickets for Old Trafford and refund cash for Hillsborough, rather than exchange Hillsborough tickets for vouchers. I accepted that and the decision was announced later that day.

Had Liverpool decided then that they could not play in the semi-final, both Everton, the winners of the other semi-final, and Nottingham Forest declared that they were prepared to carry on.

They were not the only clubs still involved in the subsequent turmoil and Bert McGee, on behalf of Sheffield Wednesday, wrote to me seeking guidance about financial help because they had closed part of the ground, staff morale was low and police costs were high for the future games. I could not, in all conscience, give any help.

After the criticisms I and the FA had fielded, it was heartening when the Archbishop of Canterbury, Robert Runcie, a Luton Town fan, expressed his admiration at the way I and the FA had handled things and hoped that some good would come out of the tragedy.

Meanwhile a lot of clubs hurried to pull down their perimeter fences and we faced a difficult decision with regard to the Cup Final. Macclesfield, finalists in the FA Trophy, were not happy that we were retaining the fences for their game as we were for the FA Vase. There was no dilemma for the England World Cup qualifying game against Albania, as FIFA demanded fences at all World Cup matches.

Forest's heart was not in a subdued semi-final at Old Trafford a fortnight after the tragedy and Liverpool went through to what was being called the 'The Requiem Cup Final'.

We dismantled the fences for the all-Merseyside final. Sadly, there were a number of crowd invasions in the later stages of the game which kept everyone on a knife edge. A large section booed and jeered the so-called fans who came on to the pitch. All but the handful of lunatics were sensitive to the occasion, and as it was an extremely hot day, the Wembley staff came round with water.

The most poignant moment was the singing of the Anfield anthem 'You'll Never Walk Alone' led by Gerry Marsden. Liverpool won the game 3–2 after extra time with Ian Rush, coming on as a substitute, scoring twice in the added half an hour. It was a match of high quality played by two top sides with a great deal of respect for each other and their supporters. The whole of Merseyside had shared the grief for over a month and I hoped that we at the FA had done as much as we could in the near impossible circumstances.

The work involved had kept the adrenaline flowing. There was nothing for it but to plough on. We had so much to do and to organise that we could not afford the luxury of stopping to reflect for too long.

It is only when I look back some years later that I appreciate how awful and appalling the whole thing was, remembering the bodies, the tears, the anguish and the grief. Just writing about the events of ten years ago brings a lump to the throat and a tear to the eye.

I have tried to recount the terrible story from my own perspective at the time. This, I know, will be little comfort to Merseysiders and the bereaved families. Some of them I met at David Mellor's Task Force meeting in Liverpool in May 1998 when they were pressing for a fresh inquiry. The police, Sheffield Wednesday and Sheffield Council had all accepted liability and settled claims, but the families felt that the matter was still unresolved. They wanted Mr Duckenfield and Superintendent Bernard Murray, who had also been in the control box, to be prosecuted.

We were heavily involved with the legal profession in the weeks following the disaster. We decided we would put in some urgent recommendations to Lord Justice Taylor's Inquiry that terracing capacity should be reduced and that there should be some minimum standards laid down for medical facilities. At the time 38% of accommodation was seated in Division One so there was a long, long way to go even for Division One grounds to become all-seater. Accordingly, we were persuaded by the Football League represent-atives to set the targets lower than our original instincts indicated.

We expressed the view that we needed more new grounds and that clubs, where practicable, should look at the possibility of ground sharing. We stressed that the reduction of the betting duty to 40% from 42.5% was compelling as it would release £16 million a year to help improve the grounds and make them safer. We sent someone to look at the fences in Nimes, but there was no room for moats in English grounds.

In my final submission to Taylor I said that football needed to exhibit a dynamic approach towards regenerating its image, not by having a national membership scheme, as advocated by the Government, putting off the casual supporter and costing the game millions of pounds it could ill-afford, but by obliging away fans to become members of the away club scheme; that we needed to get more seats into grounds; that we needed to improve facilities and be rid of the cages.

The only valid conclusion, in hindsight, is that it was a tragic error by the police to open the gates without checking where the fans would be funnelled. But they were conditioned by years of dealing with football hooliganism. As the tragedy unfolded within the stadium, the police thought they were dealing with a security issue when in reality it was a question of safety. When a policeman outside the ground asked for the gate to be opened, he did so because he genuinely feared a fatal crush outside the ground.

I had no doubts on the day, nor subsequently, that the kick-off should have been delayed.

But the legacy the tragedy has left is that England now have the best grounds in the world and, more importantly, the safest. This, too, is no consolation to the bereaved, and when the cry goes up for supporters to have the choice of standing or sitting, they should think of those 96 souls who will never be able to do either.

CHAPTER TEN

The Ugly Game

Prime Minister Margaret Thatcher was a bully who despised football, had little or no interest in sport and drove those around her who were interested in the national sport underground.

No one in the game was happy with the hooliganism which blighted football during much of her term of office, but her attitude and tactics did little to help and the fact that it was brought under control had little to do with her and everything to do with the work and co-operation of the police, the clubs and the essential introduction of CCTV cameras.

The Prime Minister did not have any feel for the game at all; nor did her ministers, come to that. There was no affinity, despite football being our national sport. She rather looked down on the muddied oafs who played the game. Those hanging onto her apron strings seemed to be rugby, golf or rowing types and you could not imagine too many of them going into the Cabinet Office the next morning and discussing the game on television the previous night.

The Iron Lady frightened those around her and they will admit there was no football lobby because she wouldn't give the game house room. I did not see Douglas Hurd or Leon Brittain exhibit any feeling for football at a time we needed understanding and help.

There were one or two who were keen – Kenneth Clarke, a Nottingham Forest fan, for one – but it was not until John Major took over at Number 10 that the football nuts came out of the closet.

The hooligan problem is one which has afflicted football

throughout my time and took me head-on with Prime Ministers, Home Secretaries and even, occasionally, Sports Ministers. We had Government reports stretching back to 1968, and in 1969 there were recommendations for detention rooms, closed circuit television surveillance and attendance centres.

The FA, it seemed, had been fighting a losing battle against something which had been despairingly called abroad 'The English Disease'. We had taken football to the world and now, it was being claimed, we had taken football violence to distant shores.

In 1971 the FA had closed Leeds United's Elland Road ground after a controversial winning goal by West Bromwich Albion effectively denied Leeds the title and sparked a riot.

Three years later there had been a death at a Blackpool – Bolton game with Minister for Sport Denis Howell setting up a working party to look into the problem. Howell, a former class one referee, at least knew what he was talking about and I always felt that it was a great pity his knowledge and expertise was denied us through the Thatcher years.

But, even with the knowledgeable and sympathetic Howell about, trouble continued and spilled over in an ugly way. There were serious troubles in Paris in 1975 when Leeds appeared in the European Cup Final against Bayern Munich, with the crowd stirred to violence by some odd refereeing decisions.

We had a very well-received report by Frank McElhone into the problem in Scotland which had recommended perimeter fences; segregation; attendance centres; more seating and restrictions on alcohol.

Howell's working party added to this by suggesting that certain high risk matches be made all ticket, but he was not at all enamoured with the concept of identification cards and that was not pursued.

The FA also set up a new Crowd Control Committee who felt that punishments were inadequate and recommended corporal punishment to the Home Secretary Merlyn Rees. Football directors were not known for their liberal views.

The violence reached a peak in 1977–78 and 78–79; 51 incidents were reported to the Football Association in each of those seasons.

The strife rumbled on from gang to gang, ground to ground and even country to country into the 1980s. There was trouble at Stamford Bridge when Chelsea played Sunderland; and there was a major riot in Luton when Millwall visited in March 1985 with police injured and retreating in the face of appalling violence. Luton had failed to recognise the risks and the game was not all ticket, attracting fans from rival London clubs to an already highly charged atmosphere.

It was so bad that the FA, considering an application to stage the 1988 European Championships, quickly and quietly tore up their blueprint in the wake of such major violence which attracted international headlines.

Millwall were fined £7,500 and Luton were ordered to put up fences but these decisions were reduced on appeal later. Minister for Sport Neil Macfarlane was horrified, as he had already been upset by the FA's adoption of 'Bulldog Bobby' as a mascot for the 1982 World Cup Final. He believed that adopting a pugnacious character like a bulldog encouraged the hooligans. Macfarlane thought the FA's penalties were far too lenient and was unhappy at the way the football authorities were handling the crisis. He cited the £800,000 Everton had paid Leicester City for Gary Lineker, saying that the money should be put to anti-hooligan measures, not understanding that the money spent internally on players stayed in the game.

We had asked the Government for a concession on betting duty in 1985 but the Chancellor, Nigel Lawson, refused. The Pool Promoters had promised to give 40% of any reduction back to football for ground improvements. £200 million went in tax every year and, shamefully, none of it came back into the game. To this day bets on football attract tax which is used to help the horse racing industry.

After the Luton incident Margaret Thatcher called us into Downing Street. It had become difficult under the Safety of Sports Grounds Act to find football clubs guilty of misconduct. If they held a safety certificate they could usually satisfy the FA that they had taken all reasonable precautions. The Prime Minister wanted us to take that phrase out of the rules and find clubs guilty if there was any sort of incident. The FA seemed quite happy to make clubs automatically responsible for anything that happened at their grounds without listening to their reasons or explanations, but, on behalf of the League, Jack Dunnett later succeeded in having the rule drafted in a more reasonable way.

The Government wanted us to accelerate closed circuit television with only half of Division One having it installed, make sure that perimeter fences were effective (they were rushing to take them down three years later), and deal severely with players who misbehaved on the pitch. They insisted that we look at membership schemes within six weeks and report back to Macfarlane.

There were few who would stand up to Mrs Thatcher. My predecessor at the Football Association, Ted Croker, was one. They had a famous exchange when Croker bravely accused her Government of inflicting the country's hooligans on football. The packed room of politicians and football administrators gave a collective shudder as she paused but took the barb with remarkable equanimity, simply saying 'Steady the Buffs.' Ted's courage stood him in good stead when he had to fight cancer at the end of his career.

The FA wanted the Home Secretary to remind magistrates about attendance orders. I recall discussing it with the Prime Minister after the meeting and she said that, as a Government, of all the issues they had to tackle, behavioural problems in all walks of life were the most difficult to get to grips with.

With a serious shortage of Ministers who owned up to any knowledge of football, the Government used David Teasdale as an advisor to Macfarlane at the time, someone I was to come across later when he also acted as press advisor to the luckless England manager Graham Taylor. In response to our request for a two and a half per cent reduction in betting duty, they said that we should find the money ourselves, with Teasdale adding that the big clubs should be levied to produce the necessary money for ground improvements. They did not appreciate that the bigger clubs were already beginning to resent the subsidies they paid the poorer clubs.

In May 1985 the problems compounded. Fifty six people died in a fire at the Bradford City Valley Parade ground, with 200 injured, and Home Secretary Leon Brittain asked Lord Justice Popplewell to look at crowd safety and control. On the same day there was the death of Ian Hambridge, a young fan from Northampton attending his first match between Birmingham City and Leeds United, who was killed when a wall collapsed during scuffles.

On 1 April the Government had decided to designate Third and Fourth Division clubs with poor records of crowd control, but after the fire they included all Third and Fourth Division clubs in the plans for more stringent safety certificates.

The Government were also becoming even keener on identity cards. The scheme would have driven scores of decent fans from the game. Moreover, faced with a problem outside grounds, the police would invariably let troublemakers in where they could be more easily controlled.

But the clubs did not assist the efforts of the FA and Football League to resist the plans when only 50 bothered to reply to Justice Popplewell's questionnaire.

Then, at the end of May, came the Heysel Stadium disaster when 39 fans, the majority Italians, died as they were attacked by Liverpool fans in Brussels before the start of the European Cup Final between the Merseysiders and Juventus. It seemed to be a bridge too far and the future of English football was plunged into doubt, certainly in terms of European and International football.

FA Chairman Bert Millichip and secretary Ted Croker flew back from Mexico where England were on a pre-World Cup tour, playing matches against the host, West Germany and, of all teams, Italy. Players from both European Cup Final teams were due to join up for the tournament.

Millichip and Croker decided, against Jack Dunnett's advice, to pre-empt any announcement by UEFA by taking the English clubs out of Europe. Liverpool voluntarily withdrew immediately, but Everton, Manchester United, Norwich, Spurs and Southampton were left feeling aggrieved. Norwich and Everton in particular objected and the five clubs commenced litigation which failed. It did not do the game a lot of good, nor did it help England's tarnished reputation.

We were summoned back to see Mrs Thatcher in June 1985 and one thing which we did have, at last, was the commitment of the Government to try and get to grips with the problem at long last. We differed on the methods and the fundamental approach to football, but at least we had the will of the Government, as Maggie assured us whenever we met.

We called for tougher sentences, having been encouraged when rioting fans in Cambridge had been jailed for five years in May 1985. We thought that was a pretty good move which sent out a strong message. We also asked again for a reduction in the pool betting duty. The Prime Minister put Neil Macfarlane in charge of a working party.

I was not particularly comfortable with Macfarlane, mainly because he did not seem to have any greater feel for football than other ministers who were not specifically involved in sport. Like most Ministers for Sport, he did not carry any real political clout. We met the Prime Minister again on 3 July and the discussions focused entirely on membership schemes. The Government wanted the FA to impose membership on the clubs through the disciplinary rules and that didn't go down too well with the League representatives.

The much-publicised Millwall riot had confirmed David Evans' view that away fans should be banned from Kenilworth Road. The club had wanted to move and build a new stadium, but Milton Keynes, a quickly growing new town, voted unanimously against Luton moving there because of the hooligan problem. The right wing Conservative MP Evans had been set on banning away fans ever since he became chairman of the club in 1984.

Popplewell had brought out a preliminary report which said that there was no single answer. He eventually came back in January 1986 and reported that there should be a membership scheme, but did not specify what sort, nor how it should be administered. He said alcohol could be allowed in executive boxes but nowhere else; powers of arrest should be widened and there should be an offence of disorderly conduct and a statutory right of search.

Back we went to see Maggie on 16 July 1986 and, surprisingly, she announced herself pleased with the progress. She had every right to be as arrests were down 46% and there was closed circuit TV in most of the major grounds. We agreed to concentrate on individual membership schemes and not on identity cards.

Unfortunately the truce between the Iron Lady and the football authorities was short-lived because of trouble on the ferries in 1986 and problems at the Odsal Stadium where Bradford City were playing following the fire at their ground. It led to the Government insisting that they were still pursuing membership schemes with David Teasdale being one of the chief proponents.

Richard Tracey then became Minister for Sport and he was wound up by continual reports from British Transport police reports of misconduct by football fans on the trains. He promptly called for another report in six weeks. This was becoming standard practice with the demand always the same: a report in six weeks.

We recommended that each club devote 70% of their ground to members, but Tracey rejected this.

So the newly-constituted League Management Committee commissioned a report from management consultants Peat Marwick. Unfortunately, the complicated 'reciprocal' membership scheme they recommended did not appeal to experienced club administrators like Les Olive of Manchester United and Eddie Plumley of Watford.

In 1986 I and the Management Committee managed to alienate the Football Association, the Government and the press in one fell swoop by throwing Luton out of the Football League Cup. The *Sun* had a wonderful headline above with pictures of the eight members of the management committee, reading 'THE SPINELESS MEN WHO CAPITULATED TO THE LOUTS AND FORCED LITTLE LUTON OUT OF THE LEAGUE CUP'. Exactly a year later they used the same eight pictures to depict the eight brave men who had stood up to the loathsome Robert Maxwell!

Initially Luton had 16,000 members. It was not a problem for League games as other clubs could retaliate by barring Luton's fans, but for a one-off cup tie we felt it would give the home club an unfair advantage.

Ted Croker was always one for discouraging away fans. He very much supported the Luton scheme, and in fact relations between the FA and the League were not helped when the FA allowed Luton to play in the FA Cup without admitting away supporters.

Despite the rules which said they had to provide 25% to the away clubs and the fact that they had opportunities to put down amendments to the rules, Luton simply said that they would not be supplying tickets to Cardiff City. The Government were perturbed, while the Management Committee were portrayed as insensitive. Even Roy Race banned away fans from Melchester Park!

Phil Carter and I saw David Evans and we agreed to refer the final decision to a vote of all the clubs. Evans agreed to abide by the vote.

On 6 October, 80 clubs supported the Management Committee, probably a record. This showed just how far Luton had upset the other clubs. John Smith, Luton's Managing Director, felt he had to resign from the Management Committee, as he believed that after the débacle his position was untenable.

Ken Bates banned Luton Town directors from his Stamford Bridge boardroom because of the away ban. Luton eventually came back into the League Cup in 1987 and said they would play away if they were drawn at home to a big club.

In that same year *Today* newspaper came up with the idea of a club, a marketing proposal linked to an identity card scheme. Chris Monckton, former advisor to Mrs Thatcher, wrote to the PM advocating the idea. I was annoyed he had written directly to Maggie on football business, but it hardly mattered as it quickly petered out.

There was a new eight-point plan put forward in February 1987 agreed with Richard Tracey and Douglas Hogg, the Home Office minister, whereby all clubs would have to prove with local plans how they dealt with crowd control; 50% of grounds would need to be covered by membership areas by the start of the following season.

Hogg threatened legislation to back up our efforts. It was decided that there would be a committee of representatives to go round the country to help clubs meet the targets.

Bert Millichip also agreed that clubs who bucked the system and failed to follow the recommendation of the committee would be in breach of FA regulations, but Phil Carter objected and it never reached the rule book.

I met the all-party football committee of MPs in March 1987 when they congratulated the Government and football on an imaginative package to help deal with hooliganism. Sir John Quinton, the chairman of Barclays who had replaced *Today* as the League sponsors, was also very supportive.

Despite the new laws relating to alcohol, arrest statistics were still down in 1987 but, nevertheless, the UEFA Executive Committee voted 8–3 to keep the ban on English clubs. Richard Tracey wrote a waffly letter to UEFA which did not help our cause. He seemed to be the latest in a long line of Ministers for Sport who sank without trace and were not a great deal of help to the national game. In that same year Colin Moynihan appeared in the role alongside Hogg. Moynihan was unhappy with the figures we produced, claiming that many of the clubs were nowhere near the required 50% membership and he took an eternity going through the files, club by club. He at least gave us eight weeks instead of six to produce a review!

The League appointed Jack Crawford, a 57-year-old ex-policeman from Merseyside, to advise on crowd control. Forty-one clubs had reached the required 50%, which was not a bad result considering that the police were as lukewarm as the clubs in many cases.

Barnsley, showing typical Yorkshire obstinacy, held out against any form of membership. They would not have anything to do with it and felt that they were the last bastion of freedom in South Yorkshire.

Jacques Georges, the UEFA President, attended the Football League Centenary Dinner and amazed us all when he said that he would like us back in Europe at the earliest opportunity!

Clubs below 40% membership had sent in letters from their local police, saying that in their view the configuration of the ground would not allow for a higher membership. Moynihan, in his wisdom, decided to challenge this and started calling in the clubs one by one, reckoning that there were six clubs he was going to shake up. The Minister for Sport also floated the idea of a breathalyser at the turnstiles which, fortunately, did not last long.

Despite all our efforts, hooliganism was not going away and at the 1988 European Championships in Germany there were some extremely unpleasant scenes on the streets of Dusseldorf when England played. The Government overreacted. I could understand the FA withdrawing their request to UEFA to readmit English clubs, but for Mrs Thatcher to say that England should withdraw from international competition was entirely wrong.

Moynihan, of course, supported her and produced his daftest comment of all when he stated: 'England should not have taken tickets.' In other words, he would have left yobs of all sorts free to go on their own and cause mayhem without any control or monitoring, a policy which had been discredited for more years than anyone at the FA could remember.

We had another problem at the Scotland match at Wembley with a skirmish in one corner in May of that year, giving Jacques Georges the opportunity of criticising England once again. Not that Moynihan was supporting a return to Europe anyway, for he castigated the FA for crowd segregation failings at the game. Amidst all this turmoil there was another stand-off over identity cards. The Government threatened that they would legislate, with Moynihan again displaying how naive he was, telling Maggie Thatcher that he would have UEFA impose a pan-European membership card scheme. He obviously had not had many dealings with UEFA.

Towards the end of 1988 the contentious identity card Bill was published. I felt that this was disastrous. Moynihan was not losing football's confidence because that presupposed he ever had it. Only three clubs, Fulham, Southampton and Wimbledon, went in to see the Minister for Sport, a bit of a pointless exercise because Moynihan then rounded on ACPO's David Phillips, demanding to know why there was not more CCTV in grounds. Phillips patiently explained that because the technology was changing so quickly, they were forced to move at a gentler pace.

The three clubs in the North, Wrexham, Barnsley and Darlington never met Moynihan. It was so much political hot air, not adding up to a row of beans.

The Minister told the Football Writers' Association Dinner that the game must move into the 90s, that supporters had a raw deal and that there was no chance of a return to Europe until clubs knuckled down.

At least he attended that function but he sent his civil servant, David McDonald, to the *Football into the 1990s* Conference at Leicester

University. McDonald read Moynihan's speech which stated that he planned a national membership scheme to which everyone must belong, as partial schemes had not worked. Legislation was threatened for the 1989–90 season.

Jim Thompson, Chairman of the Alliance Premier League (now the Conference), asked how it would have prevented trouble in Germany. 'Oh,' said Mr McDonald, 'I cannot answer that. I will take your views back to the Minister.' It just about summed up the level of understanding.

It was the farsighted Lord Justice Taylor who saved football from the membership card scheme in 1990 when he published his report into the Hillsborough disaster. He recommended all-seater stadiums, modified fences, and new offences of racist or obscene abuse, ticket touting, throwing missiles and invading the pitch.

Early in 1990 in the Budget John Major reduced the pool betting to 40% while he was at the Exchequer, giving us the two and half per cent we had been pleading for. At last we had someone in Government with a feeling for our sport, and knowing this, I, along with many like-minded football people, had written to him just before the Budget when we managed to carry the day.

I was delighted when Major took over from Thatcher as Prime Minister. The effect was immediate and our relationship as different as night and day. The whole climate was much warmer and much more co-operative towards football generally. John Major himself was a genuine football supporter who loved going to matches and was very keen to talk sport, whether it was football, cricket or whatever, when we met.

We were never hauled into Downing Street like naughty schoolboys as we had been by Maggie Thatcher. The problems had by then changed, but I often wondered how different football matters might have been, had he been in office earlier.

I felt very aggrieved when his son received so much national criticism when he was sent off and was suspended by the Hunts FA. It would not have rated a line in the local paper and it was only because it was the PM's son that it made front page news and the lead item on the electronic media's news bulletins. I feel very strongly about that. I do not believe anyone should have the focus of attention on them because they have a famous parent.

The hooligans did not disappear but they were squeezed out of the grounds in the 1990's by CCTV, increased police intelligence and more seating, especially the all-seater requirements at the top level. It was a good concerted effort by everyone involved.

But it must be recognised that hooliganism has not gone away. It has only been controlled and, at the first signs of complacency, it will be back. There are still sporadic outbursts which should serve as a reminder to everyone. England supporters caused a few problems in Stockholm at the end of 1989 and caused us to withdraw from a friendly match against Holland in December of that same year. The timing was appalling as UEFA had given their approval in April 1989 for England to return to European competitions providing our Government agreed.

Pat Smith initiated the England Travel Club (now the England Members' Club) in 1990 and tried to ensure that anyone travelling from England to watch the team were genuine supporters, because the previous policy of trying to discourage supporters from taking tickets had been discredited.

The new system worked reasonably well at the World Cup in Italy where there was massive policing. But there was a swoop by nervous Italian police in Rimini when they rounded up English supporters and put over 200 fans on a plane home, including one poor chap who was on holiday and had merely popped out for a bottle of milk.

There was also an extremely hairy moment in Turin when the police almost let the fans in without tickets for the semi-final against West Germany, but just avoided it. At that point in the competition there were a great many English spectators heading back to Italy in the hope of picking up a ticket and at one stage the FA were forced to buy up tickets ourselves because we were very concerned about the insufficient supply for our fans. It cost us an awful lot of money because we had to buy them at above the odds. We sold them back to our fans at cover price, but at least we had stopped the individual touting of tickets and the English supporters paying through the nose once again.

In July Moynihan gave the go-ahead for UEFA to admit a limited number of English clubs back into European competition for a one-year trial. I trust that trial period is not still on because I cannot remember it being lifted.

In support of his decision Moynihan promoted the facts that we had made diligent preparations for the World Cup in Italy where England had won the Fair Play Award; the Government had reduced the betting duty to allow investment in stadiums; they had extended restriction orders; arrests were down and there had been improvements in policing. All this combined to allow him to advocate our return.

After a succession of ineffectual Ministers for Sport there was a brief flicker of hope in 1992 when David Mellor combined sport with his work as Minister for the Heritage. David was a good minister but, sadly, he did not stay in office. I remember him once yawning and cutting a meeting short because he was in a bit of a rush, saying he had a speech to write. When he eventually had his much-publicised problems I remembered that yawn and thought I knew the cause of it.

During his short time at the helm he relaxed the all-seating requirements in July 1992 for Third and Fourth Division clubs providing their terracing was safe, while ensuring that the reduction in betting duty was extended to the year 2000, although it has not been worth so much since the National Lottery hit the pools business.

We did not need any help in digging the odd hole for ourselves. We could do that quite well, as we did when we discovered in 1994 that England were due to play Germany on Hitler's birthday. Not many people knew that it was 20 April, but the neo-Nazis did. Hamburg found that they were unable to guarantee security and the game was switched to Berlin, but the FA decided we could not take the risk and we upset the German FA by calling the game off just a fortnight before it was due to be played.

We thought that right wing extremists would gather from Germany and England. We did not have concrete information in this instance but we were getting very bad vibes and those on the security side were expressing concern. I do not believe the press had an influence on the ultimate decision because we were getting all our information from Germany and the more we heard, the more we worried. Quite frankly it simply was not worth the risk.

The problem continued into 1995 with the riot in Dublin and the abandonment of the friendly against the Republic of Ireland after 27 minutes, the first time that had happened. Talking to our fans outside the ground, the mood was excellent. One said: 'Do you mind if I ask you something?' 'Not at all,' I replied, expecting to be taxed on one of the burning issues of the day. 'Can you tell me where the toilets are, Graham?' he asked before turning away and gleefully yelling: 'This is Graham Kelly and he doesn't even know where the toilets are!'

But the atmosphere was soon shattered and I was deeply shocked by the extent of the violence inside the ground, something we had not experienced for a good few years.

The Irish police had refused all offers of assistance from the UK police who, in the end, did not even travel to Dublin. It transpired in the aftermath that the FA of Ireland were not given the intelligence passed across to the Irish police by the National Football Intelligence Unit. The match was called off with missiles being thrown inside the ground. The arrangements were a mess. The cordon outside the ground was ineffective with turnstiles not segregated. Fans gained access to the ground without tickets with many of them not seemingly interested in the match. There was no sterile area, little action by the police and little stewarding to any effect.

Bertie Ahern, at that time Irish Minister of Sport, criticised the FA for poor ticket distribution. This was entirely without foundation as we had carried out our normal policy and it was failing on his side of the water which caused the problems, namely the resale of 1500 tickets we returned which were put on uncontrolled general sale. I suspect someone made a tidy profit.

Both managers Jack Charlton and Terry Venables were naturally upset at what had happened but were eager to continue the game once order had been restored. However, the Dutch referee Zol abandoned it. When I went to talk to him he was adamant that he would not carry on with mayhem going on all round him. I suppose you could not blame him. That sort of violence going on around you is very numbing and it is almost paralysing when you have to go to talk about it to the media within ten minutes of the violence occurring, a very short time in which to collect any cohesive thoughts.

A handful of Irish fans sued the Football Association of Ireland for damages for the injuries they received in the fighting. The FAI tried to bring us into the argument but we simply paid a modest sum, proved we had not been negligent and all claims were dropped.

The Irish produced a very dubious report, but we had no doubts who were to blame. Our police were so aware that they were not only able to specify which ferries and planes the suspected hooligans would be on, but even which seats they would be occupying on the planes!

Such was our handling of the hooliganism problems over the years that English clubs were often used as models on how to curb the violent element in the game which was still running amok in many countries. Yet despite our reputation there were still countries whose police would not take any notice of the information we were able to provide to help them when English clubs or the national team were involved. Ireland were one, but Italy consistently ignored our advice and consequently there was always something happening whenever the two great football countries met.

It happened again in 1997 in Rome for the crucial World Cup qualifying game. Once more poor administration of the stadium, poor stewarding, poor ticket distribution with no regard for segregation, intimidation by the police and a complete breakdown in the ticketing strategy caused all sorts of unnecessary difficulties.

Some of the English fans were detained in the stadium until 1.15 am, two and a half hours after the final whistle. Pat Smith, who was responsible for the England Members' Club, refused to board the coach until the situation was resolved, I stayed with her, and it needed a hair-raising drive from a co-operative *carabiniero* to get us to the airport in time for the plane back to Luton.

After the strife FIFA attempted in the first place to fine both associations. I am certain that there was some jiggery pokery going on at FIFA as the disciplinary commission reached their decisions before Sepp Blatter got involved and called the Italian FA President Luciano Nizzola and Keith Wiseman to a lunch. He telephoned me to say that he did not want the situation to blow up out of all proportion and wanted to restore friendly relations as he expected both countries to be playing in France.

They had a cosy meal at which the subject was never properly broached. It was all smoothed over by the urbane Sepp and eventually FIFA reduced the fines on both Associations. It was a bizarre situation.

The FA should not have been in any real danger of a fine. There was no evidence that English fans had been guilty of anything much inside the ground, although some of our journalists did not like the behaviour of some Englishmen on the Via Veneto on the eve of the game.

People jump to conclusions very quickly. There were some problems with seats being thrown but they were seats which originally came from the Italian side. Initially, the police did nothing, but when the English briefly retaliated they stormed in with their batons.

There was an incident in Stockholm in our European Championship qualifying game in 1998 when we had the worrying outbreak of hooliganism from English members in stands behind the goal at the end of the game. We certainly could not complain about being fined for that.

But we appealed on the part of the fine which accused our supporters of racist chants. We could not find any evidence of the referee's allegation which claimed that our fans had been racially abusing Henrik Larsson, the Celtic striker. Of course they were jeering at him because of his dives and the fact that Paul Ince was sent off after a tussle with him, but certainly not because of his colour. The delegate who had been seated in the main tribune supported the referee who said that there had been monkey noises. That was not correct; they were boos.

We sent Nic Coward over to the appeal and I told him to take the video to prove to them that there was no evidence on the sound track. The delegate Dr Sprengers of Holland went in, warmly shook hands with all the members of the board of appeal, told them how he had heard this racist chanting and fully supported the referee. They then refused to allow Nic to show the video and we lost the appeal. He came back very chastened and learned that he needed to take a heavyweight with him. They did not know who he was and consequently took no notice of him.

To many, England's participation in the French World Cup was a riot waiting to happen and the cynics were not disappointed with the rumbles in Marseille before our game against Tunisia. By this time the England Members' Club boasted 35,000 fans, after we had embarked on a strategy of encouraging as many supporters as possible to join up and outnumber the few troublemakers.

I saw it almost at first hand as I was having a pleasant meal at a cafe in Marseille with my son when we had to grab our bouillabaisse and hurriedly disappear into the back of the restaurant because of the trouble in the Old Port. With tear gas blowing into the establishment I could not see what was going on but it became obvious from what my son was telling me that the police had stood back for far too long and then let it explode. It was the prelude to a very long night of running battles between the English and the local North Africans who were spoiling for a fight.

We came out strongly the following morning to condemn the English people involved and for the rest of the tournament I had English fans telling me that it was not them who started it and that they had been set upon. Sadly they were there and, from what we heard, some were only too ready to retaliate and take part in the fighting.

The following day Romayne, who had driven across on her own to support the team, tackled one of the English lunatics whom she caught in the act of throwing a bottle. I was already in the ground when she bravely approached him and asked him what he was trying to do, and did he want to get England banned from football forever, to which he replied: 'Fuck off, you old tart.'

There were a lot of English cars which had their windscreens broken during the match. The incidents set an unfortunate tone for the tournament because we had to work hard to convince everybody it would not recur in Toulouse, while Lens was a no-go area. You just could not reach the centre of Lens even if you wanted to.

It is strange how the atmosphere can change so quickly. Generally speaking the fans were marvellous. There were thousands and thousands in the ground in Marseille, even though we had only a handful of tickets. They had to pay well over the odds, but inside the ground they behaved properly and gave incredible support to the team. They continued to support their country and there was no trouble in any of the grounds, apart from the merest flicker, which was quickly doused, in the highly charged game against Argentina.

FIFA were magnificent over the problems in Marseille. I spoke to Keith Cooper, their British-born Media Director, on the Monday morning, the day of the match, and told him the latest information we had and he came out strongly in support of our efforts. Sepp Blatter echoed his comments and I thanked them later for their solid support.

We were never in any danger of draconian punishments or, indeed, any punishments at all as some newspapers back home delighted in suggesting.

I took a lot of time out walking the streets of Marseille and Toulouse. Obviously my face is known to the fans from television and I enjoy the banter but once it gets to five or six o clock it becomes virtually impossible to have sensible discussions because of the risk of coming across someone who has had too much to drink.

I walked back to the coast after the opening game against Tunisia in Marseille to catch a bus back into town. Just on the corner, near the large screen on the beach, there was a large group of lads outside a pub and one of them was particularly obnoxious, screaming at me: 'What have the FA ever done for supporters? All you ever do is slag us off.' The problem is that much of the time I am prepared to argue the case, I rarely walk away, but sometimes you reach a stage where it is impossible to have a reasoned argument and such was the case on that day. In the end I turned on my heel, after letting forth with an epithet of my own.

There was another incident on the streets of Toulouse. I was suddenly met with a stream of foul-mouthed abuse from a young man. I went across to have a quiet word with him but he was not even capable of standing up, never mind carrying on a sensible conversation.

Executive Committee member Frank Pattison commented on the rowdy behaviour of the England members he sat among at the Colombia match at Lens. He seemed not to have appreciated the problems our staff faced in keeping everyone happy in a finals tournament. Pat Smith's colleague Jill Smith worked tirelessly for the fans on all the away trips.

I secured the services of retiring Deputy Metropolitan Police Commissioner Sir Brian Hayes for the World Cup. He did a sterling job, liaising with the French authorities and generally adding professionalism to our operation. Sadly, when he went to Spain on a pre-arranged trip in the week between Marseille and Toulouse matches, he was vilified by the *Daily Mirror* for 'going on holiday'.

Under certain circumstances, with that type of person who wants to travel abroad and does not mind drinking too much and creating havoc, the potential for violence is always there. We have seen over the years that the England team has become the focus for some very objectionable people. It still happens at Wembley if you believe the accounts of certain writers who sit in seats surrounded by obnoxious people who will not sit down or stop swearing.

Basically they are ignorant yobs with little love for the game.

I have even seen it myself in areas at Wembley which are reserved for family groups. I became increasingly agitated when I looked down on the seats in front of the box at one Final where two groups were yelling obscenities across the divide, one of them gesticulating with one hand while holding onto a four year old boy with the other.

I do not know if I am qualified to understand them or if anyone is. Why is the problem still there? Everyone has different tolerance levels. I began to find mine was becoming quite low and I started rushing down from the Royal Box to confront these people at Wembley. Pat Smith became concerned at one of the lesser club matches when the stewards were taking no notice of a particularly foul-mouthed individual and the fact that this lout was standing up making a nuisance of himself amongst the families.

Having seen and heard enough, I sought out a security man and asked him to do something about it. Pat thought I was only inciting abuse, but suddenly I had had enough of sitting there watching him misbehave.

Eventually the security men discovered who I was on about and hauled the offender out. As the ground was not even half full, I could not understand why the problem had been allowed to develop. Generally people are very tolerant at football and it appears to be accepted that certain individuals will let off steam. I suppose fear comes into it if you are confronted with three great hairy youths in hob nail boots and reeking of lager. But there is no doubt that, collectively, we accept too much.

Community schemes have played a large part in improving things and it is now fashionable to support football, whereas in the eighties too often I felt compelled to apologise for being a supporter, particularly an Englishman abroad. On one memorable occasion, I was introduced as the Chief Executive of the Football Association to the Duke of Edinburgh. He replied: 'What have you done to deserve that?'

Despite the improvements, a handful of idiots are still able to transform Pele's Beautiful Game into the Ugly Game.

CHAPTER ELEVEN

Shearer Madness

A lan Shearer, captain of England, is an outstanding goalscorer and a very fine footballer. He is also an extremely obdurate man and I feared at one stage that the Football Association's disciplinary machinery was going to force both him and coach Glenn Hoddle out of the World Cup Finals in France in 1998.

There were thousands of words written and spoken over the Newcastle striker's alleged kick at Leicester City's Neil Lennon in an FA Carling Premiership match, but none of them revealed the true drama behind the issue as Shearer threatened, quite seriously, to turn his back on his country if he was charged by Lancaster Gate – and, what is more, Hoddle threatened to follow him.

Not only was England's most expensive footballer threatening to cause international, front page headlines, he also warned me that I could be driving him out of the country altogether! The inference was that he would not only refuse to play in France but would also leave Newcastle United for a club abroad.

There was I right in the middle of a disciplinary dilemma which had greater ramifications than the infamous Eric Cantona affair and would undoubtedly have made me the most unpopular figure in English football, if I was not already!

The date was 29 April 1998 and I was in Dublin for a UEFA Congress. I attended a welcome dinner given by the Football Association of Ireland, where I met Prime Minister Bertie Ahern. At the end of proceedings, I returned to my hotel room, switched on the Sky news, and there was footage of Alan Shearer appearing to react angrily to a foul by Neil Lennon in the Leicester City–Newcastle United match played at Filbert Street earlier that evening.

It looked a terrible incident on first showing and it seemed that Shearer clearly aimed a kick at Lennon. When I returned to London two days later on the Friday afternoon, I discussed the incident with Graham Noakes, a member of the management team responsible for disciplinary matters. The referee's report from Martin Bodenham was non-committal and Graham and I reached the decision together that it would probably be appropriate to charge Shearer with misconduct.

Shearer had already protested his innocence publicly while Lennon had stated that he wanted to forget about the whole affair. But I let it be known over the weekend that we were likely to charge Shearer.

Monday was the Bank Holiday so the charge letter was not sent until the Tuesday, 5 May. I could not see how we could avoid taking action in what seemed to me to be a fairly clear-cut case.

I had a meeting that day at the FA's National School at Lilleshall before driving back to London for a House of Commons meeting on World Cup 2006, returning to Lancaster Gate at 6 pm for a meeting with officials from Saudi Arabia. But as soon as I arrived I encountered an extremely agitated Glenn Hoddle waiting for me.

According to Glenn, Alan was seriously threatening to pull out of the World Cup because his employers for the World Cup, i.e. the FA, did not believe his explanation of events at Filbert Street. Glenn was supporting Shearer and said that he felt that the incident was accidental.

This was more than a bit tricky. I had the England captain threatening to pull out of the World Cup and the England coach supporting him. The media were already expecting a charge and morally I felt that, at the very least, Shearer had a case to answer. If he could satisfy a commission that he had not done anything wrong, then fine by me. But I did not think we should be party to sweeping it under the carpet because he was captain of England and because the World Cup Finals were looming. The word 'charge' seemed to cause particular offence to Alan.

David Davies knew of the incident and of Glenn Hoddle's disquiet. He telephoned Russell Cushing, the General Manager at Newcastle United, and asked him to slip our fax notifying the player and club of the pending charges into a drawer in his desk while we had further discussions on the matter. Fortunately, Russell agreed to do so.

The dilemma was that I was not qualified to argue with Glenn on technical matters and would never seek to overrule the England coach on any matter remotely connected with playing the game. I never had with any manager and never would. If he said it was accidental, it was difficult for me to say that it was not.

I tried to explain to him that it was in everybody's interest that the case be properly ventilated in a commission and that, in any case, the letter had gone and he was too late. What is more, the entire country had seen the incident on television and everyone had a view on it.

However, I promised to think about it overnight. I spoke to Graham Noakes again to be sure that we were right to be bringing up the case and it complied with previous precedents. I asked him and myself if there was clearly a case which needed to be answered. He was more certain than ever and was of the mind that just because it was Alan Shearer, we should not shirk it.

At that point I broke one of my own unwritten rules. I had always been at great pains to establish the principle that only the Chief Executive had the authority to issue charges. It was important for the integrity of the whole disciplinary system that someone totally independent commenced proceedings. But this time I thought to myself, 'This just isn't a normal FA charge'. It was a matter of policy if the country were to lose its captain and possibly its coach five weeks before the first World Cup match against Tunisia in Marseille.

I telephoned Chairman Keith Wiseman and told him what I planned to do. He agreed without hesitation that I had to do what I thought best. Players and managers become upset about these things, but you have to do what you think is right, regardless of who it is.

That resolved my determination and I went to bed that night with my mind made up. When I telephoned Glenn the next morning I had a bad line, he was out of doors somewhere and I could hear the wind whistling. It was not the ideal way of telling him that I was sorry but I had to go ahead with the charge.

Glenn asked me whether I had spoken to Alan Shearer because the player was determined that he would not go to France if he was charged. He then followed up with a double whammy as he went on to say: 'If that happens, I will have to consider my own position.'

I was immediately in touch with Alan on the telephone and argued for some time over the rights and wrongs. He was clearly upset that we did not believe him.

'If it was anybody else, you wouldn't be charging me,' Shearer said.

'Yes, we would,' I replied. I thought to myself, yes, like Paul Gascoigne or Eric Cantona, or anyone else in the spotlight. Shearer did not have the sole claim on fame.

He claimed that my actions had been influenced by the negative press coverage. I refuted that categorically. 'Besides,' I continued, 'I made the decision before all the hullabaloo in the papers over the weekend.'

He found it difficult to accept this. 'If I don't have the trust of my employers,' said Shearer, 'I will not go to France [for the World Cup] and will consider leaving Newcastle United and English football as well.'

This was heavy stuff and I did not want to be the unwitting cause of such a severe blow to our World Cup hopes. I found it quite staggering, and frankly it was childish behaviour for the England captain to threaten to give up the job of captaining his country. It lacked the maturity I had come to expect from him. I was surprised that he was sticking his neck on the line like that, especially in view of the advice he would have been getting from his agent Tony Stephens. Was he using this incident as an excuse for leaving Newcastle and the Geordie fans? I did not know whether he would go or not. But I had to believe him because it was said in his usual downbeat, matter-of-fact way.

Shearer is a good captain when things are going well, but if he is not getting the service you can tell from his body language – shoulders dropped and gestures to his team-mates – that he is not the most inspirational player to lead the side. In any event, I've always believed that playing up front is not the best position from which to captain any team.

I sent Glenn a note after speaking to the England captain. I told him I could not argue with him on the playing side of the game but that there was a case to answer, just as there had been in many other recent precedents, and Alan would have the opportunity to explain himself, hopefully as soon as possible. I added that no Football Association can deal with their own international players' club situations any differently from other players. It would not be fair. I also explained that I believed he was wrong to take sides with Alan in claiming that I had taken action because of the press attention on the case. I told him that I had made up my mind very soon after the incident, that the letter had already gone to Newcastle before I was aware of his disquiet and that I could not withdraw the charge at that stage.

The entire affair was fast getting out of hand. As if I did not have a big enough problem, I was also upset on two other counts. Glenn put out a press statement saying that the kick was unintentional and that people should get off Alan's back. I was upset at that, but even more so that our own media department had put out the statement for him.

I felt that, in effect, I was being criticised by my own staff. The matter was raised at the regular management meeting the following Friday and colleagues were horrified that the media department had put out conflicting views on the same incident, mine on one day and Glenn's the next.

The press had picked up on the difference of opinion, as one would expect them to. Strictly speaking it was a breach of contract by the England coach to cast doubt on an action by his employers.

The Professional Footballers' Association became involved when Gordon Taylor rang me at home on the following Sunday evening. He was with Shearer at the Tickled Trout Hotel, by the M6 in Preston, and they were requesting that the commission be fixed fairly quickly for the following Tuesday so that it would be out of the way before the Cup Final in which Shearer was due to play for Newcastle United against Arsenal. I promised to do what I could but I could not guarantee when the commission would be ready. In the event, the Disciplinary Department at Lancaster Gate pulled out all the stops and organised the commission for the day that Taylor and Shearer had requested.

The final verdict after all that was 'Not Proven'. It has to be said that the commission were not aware of the threats of the captain or the coach and made their own judgement on the evidence in front of them. I did not attend the meeting, nor did I have any input into it. That would have been equally wrong.

It was altogether an unpleasant affair. I suppose I could have perpetuated the argument, but as far as I was concerned Hoddle and Shearer had backed down. How much worse it would have been for them, and the FA, if we had backed down rather than them. What sort of accusations would have been made against all of us?

An article by Henry Winter in the *Daily Telegraph* said: 'The FA's statement about the charge made considerable reference to the desire of Graham Kelly to tackle the issue. Graham Kelly believes it is in the interests of the game that Alan Shearer receives the fullest opportunity to explain to a commission what happened. There is obviously a divide within Lancaster Gate.'

In fact the only divide was between the Chief Executive and the England coach.

Gordon Taylor, rather unfairly, had said before the hearing that the FA were shooting themselves in the foot. He also believed, because of the long weekend and then the further delay, that we had been pressurised by the media. He said that we were going down a dangerous road in taking action when there was no formal complaint from the other player.

It was, however, not always player on player and, indeed, the most notorious disciplinary case was one of player versus spectator!

It was the night of 25 January 1995 and I had worked late at Lancaster Gate before driving home. I had a quick bite and switched on the television to see that the lead story on ITV's *News at Ten*, with graphic pictures, was Eric Cantona jumping over the fence at Selhurst Park following his sending-off in the Crystal Palace–Manchester United match earlier that evening.

I was quite staggered by what I saw on the screen as the Frenchman jumped over the wall into the crowd with a two-footed assault on an individual. I believed at the time that it was unprecedented, although I have since learned that there may have been one or two cases earlier where players had become upset at fans and taken the law into their own hands. Dixie Dean, Everton and England's famous striker, was supposed to have been involved in a similar incident, but everything was anecdotal and I could find nothing in the records. There had been nothing as high profile as this in modern times.

My role at the FA in disciplinary cases was to decide whether there should be a charge laid, alleging breaches of FA rules. I was very rarely involved in the later stages of disciplinary proceedings, because I managed to have it agreed by the Council fairly early in my time that it should be a professional independent view as to whether there was a case to answer. I could not have people pre-judging the case by chatting about it beforehand.

It was fairly obvious that night that this would be a disciplinary case. It did not need a lot of grey matter to work that out and, indeed, it also became a criminal case. When I reached the office at 7 am the next morning, Sky cameras were waiting and I spoke to the reporters live half an hour later, saying that charges were inevitable, even though I had not seen any reports by then.

The Cantona case led to a couple of changes in procedure at the FA. Firstly, we made it a requirement of referees that if they witnessed an extraordinary incident, they should fax in the report to the FA from the ground so that we were in possession of the outline facts immediately. This arose because we spent much of Thursday trying to reach referee Alan Wilkie to find out what was going to be in the report. Were we going to charge Cantona on his or the linesman's report, or would we have to rely on video evidence? They were questions which needed answering quickly.

Secondly, it was so clear-cut that there had been a breach of rules, I also recommended – which was later accepted – that we introduce an amendment allowing for immediate suspension in such obvious cases, so that we could be seen to be taking decisive action, rather than being perceived to be dithering about a case in the period before it was due to come before commission. We changed the rules so that, providing the League and the PFA agreed with us, we could suspend the player immediately in any extraordinary or unusual circumstances which merited such drastic action.

Our statement that day said that the FA were appalled by the incident which brought shame on those involved, as well as upon the game itself.

Controversy immediately raged, many calling for Eric Cantona to be banished from the English game for life. We issued the charge letter fairly quickly, having finally contacted the referee later that day.

Everyone had their say, with television pundit and former Liverpool player Alan Hansen urging him to go home to France.

Manchester United were quite shocked when they realised the gravity of what he had done and they seriously considered whether he had a future with them. They were definitely wavering at one point, before suspending him until the end of the season.

Trevor Brooking, writing in the *Evening Standard*, said that it was the most horrendous incident he had ever witnessed at an English football ground. It was hard to argue with that view.

Cantona wrote back and gave the background to the incident. He said that he was walking along the touchline after being sent off for an offence which he did not contest, when he noticed a man wearing a Crystal Palace tie whom he assumed was a security man because he was so close to the perimeter barrier and was standing up. He saw that the man was speaking to him but did not at first hear what he said; then the man addressed him in an extremely insulting and racist manner, causing him to react instinctively and emotionally. He deeply regretted the incident but claimed that the abuse was extremely upsetting. He understood that he would be losing the captaincy of the French national team and had been subject to considerable hostile publicity.

He wanted to have the chance of rehabilitating himself in English football and asked the FA to take into account his sincere regret, the nature of the provocation, the severity of the punishment already given him by his club and the fact that he was also facing a criminal court case.

The penalty that Manchester United had quickly imposed was generally welcomed, with most people of the opinion that the club had got it right. Gordon Taylor felt that, whilst he did not condone what had happened, he did not believe a life ban would be appropriate. That would be too much.

The view of the players' union was interesting. They came out more strongly against drugs than a flash of violent temper like Cantona's. I would probably agree.

The hearing was eventually fixed for 24 February. In the meantime I was concerned that the Commission might be pressurised into going over the top and I was also worried about Eric's likely reaction to appearing before them. He had distinguished himself in France by walking up to each of three members of a similar disciplinary commission and saying 'Idiot' in their faces, one by one. Any similar display of emotion in the FA Committee room would not serve him well.

I had huge regard for Eric Cantona as a player. I thought his skill was sublime and did not want to see him lost to the English game. I did not even want him out of the game for a particularly excessive period. I had met him during the World Cup in the USA the year before and chatted to him about the game. I felt I knew him well enough to approach him privately and give him some advice about the commission. I took his telephone number from Manchester United manager Alex Ferguson and called him at home; his wife Isabelle was acting as his shield but called him to the phone.

We had a chat and I told him that one thing was paramount and that was he had to apologise. I told him that he had to say how sorry he was for attacking this man, even though he was a foul-mouthed yob. He listened, said that he understood and would follow my advice. He was clearly surprised that I had called him, but also sounded grateful.

The hearing was held at Sopwell House Hotel in St Albans with Eric arriving amid a considerable entourage including his manager Alex Ferguson, United director and lawyer Maurice Watkins, Gordon Taylor from our own PFA, a representative from the French players' union and also his own agent/lawyer. All of his team were ranged alongside one side of the table with the commission members, Geoff Thompson the chairman, Ian Stott and Gordon McKeag on the other side of the table. Margaret O'Brien, the disciplinary secretary, and I sat at the end of the table. I did not normally attend these commissions, but because of the high profile nature of this one I was allowed in as a silent observer of the evidence, unable to speak or influence the commission in any way. I would be expected to announce their verdict to the press.

The hearing lasted for over three hours with everyone having their say and then it came to Eric's turn to speak. He was squashed in two-thirds of the way along the table. He turned to Geoff Thompson and said:

*'Mr Chairman, I do not want to say very much. You have heard my explanation through my representatives here today and you have read my letter. I just want to apologise to everyone concerned. I want to apologise to Manchester United Football Club; I want to apologise to my team mates; I want to apologise to the supporters of the club; I want to apologise to the Football Association...**And I want to apologise to the prostitute who shared my bed last evening.'***

I was stunned but clearly not everybody in the room heard or took in what he said; certainly not all the members of the commission were aware of how deeply and sardonically he had expressed his regret to everybody. Maurice Watkins was aware, as he was sitting next to Eric and because they were cramped he was half-facing away from him when he spoke. Maurice turned, his mouth dropped open and he almost fell off his chair. For the first time since I have known him, Alex Ferguson was totally speechless too.

I thought to myself, 'Oh no, will I ever try to help anyone again?'

Cantona's point was that he was going to express regret for the incident, but he did not intend to humble himself on his knees before everybody. He was going to keep his pride and that sardonic line was his way of saying that, while he recognised he was in the wrong, he was never going to prostrate himself in front of anyone.

Geoff Thompson was certainly within hearing but said simply: 'Thank you. Mr Cantona, you had better retire now and let us consider our verdict.'

We all trooped out and Ian Stott picked up the blotter that Eric had been doodling on. I never found out what was on it, something surreal I have no doubt. Ian wanted the blotter for his daughter. She is probably a millionaire by now, having sold this exclusive work of art penned on such a momentous occasion.

The Commission duly gave him a ban until 30 September and a fine of £10,000. I think the Commission felt that they did not want to be dictated to by Manchester United and they might have needed to make a point by extending the suspension until beyond the end of the season. Alternatively, they might just have felt that he deserved to be out of the game for longer because of the serious nature of his crime.

Certainly Manchester United were very upset that they would be starting the 1995–96 season without him. When the decision was announced, Alex Ferguson left the room incandescent with rage. He needed to be out of public earshot and I took him, Maurice Watkins, and David Davies into a room in the hotel to talk about it privately.

Alex believed that pressure had been put on the club by the FA to suspend Cantona until the end of the season and that, by reneging on this we were succumbing to outside pressures. It took quite a while to calm him down sufficiently to go and meet the outside world.

I assured him that there had never been any suggestion of a deal, that the commission was independent and reached their decision purely on the facts of the case as they saw fit.

I could understand the sentiments if not all the words. Maurice was not quite as animated, but he was equally upset deep down. Nevertheless he could understand that the commission had done the job honestly and to the best of their ability, even though he did not necessarily agree with their findings.

Cantona went on to be found guilty by the court in Croydon and ordered to do community service, which he buckled down to and did faithfully and properly, thrilling a lot of kids in the Salford area.

The prostitute got off scot free !!

Cantona was a one-off. His temper was terrible, but he controlled it in his last years in England and was especially good with the Manchester United youngsters. He surprised everyone by retiring so suddenly and I wondered if he felt that by his own high standards he was having a difficult time. I suspect he probably did. His touch that final season was not quite what it had been the previous season. He was also probably disappointed that he was so ineffectual at European level. His departure left a big gap.

Disciplinary action has always played a big part in my footballing life and, of course, brought me a high profile. I was often accused at these times of being dour and boring, but I could hardly do a song and dance act in front of the television cameras when some poor player's career was in the balance or, even worse, after there had been some tragedy.

Even before I went to the FA we had cases where the public authorities or police had become involved in prosecuting players for onfield incidents. There was one case where a policeman had marched onto the pitch at Colchester and cautioned the goalkeeper for using offensive language and then, in 1987, the Glasgow authorities charged Terry Butcher, Chris Woods and Frank McAvennie for an incident in the Old Firm derby between Rangers and Celtic.

Gordon Taylor and I were very concerned about these developments. We felt that the game risked becoming a farce if a policeman marched into a dressing room at half time and insist that a referee red card a player or, even worse, if he went in and arrested a player and carted him off to the nick.

A lot of people thought we were trying to put football above the law but that was not the case. We were trying to ensure that the game progressed without interference or undue influence from police or public authorities and we needed to be able to show that, if a player did step out of line, the justice meted out by the FA was quicker, possibly fairer, and certainly cheaper. In any case, football could often impose more substantial penalties than the courts on players guilty of misconduct.

We reached agreement with the Association of Chief Police Officers' David Phillips, the assistant Chief Constable of Greater Manchester, that if the police had any complaints about player behaviour, they would draw the matter to the attention of the referee at the end of the game and would submit a report to the FA who, in nine cases out of ten, took disciplinary action against the player concerned.

We would not wish to prevent the police taking action in serious cases, such as that of Cantona, but by and large we felt that an agreement of this nature would best serve both the game and the law. The police were very co-operative and the system is still operating. The only problem is when the police pass on to us a complaint from a very small number of spectators where they might have an axe to grind against a particular player or club. Sometimes the same supporters figure more than once.

I had only been at the FA a few weeks in September 1988 when an incident was highlighted on the television news of Paul Davis of Arsenal punching Glen Cockerill of Southampton, clear to the camera's all-seeing eye but surreptitiously behind the backs of the officials. This was the first case where the FA took action solely on television evidence.

I felt we could not ignore a fairly blatant and serious offence, albeit that none of the three match officials had reported it to Lancaster Gate. The hearing was held and Paul Davis was suspended for nine matches. It established a principle that, just as players could, under exceptional circumstances, clear themselves of charges with the use of video, so the FA were allowed to rely on television evidence where they had received no misconduct report from the match officials.

Only a couple of months after the Davis case there was another incident which captured a lot of attention. Wimbledon were playing Manchester United at Plough Lane and Alex Ferguson claimed that after the game United defender Viv Anderson had been assaulted in the tunnel by a Wimbledon player whom he declined to name.

I thought when I read the comments the next day that this seemed to be a serious case which merited action, but we couldn't do anything unless Manchester United complained. I told Alex that he was bringing the game into disrepute by making these comments if he was not prepared to substantiate them. I also told him he had to put up or shut up, and that he might well be charged himself for shooting off his mouth and then not naming names.

Secrets are hard to keep in football and it soon came out that the player concerned was the big striker John Fashanu. Wimbledon's colourful chairman Sam Hammam rang the next morning on Friday 4 November and said that they had carried out an investigation to the best of their ability. As a consequence they alleged that Fashanu was assaulted and fell. But, surprise, surprise, he did not want to press charges.

Sam said that he felt that both clubs wanted the matter closed and that he did not want to embarrass Manchester United because Alex Ferguson would be proved to be a liar if the case was pursued. Sam said that Alex had lost his head and gone completely insane, adding that if he had held his tongue and waited, none of the publicity would have been attracted.

Sam was in full flow and claimed that Alex was backtracking and then asked me why I thought that the referee asked for an escort off the field of play. He answered for me, saying that it was because of the Manchester United players.

I spoke to Gordon Taylor about it on the same day and he was very upset at the attitude of Wimbledon, thinking that Sam was trying to wriggle out of it. Bobby Gould, the Wimbledon manager, was next to call and asked what they should do. I told him that my best advice after what Sam had said was to keep their heads down.

In the end Alex Ferguson promised to co-operate. I spoke to his chairman Martin Edwards early the next week and he wanted it dealt with as quickly as possible, but I explained that if we issued charges he would have to wait for the usual 14 days in which the player could formulate his defence.

Ferguson had clearly told the press that he had seen the incident, while referee Brian Hill had not seen anything. We held a commission and Fashanu was found guilty, with Anderson found to have committed a lesser offence.

Another unusual case was in 1989 when Brian Clough cuffed some lads who encroached onto the pitch and was charged with misconduct. The police and everyone stood up for Cloughie and told us what a fine upstanding fellow he was, but then he went and sold his story to the *Sun*.

I rang the paper's chief football writer Alex Montgomery to ask how much Clough had been paid for it. Alex played a straight bat, saying that Clough wrote for the paper anyway and perhaps it was part of that deal. I thought 'Pull the other one, this is a front-page story explaining why he took the law into his own hands.' We had a hearing and Clough came up to me beforehand and said he was very disappointed. Why had I not asked him instead of going behind his back to ask about the paper and his money? He then tried to charm Geoff Thompson, asking him how his wife was and that Barbara (his wife) sent her love. It did him no good. He was fined £5,000, probably around the amount he would have received for his story.

I became very concerned about mass brawls in 1989. On 5 November George Tyson refereed a game between Arsenal and Norwich and there was an incident which involved most of the players on the pitch. It became apparent to me that if an incident went off, managers could quite easily instruct the players to pile in and make it impossible for the referee to ascertain who the real culprits were. No referee was going to send off half a dozen players over the same incident and ruin the game for the spectators.

I felt that we should make the clubs responsible for the players. We already had a rule saying clubs were responsible for the behaviour of their players, so we fined Arsenal £20,000 and Norwich £50,000. Norwich were adjudged to have been the more guilty party and had more players embroiled. George Tyson could not identify who the guilty players were, so it came down to collective responsibility.

There was another melee involving West Ham United and Wimbledon and they were both fined £20,000. In the same month I persuaded the Executive Committee to issue a warning saying that we would consider deducting championship points if clubs failed to stamp out this unhealthy trend. Then, the following year, there was a major incident in the Manchester United–Arsenal match.

This was the first one after the warning and the commission took two points off Arsenal and one from Manchester United. I had about a thousand letters from Arsenal supporters complaining about the decision. It is always the case when a club is disciplined, everybody involved is alleged to have been biased against their club. It took an age to reply to everyone, painstakingly pointing out that I did not have a grudge against Arsenal.

The Chairman Peter Hill-Wood told George Graham to fine his players heavily which he claimed to have done, but I suspect that maybe they forgot to deduct it from their wages. Who knows? But clearly it was an effort to pre-empt our decision and it failed.

It was a common misconception that the Football Association disciplines players and managers whenever they speak out of turn. I became very cross about this on a number of occasions, because I believe in the principle of free speech and, providing an opinion was honestly expressed, it should not automatically result in a charge of bringing the game into disrepute. I thought that if these outbursts did anything, they brought the player or the manager who was shouting off his mouth into discredit, and that the game was big enough to withstand the expression of personal opinions.

There were, of course, exceptions to this loosely-held rule. The Football Association as a body did not tolerate criticism of referees and sometimes I had to charge managers with misconduct for criticising referees in the press.

This was poor sportsmanship and managers, in any event, had an avenue to express their views on referees through the official report to the League or the FA.

There were also cases where a player sold a story based on a personal attack on someone else. This would result in a complaint from an injured party and an action would probably follow in those cases. One such was when Paul McGrath moved from Manchester United to Aston Villa and sold a story to a Sunday newspaper, saying that the job at Old Trafford was too big for Alex Ferguson. He was fined after United complained.

Even this case, so many years later, tends to support my view that it is the perpetrator himself who is discredited, rather than the game. After all, Ferguson has proved McGrath wrong many times over.

We took action against Vinnie Jones when he allowed himself to be used to promote his video, *Soccer's Hard Men*. Sam Hammam called his erstwhile captain a 'mosquito brain' and the FA fined the player £20,000.

I suppose it is ironic that my belief in freedom of expression contributed in a limited way to my losing my job when so many people at the FA became upset about Glenn Hoddle's diary which I sanctioned in 1998.

One of the more infamous cases we had to deal with was the Ian Wright–Peter Schmeichel business in 1996–97. In the first game at Old Trafford there was a brief flare-up between the Arsenal forward and the United goalkeeper. Wright had challenged Schmeichel for a through ball and, according to lip readers quoted in the press who had seen the incident on television, Schmeichel referred to Wright in racist terms. In the second match at Old Trafford Wright lunged in late on the goalkeeper and this led to angry words between the two internationals at the end of the game.

After the first incident I had asked Schmeichel for his observations, but he failed to concede that he had made the comments complained of.

I was not keen on trying to charge a player on the evidence of lip readers' comments to the press. I thought it was a bit tenuous, but nevertheless, when the second incident occurred, it highlighted a very real dilemma in an issue which had overtones of both discipline and racism, something that the FA were particularly keen to eradicate.

The police had become involved following the first match because complaints had been made to them, and after the second game Wright complained that he was racially insulted by Schmeichel. Alex Ferguson categorically denied that his goalkeeper had done this. The file on the first case had already been passed to the Crown Prosecution Service, although after all that time it did not seem as though anything was going to happen.

Schmeichel clearly confronted Wright at the final whistle at Highbury after the two-footed tackle which Wright had perpetrated. Wright had to be restrained by Arsenal physiotherapist Gary Lewin. Wright claimed he had to be restrained because Schmeichel made a racist insult.

Neil Harman, writing in the *Daily Mail* under the heading 'NO SIGN OF STIRRING AT THE FA,' said: 'Graham Kelly, who jumped so quickly when he discovered three years after being told that the Germans were Europe's candidates to stage the 2006 World Cup, cannot raise himself to address the Wright–Schmeichel débacle.' Thanks, Neil.

I said that we would investigate the reports of the police and match officials and decide whether to make any charges against either of the players after the Highbury incident. Significantly referee Martin Bodenham did not caution Wright for the challenge at Highbury.

I invited the two managers Alex Ferguson and Arsene Wenger to bring the players into the FA to try and resolve the situation. I was also awaiting a report from the police because they were on duty in the tunnel and we could not do anything until I saw what the police had to say.

Wright, a regular contributor to the newspapers, became a little upset about a piece on him by former Spurs striker Jimmy Greaves.

Wright claimed: 'Sure enough, there was a scene, a bit of a fuss but no physical contract between us and nothing happened between us and by the time I walked down the tunnel Peter was already in the visitors' changing room. These things happen and I want to put an end to the whole thing right now.'

With disciplinary charges hanging over both players, we eventually managed to bring the two clubs together in a meeting at a Manchester Airport hotel. It was a particularly difficult case to resolve and whilst David Dein, on behalf of Ian Wright, was prepared to make certain acknowledgements and apologise for Wright's part in the episode, it proved very difficult to wring anything like an apology out of Maurice Watkins, who was representing Schmeichel.

David Davies and I talked to them for more than an hour and eventually agreed a form of words which we hoped would put the incident behind us. David Dein stayed at the hotel while Maurice Watkins went to see Schmeichel at the end of training to consult him about the joint statement which we hoped to put out. To our dismay it became apparent that Schmeichel would not agree to anything which approached an apology for racist comments, as he continued to deny making them. Dein wanted to know why it was that Arsenal were prepared to compromise while Manchester United were not. An irate Watkins retorted that it was a fairly serious issue which could still involve criminal charges and Peter was adamant that he had not done anything wrong.

The talks dragged on throughout the day and broke up without a resolution. The original statement, which went near enough to having Schmeichel admitting to making racist comments, was scrapped.

We were being attacked from every angle, with the Commission for Racial Equality on our backs, saying that we had not done enough. We also involved Gordon Taylor from the PFA and Peter Leaver from the Premier League, but the best we could do was to issue a statement which said that both players and the clubs assured the FA that there was no feud between them.

I received expressions of regret from both sides and a recognition of the wider interests of the game. Ian Wright was still deeply upset that what he insisted had been genuine attempts to win the ball were being misinterpreted. Manchester United had said Peter Schmeichel was not a racist and never would be. That was the best we could do. Neither would apologise.

I was very disappointed. I learned a lesson that, if you become involved in something like that, you have to be confident that you are going to settle it, and quite clearly we had not been able to reach an agreed position to which both sides could put their signatures. It was our statement which came out and that was a watered-down version of what we had hoped to achieve when we first looked at the incident.

I could quite clearly see that Ian Wright would have been prepared to apologise for being over-exuberant or getting carried away, but the issue with Schmeichel was a much bigger one, going to the heart of a major national concern at a delicate time.

It surprised me that Wenger and Ferguson, two experienced club managers, didn't step in earlier to prevent the feud escalating. The fact that they didn't meant the problem landed on the FA's desk. I found it distasteful that the Football Association needed to become involved in the first place.

As far as I was concerned, I was not going to charge Schmeichel on the evidence of a lip-reader's examination of the video recording of the incident. It would have been farcical, had I done so. It was one of the least satisfying results during my tenure at the FA and left more questions than answers.

Another case – which threatened to be the biggest, certainly since the bribery scandals of the 1960s – was when former Liverpool goalkeeper Bruce Grobbelaar was accused, with others, of match fixing. However, despite the magnitude of the case, we at the FA had surprisingly little to do with it, as it was immediately taken out of our hands by the Hampshire Police.

Like most other people in football, I had heard the rumours that a goalkeeper was about to be exposed in a newspaper, but when it broke in the *Sun* on 9 November 1994 and the colourful Zimbabwe international Grobbelaar was the focus of attention, I was surprised and shocked to read the revelations.

Ever since that betting scandal in the 1960s English football, for the most part, had been free of suspicions. Everyone in the game was startled by the story in the *Sun* and the newspaper passed on to us the material they had gathered. On the strength of that, I decided to charge Bruce Grobbelaar with misconduct on the charge of fixing matches.

We were in contact with Southampton, his club, via the Premier League. They found themselves in a difficult position, particularly as Sepp Blatter demanded that the goalkeeper should be suspended immediately.

I wrote back and said that in England a person was considered innocent until proved guilty and that we had no provision in our rules for immediate suspensions. Even had we been able, I doubt whether we would have done so in this case, because it was far from clear-cut right from the start and unless Bruce Grobbelaar's continued presence constituted a problem for the game, I would have felt very uneasy about suspending him immediately.

Southampton also concluded that they had no legal grounds to suspend him and they continued to play him and to support him, much to his relief.

The police in Hampshire investigated the allegations, and charges were laid by the Crown Prosecution Service against Grobbelaar, John Fashanu, Hans Segers and a mysterious Malaysian businessman.

The first jury could not agree so, surprisingly in the circumstances, a re-trial was ordered. Three years after the original accusations, verdicts of not guilty were brought on all of the accused in August 1997.

In the meantime we had been asked by the police not to proceed with our own charges. We could not get involved to any great degree while there was a criminal investigation going on.

However, it was not the end of the matter for the FA. The court disallowed applications for costs by Segers and Fashanu because they thought that they had brought suspicion on themselves. There was sufficient concern about some of the statements made in the trial that we wanted to take a further close look at all of the evidence before deciding whether to proceed with breaches of the FA rules.

We asked Sir John Smith, former deputy commissioner of the Metropolitan Police, to look at the evidence urgently and to examine whether the rules on betting needed to be reinforced. Should there be a rule prohibiting forecasting activities? The actual charge we originally laid against Grobbelaar was accepting a consideration with a view to influencing the result, and also with bringing the game into disrepute.

When the case surfaced I called for anyone with any information about betting or bribery to let us know. Anything that the FA did while criminal investigations were proceeding could have been reported and might have prejudiced the trial. The worry was – and it was a very real worry that was subsequently borne out – that the trial would drag on for ages. We could try to keep our activities confidential but the source of the story, Chris Vincent, appeared to be a loose cannon who would not hesitate to talk.

I suspected that Grobbelaar, a noted prankster, was merely stringing the guy along. We asked the Asian football authorities if they had any useful information for us but they could not find anything helpful and not one person came up with a single item from our appeal for information. There was not a call, not a letter, nothing.

At the police's request I asked Jimmy Armfield to view the matches in question: Liverpool v Newcastle; Norwich v Liverpool; Liverpool v Manchester United; Coventry City v Southampton and Manchester City v Southampton over the two seasons 1993–94 and 1994–95. Jim played the videotapes over and over and spent hours in front of his television set but could not point out anything that was suspicious or untoward in Grobbelaar's actions. He could never say categorically that it was inconceivable for a goal to be conceded under any of those circumstances.

Bruce's goalkeeping was sufficiently eccentric to cast at least an element of doubt over the proceedings, as he tended to be a bit careless with his distribution of the ball and it was not unknown for him to make a mistake, the way he played.

When the players were charged by the police in July 1995, we once again came under great pressure from FIFA to suspend them which we had to resist yet again.

We received Sir John Smith's report early in September 1997 and decided to drop the match-fixing charges against Grobbelaar, but as Grobbelaar and Segers both said in court that they were forecasting matches we charged them for contravening FA rules by assisting in betting. By this time Segers had moved on to Wolves and Grobbelaar had signed a short term agreement with Oxford United.

We also obtained transcripts from the courts and forwarded them to FIFA as they were considering Fashanu's request to become a players' agent.

The disciplinary commission eventually took place on 11 and 12 December 1997 in front of Geoff Thompson in the chair, Barry Bright of Kent and Frank Pattison of Durham. Both players requested personal hearings and at the meeting Grobbelaar pleaded guilty to the charge of contravening FA rules by assisting in betting and after two preliminary issues were adjudicated, Segers also pleaded guilty. The commission suspended both for six months and fined them £10,000 each, both orders suspended for two years. They were ordered to pay £4,000 each towards the costs of the commission.

'SOFT LINE', said the *Guardian* headline the next day, but what else could be done in the circumstances? We re-emphasised the prohibition of betting in any match under the FA's jurisdiction other than the pools. This was an absolute. Any bet by the managers or players was against the rules, but it took a long time for them to understand because there appeared to be a culture of betting within the game, maybe in the country as a whole. Spread betting produced bets which affected the game. Players were alleged to be kicking the ball into touch for the first throw-in and minor things like that. Maybe it did not affect the result, but it was still totally wrong.

We were glad to put the Grobbelaar affair behind us after more than three years of worry and concern for the game. Bruce went on to win libel damage over the original newspaper article.

It was very much like the Australian cricket betting business which saw Mark Waugh and Shane Warne fined for giving information to a bookmaker on inside information. Grobbelaar did not forecast results of matches in which his teams Liverpool and Southampton were playing, but he did give information about their matches.

When I watched the videos of the games, I was worried that the wrong construction could be placed on any mistake made by Bruce.

There are cases of civil liability when one player sues another after a bad tackle and each side have expert witnesses ranged against each other. Such a situation arose during the OJ Simpson trial in the States. I was worried that the same thing could occur here and the result could go the wrong way. Had this disaster occurred it would have cast a blight over the whole game in this country.

I became embroiled as an 'expert witness' myself in 1992 when Gary Blissett of Brentford was prosecuted for grievous bodily harm after an aerial challenge at Torquay United which had left defender John Uzzell with a shattered cheek bone.

The story of the case began shortly after the match when I became aware of concern that Blissett had deliberately elbowed Uzzell, causing horrific injuries. Torquay were outraged about the incident and determined to bring Blissett to book.

I looked at the referee's report and decided that it was serious enough to warrant a charge of misconduct in addition to the standard punishment of a three match suspension which Blissett would be certain to suffer for being sent off by referee Arthur Smith. There had been a precedent when Mark Dennis in 1988 had been fined £1,000 on top of the suspension, having been sent off for spitting. Mark was something of a disciplinary regular and this seemed a bit like the tax charges which eventually sent down Al Capone!

There was clearly scope under our regulations to issue charges in particularly serious cases. The Disciplinary Commission sat on 20 January 1992. Jack Hayward of Essex, the Vice Chairman of the disciplinary committee, took the chair, along with Alan Burbidge of Cheshire and Noel White from Liverpool. They were not satisfied that Blissett was guilty of misconduct under FA rules and decided to take no further action against him.

At first I was a little concerned about this. How could we have had such outrage over the incident and yet a three-match suspension was considered sufficient? I viewed the video myself and reached the view that the commission were right. It was a nasty injury, no doubt, but I did not believe that there was any malice on the part of Blissett when he went up for the ball. I was quite happy for the referee to have sent him off, but also that the commission had reached a proper verdict. It was mere curiosity on my part to look at it all again. There was nothing I could do to change things as there is a cardinal rule at the FA that is never, ever breached in that no one interferes with the decisions of commissions or appeals. They are sacrosanct once they are finished, even if it was discovered at a later date that black was white. Jack Hayward himself had pursued a case for years on behalf of a group of lads he called the 'Clacton 57'who suffered what he perceived as a grave injustice at the hands of the Essex County FA. He kept writing letters but never managed to get the case reopened.

Although the incident with Blissett had happened in a lower division match, it still attracted national publicity both in the newspapers and on television and because of the controversy Blissett was charged with the very serious offence of grievous bodily harm.

I was approached by his solicitor Charles Newman to attend the court hearing to explain the FA viewpoint and our disciplinary proceedings. I also felt personally that, while I had lots of sympathy for Uzzell's injuries, which subsequently ended his career, I also felt sorry for Blissett who faced a prison term for an on-the-ball incident. There was no way I could condone mayhem on the pitch by players indulging in off-the-ball incidents, but this was a challenge for the ball between two players.

Jack Hayward, as chairman of the disciplinary commission involved, and Terry Evans, a centre-half with Wycombe Wanderers also gave evidence on the defendant's behalf.

I was asked, was it reasonable to try and win the ball? Was there anything improper in the way he used his arms? How would I characterise the challenge? Could I give an idea of the frequency of such challenges? I was also questioned as to why I was there, to which I answered, in all honesty, because I believed in fairness.

They were all straightforward questions to which I gave straightforward answers, as did the other witnesses. Charles Newman thanked me and offered to pay my expenses which I turned down because it was something I felt I had to do personally. But while Hayward's responses were not picked up at all, mine had the full treatment and I was plunged into a maelstrom of controversy, the like I had never experienced before. I had told the court that the incident was an ordinary aerial challenge, the like of which I saw fifty times in every match.

Mike Bateson, the Torquay Chairman, demanded that I should be charged by the FA for bringing the game into disrepute, adding that I should have stayed out of the case. He took his complaint to the Devon FA.

The Association of Football League Referees and Linesmen added their weight to the row by expressing their outrage, claiming that I had gone against the evidence of the match referee, that I had done a great disservice to the game and that I had condoned the use of the arm and the elbow. They also demanded action.

However, Peter Willis, President of the National Referees' Association, came to my assistance. He was very understanding, particularly when I explained that I wanted to keep discipline within the game. In football, referees' decisions are always final, but I explained that this was a court of law and that I had never set out to undermine the referee.

The Devon FA duly complained to the FA and it was discussed at length with Sir Bert Millichip and Jack Hayward. As a result Sir Bert replied to Torquay that I was acting within the scope of my authority, that I gave evidence on oath and he agreed with my views. Welcome support on this occasion. Hayward had given similar evidence to the effect that Blissett did not intend to cause injury to Uzzell.

But it rumbled on with letters to the *Daily Telegraph*. There were also questions at the Executive Committee, raised by David Henson of the Devon FA. I was a bit surprised and annoyed at his attacking me after I had spoken at a dinner organised by his wife, the then Mayor of Exeter. He then followed this up with comments aimed at me in a regional newspaper in the South West, cuttings of which were immediately sent to me by John Ryder from neighbouring Cornwall, warning me to be aware of the 'rubbish' being written in the local press. There was no love lost between the two counties.

Henson and Bateson were determined not to let it rest. Henson wanted a vote of no confidence put on the agenda for the upcoming Council meeting and claimed in the *Northern Echo* that what I had said in court had caused immeasurable harm to the game, while the opposite view came from Frank Pattison, who expressed the view that he was delighted that I had volunteered to attend the hearing and that, in any case, I should have attended on behalf of the Football Association because if the verdict had gone against Blissett, it would have been catastrophic for all contact sports.

I had no regrets and, despite the furore, I would do the same thing in exactly the same way if it arose again. But I learned that, as with the Alan Shearer case six years later, disciplinary cases invariably attracted all the headlines, usually unwelcome.

CHAPTER TWELVE

England, My England

G raham Taylor was mortified when he failed to steer England to the 1994 World Cup after the team had reached the semi-finals four years earlier. It was clear that he was going to offer his resignation after the controversial defeat in Holland before the Football Association made the decision on his behalf. But I was not ready for his amazing ultimatum.

I was stunned when he insisted that he would only resign on the proviso that his assistant Lawrie McMenemy did not succeed him.

It was not going to be a problem as far as we were concerned as Lawrie's name had not been mentioned in connection with the impending vacancy, but it was particularly staggering as it was Taylor himself who had forced through McMenemy's appointment against the feeling of many of the International Committee.

It was quite obvious during the final year of Graham's reign that their relationship had cooled, but I was unaware just how seriously they had drifted apart. Taylor obviously had his finger on the pulse because, after he had resigned, Lawrie telephoned me to offer his services.

It is never an easy thing to walk away from one of the most prestigious positions in the world of football and nothing has changed since Sir Alf Ramsey, after winning the World Cup, was dismissed. Sir Alf was understandably bitter at the way he had been treated and I was sorry that it was not until the final months of his life that I was able to help him in a small way. More recently Terry Venables did not like the fact that his successor Glenn Hoddle had been offered a four-year contract.

Perhaps the one exception to the rule was Bobby Robson, who left after eight years as England coach, having lost only one qualifying match and reaching the quarter-finals in Mexico and the semi-finals in Italy, the best England had done in an overseas World Cup in history and just a penalty miss or two away from the World Cup Final itself.

The writing was clearly on the wall for the former Ipswich manager when, in March 1990, Bert Millichip, not for the first time, was caught off guard in the Executive Lounge at Heathrow Airport on the way to a World Cup workshop. One or two journalists approached him and he said: 'What happens in Italy will affect our decision about Bobby's contract.'

Bobby's contract was not due to expire until 1991, but Bert made it clear that the FA's thoughts were on possible replacements when he went on to add: 'I have an open mind. I have some names in mind. There are three candidates. Every man has his time and we have to know when that time comes.'

Bobby Robson was taken aback by these comments when he learned of them from the next day's newspapers and, not unreasonably, he came to the conclusion that his future in the job he loved was limited. He had suffered a torrid time with allegations about his private life and the team had performed poorly in West Germany in the European Championship Finals in 1988. He was dependent, it seemed, on how the team played in Italy to see whether he could have his contract extended.

It was the FA's policy to end the manager's contract a year after the World Cup in anticipation of discussions coming up. It had become the practice for the FA to regard that extra year's salary as a golden handshake.

I had persuaded the Executive Committee earlier in the year to delegate authority to the Chairman of the Council; the Chairman of the International Committee, Dick Wragg; the President of the Football League, Bill Fox; and myself, to deal with the position of the England manager.

The original story was followed up in April 1990 when there was speculation in the Sunday press as to who would be appointed England manager after the World Cup. Bobby telephoned the journalist to find out what was going on, but it didn't prevent further speculation on his long term future. Assuming he might be available,

Dutch club PSV Eindhoven approached him as they were looking for a top-class replacement for their incumbent manager, Guus Hiddink.

The first I knew about it was on 25 April at Wembley at the England friendly game against Czechoslovakia when the grapevine was in full flow. A few days later the gossip became reality when Robson was contacted by Eindhoven's General Manager Kees Ploegsma by telephone. They met in Cambridge in early May and discussed a two-year contract. Robson was keen to pursue their interest but could not do so until he had discussed it with the FA.

Bobby reported the situation to Bert Millichip on 11 May because at that time the England manager reported directly to the Chairman, rather like at a League club. I was keen for future managers to report direct to the Chief Executive in the same way as other key management personnel would.

Robson told Millichip that he wanted to see him because of the press reports, one of which quoted Millichip as saying that unless England won the World Cup Robson would be out of a job, and subsequently another which said he would definitely be out, whatever happened. He wanted to know exactly where he stood as these reports put him on offer. That was how Eindhoven had discovered his availability. Bobby loved the England job and wanted to continue. He clearly hoped that the FA would extend his contract, but Bert refused to offer him any guarantees, pointing out that if we did as badly as we did in West Germany he would have to leave. Bobby predicted then that England would not only do well, but could win it.

Bobby said that he would have to consider his future and asked for permission to further his talks with the Dutch club. Bert granted his permission and asked to be kept in touch. The relationship had always been cordial between the two and, despite the disparity in their thinking, this did not seem to change.

Talks progressed and Robson was very interested, but Eindhoven could not wait indefinitely. He was told that he had to make up his mind or they would be forced to look elsewhere. He promised he would let them know by 17 May. He arranged another meeting with Bert nine days before the deadline and told him that he was prepared to accept the offer if Bert could not give him any assurances, which he was not prepared to do. It was at this point that Bert called me into the meeting. He had already warned me that Bobby was in talks with Eindhoven and it became a matter of when his leaving was going to be announced.

Bobby wanted it to wait until after the World Cup. He had not signed anything and it appeared to me that he was still waiting for someone to ask him to stay, even though it seemed to have gone so far when I came into the meeting that it was irreversible. I thought the matter should be dealt with quickly if he had decided to go.

Bobby told PSV that he was free to sign for them but he did not want to divert from the World Cup preparations to discuss terms. He was so focused that he did not even want to go to Holland to meet them. He told me he would keep me in the picture as he sent his advisor John Hazell to negotiate for him on 19 May.

PSV, understandably, did not want to wait once the contract had been drawn up, as they had season tickets to sell and wanted to be able to use Robson's name.

Bobby then became aware that the press were planning to give further publicity to matters concerning his private life. One lady was negotiating with several papers about her story being published, along with a book which was supposed to come out on the opening day of the World Cup.

Bobby felt that the media were confusing two strands of the story as word of his arrangement with Eindhoven had begun to surface, allied to the rumours that he may have to resign because of this lady's story.

I spoke to Gordon Taylor about a possible successor and he agreed that Graham Taylor would be an ideal choice. I also spoke to Bert Millichip and Bill Fox about Taylor and two other names which had been canvassed, Howard Kendall of Manchester City and Joe Royle of Oldham. Bill Fox felt that Kendall was a real winner and wanted us to speak to him. He also thought that Royle was one for the future, having gained a reputation with Oldham for his refreshing attacking approach.

One person I did not consult was the Vice Chairman of the International Committee, Peter Swales, even though the chairman Dick Wragg was ill at the time, because of a conflict of interest with Kendall being at Manchester City. Swales was upset about it when he found out. He could not accept that we were talking about his manager without telling him, and I had to write to him explaining that he could not wear two hats.

Doug Ellis also became aware of the fact that Graham Taylor was in the frame. I do not know whether he made efforts to get Graham to sign a new contract or not, but his first thought was for the FA to pay Villa £1.5 million in compensation!

Bobby Robson telephoned me on the morning of Tuesday 22 May from England's training camp at Burnham Beeches in Buckinghamshire. His lawyer had finalised terms with the Dutch club and we arranged for him to come to Lancaster Gate to discuss the timing of the press release. When we met he gave me a handwritten press statement because PSV were pressing for an early announcement. Bobby still wanted it to be made in Sardinia when everyone had arrived at the camp on the Italian island. I wanted it to be announced sooner because I did not think it would hold.

He also expressed his concern that the stories about his past private life were circulating again. I thanked him for telling me but told him that he had ridden it before and that he would just have to ride it again. I told him that there was no difficulty as far as the FA was concerned, as there was nothing new about to come out, and I gave him no indication that any publication should lead to his resignation.

It was quite clear that he was resigning to take over PSV, because he was not sure he would get a new contract with the FA. Given a choice between the two, there was no doubt at all which he would have chosen.

The Council meeting was due next day, as was the FA's AGM. Senior FA official Glen Kirton and Bobby Robson arrived at lunchtime at the end of the Council meeting and spoke to me and Bert. Bobby wanted to agree the timing of the press release. He and Glen suggested 28 May when they were in Italy and after the players and coaching staff had been told.

Both Bert and I hoped they were right and that the story would not break until then. I had a letter prepared already to inform the members of the Executive and International Committees, in confidence, of Bobby's departure. I gave it to them that day. Later on in the evening journalists already in Sardinia began ringing me and Bobby to find out what was happening. The *Today* newspaper were going to run a story saying that he had resigned and that he had been seen that afternoon handing out envelopes to the FA containing a hand written letter of resignation. He was supposed to be going because of allegations about his private life.

Bobby himself told the journalists, including the one from *Today*, that the story had little truth in it and should be killed, but it still appeared next day and all hell was let loose.

Bobby was being doorstepped by hordes of the media at his Ipswich home where he had gone to pack, ready for his departure to Italy. He rang me later that day and we had a tense and angry press conference at Lancaster Gate at 4 pm. He was understandably dismayed that *Today* wrongly portrayed him as a 'liar, a cheat and a traitor' when, in actual fact, he had done everything possible to safeguard the interests of the England team at a difficult time during the build-up to the World Cup. I had never seen a man as angry as Bobby was when the press photographers refused to allow us to start speaking.

We interviewed Graham Taylor on June 1 and had further discussions with Doug Ellis. Joe Royle declined the interview on the grounds that he would miss the day-to-day involvement at club level and still had a lot to learn after only eight years as a League manager, while Howard Kendall also turned down a meeting. He didn't say why, but I suspect it was because he believed the decision was cut and dried and did not want to waste his time. Bert refused to discuss the compensation for Graham Taylor with Ellis until after the World Cup.

It was not a good time for Ellis as his yacht broke down on the way to Italy and he had to be picked up in Palma, Majorca. They eventually agreed a £250,000 compensation at a Council meeting in Blackpool on 14 July.

We finalised a four-year contract with Taylor, agreeing that he should have authority over the full England team, the 'B' team and the Under-21s. He did not particularly want to become too involved with the coaching department and international teams at a lower level.

Italy was my first working experience of a World Cup, and what an experience it was. It was a fascinating journey with England getting stronger and stronger after a fairly average first round. We really felt that we could go all the way.

The World Cup was condemned by many as a cynical tournament riddled with negativity and foul play. This was true, but we did not see it that way, following England around Italy. Probably everyone in the country remembers where they were when we lost the dramatic penalty shoot-out to West Germany in the semi-final in Turin on 4 July.

For my part I said goodbye to Bobby Robson. He had come so close to taking England to the World Cup Final, one we could have won if we had converted those penalties, as the final was a dreadful affair between Argentina and West Germany.

Bobby went off to manage PSV, Sporting Lisbon, Porto, Barcelona and PSV again with massive success and never at any time did he have a bad word to say about the Football Association or any of his successors in what became known as 'The Impossible Job'.

He never thought of it as that; indeed, he thought of it as a privilege to manage England's best players and at any time subsequently would have come back like a shot to help out. A gentleman who loved his country and the team, Bobby unfailingly offered his help whenever I asked in later years.

Almost everybody at the FA was sorry to see him go, especially after we had done so well – except Peter Swales, who became Chairman of the International Committee after that World Cup. It transpired subsequently that he was not sorry to see Robson go. He told the press after Graham Taylor's England qualified for the European Championships in Sweden in 1992 that he was the most relieved man in England when we did not win the World Cup in 1990.

It was an incredible statement coming from the man who ostensibly headed up the England international set-up, but he explained that, had England beaten West Germany and then gone on to beat Argentina, the pressure to keep Bobby Robson would have been irresistible and that he had not thought he had been a good England manager because he could not handle the press.

I liked Peter a lot. He was amusing company, an excellent host at Maine Road and usually very kind in his comments. Just occasionally, he startled us with some sudden and surprising criticism.

It would be interesting to speculate what Robson would have done with a contract in his back pocket.

Graham Taylor officially took over on 16 July. At that time I had not fully appreciated the strength of Terry Venables' qualifications to do the job and did not particularly advance his cause within the FA. Not that I spoke against him. It was just that nobody in the group considering the replacement had particularly advocated either Venables or Howard Wilkinson, whose name was also being mentioned at the time. Although I had been acquainted with Terry from the early days of the Professional Football Negotiating Committee in the seventies, sadly I did not know him well enough and thought perhaps he was a little too cute for England.

I was keen on Graham Taylor because I saw him as someone who would not be diverted by pressure. Bobby had been driven to distraction by talking to the press and suffering the campaigns of the tabloids to have him sacked, all in the cause of their circulation war. I thought Graham had a clear mind and would be able to handle the job with ease. He had a decent record, having done well with Watford, whom he took from the Fourth Division to second in the First

Division, the FA Cup Final and a place in Europe and again with Aston Villa after a tricky start. I also felt that he was the right age.

It was Taylor himself who recommended the appointment of Lawrie McMenemy as his assistant, wanting him to be his eyes and ears and to act as a buffer between him and the world at large. Lawrie would also look after the Under-21 team and blood younger managers with the team.

Graham was quick to be rid of goalkeeping coach Mike Kelly. I do not know what it was, but he had a bad feeling about him. I thought Charles Hughes could continue to use Kelly as a national goalkeeping coach, for they enjoyed a good rapport and Kelly had done a good job at the Lilleshall school where he had a reputation as a disciplinarian. We made him what I considered a good offer, but he did not accept it.

Apart from not being wanted by Taylor, Kelly also felt aggrieved that, as a full-time member of staff, he did not get the same level of payments as the part-time staff for the performances of England in Italy. We had put Don Howe, Doc Crane and the physiotherapists on a good fee per game which had an element of bonus in it and amounted to a tidy sum when we reached the semi-finals.

The International Committee were a bit surprised at the appointment of McMenemy; no one had forecast or even suggested that he came in and Bobby Robson had been refused in his efforts to have Howe appointed as a full-time assistant.

Taylor soon stamped his authority on his new position. He raised a few eyebrows when he said that he did not want the vastly experienced Don Howe, because he would be doing the coaching himself. Don had been the right-hand man not only for Robson but also for Ron Greenwood.

Taylor brought in the relatively unknown Steve Harrison who admitted he was not even a bread and butter coach, more a crust and jam man! He also used Peter Shilton as his goalkeeping coach for a time. Ian Stott at Oldham was happy for his manager Joe Royle, to be involved with the Under-21s, as long as it was not for all five games per season. At the same time Liverpool's Noel White took over as Vice-Chairman of the International Committee.

It started well enough for Graham Taylor in the first couple of years as England qualified for the 1992 European Championships in Sweden. But the honeymoon was showing signs of being over as far as the press were concerned when his tactics gave cause for speculation. We drew 0–0 with Denmark and 0–0 with France and he finally brought down the wrath of the press when he substituted Gary Lineker with Alan Smith in the 2–1 defeat by Sweden. The popular Lineker had laid on the first goal for David Platt before being taken off with thirty minutes to go to mark the end of a marvellous international career. It was a sad way for him to go, one short of Bobby Charlton's all-time goalscoring record for England, especially as he had come to Taylor's rescue on previous occasions.

There were suggestions that Graham Taylor could not handle superstars and he had already caused controversy when he talked about Paul Gascoigne's refuelling habits. It was a disappointing end to our challenge. Many believed that it was a tournament we could have won.

It was during this time the relationship between Taylor and McMenemy cooled. I do not know when precisely it occurred, or why. But it became increasingly obvious when Taylor made it clear on his resignation that he would not do so if there was any danger of Lawrie being named in his place.

After Sweden, Taylor attended the summer meeting of the Council at Windermere. The press reported that he received a round of applause, but that was not true. He was merely received politely when he gave his progress report.

Peter Swales had said in Helsinki before Euro '92 that Graham Taylor was the best manager England had ever had in his football career, better than Don Revie or Ron Greenwood and easily better than Bobby Robson. It was then that he made his disparaging remarks about Robson. He was already talking publicly of extending Graham Taylor's contract beyond 1994.

Bobby Robson complained to me privately about Swales' comments and I suggested to Bert Millichip that he asked Swales to stand down from the chair for a while, but nothing happened. Peter Swales eventually wrote to Bobby to try and smooth things over.

All went well for a while after Sweden. We beat San Marino 6–0 and Turkey 2–0 in Izmir in a very hostile atmosphere. Then we drew 2–2 with Holland at Wembley when Paul Gascoigne was elbowed in the face by Jan Wouters, fracturing his jaw, as we lost a 2–0 lead. We managed a 1–1 draw in Poland thanks to a late Ian Wright goal. Taylor made comments after the game about the players 'running about like headless chickens '. Personally I didn't think it was a bad result, drawing 1–1 in Katowice in front of a hostile crowd. These results have to be placed in context.

However, we reached our nadir in June when we lost 2–0 to Norway in Oslo, a disastrous performance with great ramifications. David Teasdale, a former government advisor, had been brought in to ease the press burden as relations had declined alarmingly. But there was not a lot he or anyone else could say in defence of the tactical approach which was roundly condemned by all and sundry.

It did not improve when we went to the USA for what was supposed to be a warm-up for our appearance in the World Cup the following year. I was at Foxborough in Boston and watched the game against the USA from a box when an electric storm wiped out the electronic scoreboard. It would have been better if it had put out the lights, because ours were going out on the pitch as we lost 2–0. There was I, Chief Executive of the mother nation of football, with eleven American guys who didn't really know what was going on or how they had achieved their victory. We redeemed ourselves with a 1–1 draw in Washington against Brazil as Tim Flowers made his debut, but then lost 2–1 to Germany in Detroit on a portable grass surface.

Thankfully, I had left for a UEFA meeting before Detroit, but it was a grim tour which did not bode well for qualification. I took the unusual step of attending a press briefing in Washington where I told the press categorically that Taylor would still be in charge when we played Poland in September. The turnround was incredible because exactly a year earlier Peter Swales had lauded Taylor to the heavens. Swales was an unpredictable character who made some errors of judgement in his time at both club and country. I recall him tearing David Davies off a strip when he went round the FA expressing the need for coordination in all our comments to the press.

Everyone seemed to accept it was a sound idea except for Swales, who took great exception and tore into the surprised Davies, accusing him of acting like Goebbels.

All was not lost and we could still have made it to the finals, but after beating Poland 3–0 in September we had the infamous game against Holland in Rotterdam when we controversially lost 2–0. The Dutch captain Ronald Koeman stayed on the field when he should not have done, courtesy of the German referee Karl Joseph Assenmacher. Koeman had clearly brought down David Platt as he went for goal and, not only did the referee give the free-kick outside the penalty area, he did not send Koeman off for the very blatant 'professional' foul.

Graham Taylor had his unforgettable exchange with the linesman when he said: 'Tell your friend out there that he has just got me the sack. Thank you *very* much.' When I watched the video recording of the game it reminded me of Basil talking to Sybil in *Fawlty Towers*.

We had sanctioned the controversial television documentary on Taylor, confident in the belief that we would qualify, but when we didn't, it turned out to be an even better programme for the producers. I still laugh when I recall Carlton Palmer mimicking Graham Taylor to Gascoigne, saying: 'You have had too many Mars bars, your knees are fucked, your belly's fucked and so is your brain.'

Some of the Council members were quite upset about it, but I managed to placate them. I guess the FA will not be too keen to sanction any more videos or books from future managers or coaches. It was David Davies who advised me later never to undertake any fly-on-the-wall documentaries.

Despite the rumours, at no stage had we discussed sacking Taylor. We had been pursued across America by the press pack howling for his blood, but we stuck by him.

This was my first and only experience of doubts being cast over the England manager because of results. We were confident he had a chance of getting it right, even after the fiasco in Norway. In retrospect, we should have looked more closely at the position following that Norway game, but we considered that a one-off. In any event, Graham suffered more than his share of bad luck, as evidenced by both games against Holland.

In our final game against San Marino in Bologna we needed a bucketful of goals and for Poland to beat Holland on the same day to sneak in by the back door, but the omens were bad when we conceded a goal to the minnows of the competition within seconds of the start. It all happened so quickly that Jonathan Pearce on Capital Gold was still in the middle of his introduction and his sponsors' check when Stuart Pearce gave the back pass which led to the embarrassing goal. We overcame that setback to win 7–1, with Ian Wright scoring four times, but it was too little, too late.

We were resigned to the fact that Graham Taylor would be going after the Holland result. He finally quit after the end of the campaign. He made his decision before we made it.

Peter Swales stated that Don Howe would be appointed as caretaker manager, despite not having spoken to anybody. He was clearly not going to take any notice of David Davies' call for unity. He was under pressure at the time at Manchester City where his position was becoming increasingly difficult, firing goodness knows how many managers and having the supporters on his back demanding that he resign.

Bert and I advised him not to sit on the selection committee for the new manager as his credibility was not high at that time and that would damage us. He understood, as he had had a belly full of Maine Road at the time. There was no excuse for the City 'fans' to involve Peter's family.

The Executive Committee appointed Bert, Ian Stott, Noel White and me to search for the new man for the job. I could foresee the headlines quite easily about the non-qualified amateurs choosing the next England manager and, for sure, the four of us would have been open to criticism. With this in mind I looked around for someone to help us and spoke to Jim Armfield who was working for the *Daily Express* at the time. I thought he was ideally qualified, he had a good reputation and was still close to things with his work for the *Express* and BBC radio. He had appeared 43 times for England, had been captain and made 568 appearances for Blackpool, before going on to manage Bolton and Leeds. I generally thought he could act as a conduit between the FA and people who would be expressing opinions within the game, namely managers and coaches. Jim has always impressed me as a radio summariser with his knowledge and dry humour.

He gave up his *Express* job and came to work for us after I had taken him for dinner in Manchester before a United game. He became very enthused about the project and the FA gave their full approval to my decision to appoint him as technical consultant. Six years on, the canny Jim owes me quite a few dinners; he even kept his wallet well hidden on his ruby wedding anniversary! Gordon Taylor called the appointment 'tokenism'. Thankfully, his reservations were dispelled sufficiently by 1996 when Gordon agreed to second Jim from the FA to head up the PFA's regional coaching scheme.

There was the usual media field day canvassing prospective managers. The Leeds chairman Leslie Silver said 'hands off Howard Wilkinson'; Sir John Hall said even more loudly 'hands off Kevin Keegan' at Newcastle United. Interestingly in respect of future events, Jim Armfield really fancied Keegan for the job at that time.

The Argentinian Ossie Ardiles criticised the preparation time for England teams, while Brian Clough advocated Ron Atkinson on the grounds that Wilkinson was too conceited.

In truth we were in quite a deep hole, with disappointment at not qualifying for the World Cup for the first time since Argentina 1978 immense. Gordon Taylor led the attack because he was always critical of the coaching side of the FA under Charles Hughes. He said: 'We are the laughing stock of the world. The FA are incapable of reform. Desperate football fans are begging me to do something about it. I would accept the job of director of football, but I would rather John Major set up an independent inquiry.'

In a remarkable foretaste of things to come, Sir John Hall eventually offered Kevin Keegan to England on a part-time basis with Keegan having just signed a new contract with Newcastle. It makes you wonder, doesn't it?

I thought at the time that it was a full-time job – and I still do. Anyone close to the England manager's job will quickly see that the demands on time would preclude anyone doing it part-time on a long term basis, even someone with the unquenchable enthusiasm and energy of Kevin Keegan. Kevin soon realised this.

At the same time Peter Swales quit at Maine Road and announced that he would be stepping down as Chairman of the International Committee in the summer. Bobby Robson must have been laughing up his sleeve, if he was not too sick at having watched his semi-finalists from four years earlier fail to make the grade this time. He was too much of a gentleman to gloat, certainly in public and he never said one bad word about Graham Taylor or the FA.

It soon transpired that Terry Venables was clear favourite with only Joe Royle coming out against the appointment, presumably regarding him as the darling of (some of) the southern press.

Jim brought these observations to the Sub Committee meeting on 21 December.

Noel White wanted us to look more closely at former England captain Gerry Francis, but the committee met Terry Venables early in the New Year. We were joined in our discussions by Rick Parry because of widespread concern at the contents of the FA Premier League inquiry into the allegations arising from the dispute between Venables and Alan Sugar at Tottenham Hotspur.

It was only the previous month that new examples of breaches of football regulations came to light. Spurs were said to have made unauthorised loans over a long period of time to players. As far as we could tell from the discussion, Terry was not directly implicated in any major way in any of the issues. When we questioned him closely, he assured us that everything was above board and nothing would

bove: Bobby Robson, shadowed
y Glen Kirton, listens patiently to
ress questions. Rather ironic that
e was later hounded out of a job
y the very same people.

Above right: FIFA President
Joao Havelange and the
ultimate prize, the World Cup.

Right: Brian Clough getting a
point across in his usual
unique manner.

Scotland v England, Euro '96. I'm in pre-match negotiations with the Scots fans
for the return of the Wembley goalposts.

Keith Wiseman *(sixth right)* an
Peter Leaver *(second left)*, of
the FA management and the
Premier League, meet
Havelange at Lancaster Gate.

Receiving a Euro '96
commemoration medal
from UEFA President
Lennart Johansson.

Meeting FA President the
Duke of Kent before the
Euro '96 Final, with UEFA
General Secretary Gerhard
Aigner looking on.

FIFA General Secretary Sepp Blatter conducts the World Cup draw in inimitable fashion with film star Sophia Loren.

'Tell your colleague to ...' Graham Taylor boils over in Rotterdam as England lose to Holland 2-0 and fail to qualify for World Cup '94.

With FIFA Vice President, Julio Grondona and the infamous Antonio Rattin in Buenos Aires, 1998.

The other corridor of power. Meeting
Prime Minister John Major at No.10.

Rick Parry, chief executive
of the Premier League.

Keith Wiseman and Arsenal's
David Dein sharing a joke at
a league match.

Geoff Thompson, who succeeded Keith Wiseman as FA Chairman in June 1999.

Gordon Taylor, chief executive of the PFA, talks to England 1966 World Cup hero Nobby Stiles.

David Mellor's duties as Minister for Fun include overseeing the Ken Bates look-a-like competition!

Old and older Labour! Tony Banks, Minister for Sport, and an archive picture.

Sepp Blatter takes cent
stage among world footb[a
luminaries, Michel Plati[n
Pele, Bobby Charlton a[n
Franz Beckenbau[e

Campaigning for World Cu[p
2006 at No.10. Prime
Minister Tony Blair meets
Franco Carraro of Italy.

The Football Trust.
From left to right (back row[)
Susan O'Brien, Peter Lee,
Colin Thwaite, Bob Booker[,
Brian Ludlam, Gordon
Taylor and (front row)
Tom 'Tiny' Wharton,
Richard Faulkner, Lord
Aberdare, Gordon McKeag
and John Reames.

Glenn Hoddle with the spectre of
David Davies at his shoulder!

Eileen Drewery, faith-healer and a
prime (unwitting) cause of Hoddle's
downfall as England coach.

World Cup 2006 campaign trip, Asuncion, Paraguay. Alec McGivan and I
pay attention whilst Tony Banks and Sir Bobby Charlton feign disinterest.

Instant retribution for a yob.
Eric Cantona loses it at
Selhurst Park, 1995.

Shearer the solicitous. England's captain
extends a hand to the fallen Neil Lennon
of Leicester City during the infamous
incident in April 1998.

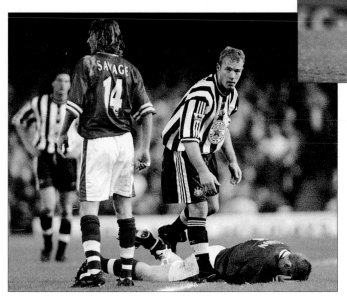

Above: Gary Blissett
of Brentford. Source
of one of my major
controversies.

subsequently come out which would seriously embarrass either him or the Football Association.

We also talked to him about his ideas for the job. He was very keen to give it a go and impressed us strongly with his views generally. He said he was prepared to blood a successor while he was in the job. Just as he was getting into his stride I caught sight of a woman outside the window threatening to jump from a ledge. We were in the Football League's office in Winchester House, Old Marylebone Road and just about ten yards away across the roof this woman seemed to be about to plunge 200 feet. I had a quick look to make sure that the authorities were in control and that she was going to be safe before settling down again. I commented that she had more problems than any of us. No one replied, but Terry was no doubt thinking that he could give her a run for her money.

The upshot was that we were very keen on appointing Terry and he was very keen on us, although he kept reminding us that the Welsh FA wanted him as well. We were on the verge of deciding in his favour but not because we were worried about the competition from over the border.

I happened to be in Helsinki for a meeting of the Scandinavian and British Associations, a meeting held annually, when Peter Swales telephoned me, saying that he was very concerned about the possibility of appointing Venables, adding that he hung out with a funny crowd and that while he was a good talker, he was dangerous. I said I would pass on his views to the committee, although I was sure he would have already made the point to his close friend and former business partner Noel White.

In the middle of January, Noel rang and asked me to see Martin Bashir who had been instrumental in the *Panorama* programme called 'The Manager' which had cast serious doubts on Venables' business practices. Bashir, who also featured in the Princess Diana interview, was thinking of doing a follow-up programme on Venables. He told me that there had been no writs issued against the BBC at that point and he alleged that Venables had raised the money to invest in Spurs by virtue of a sophisticated £1 million fraud which the Inland Revenue were investigating.

He also showed me the draft of an article he had written for the *Financial Times* for the following weekend. This set me back a bit because I thought that a front page article in a respected paper like the *FT* was a bit difficult to live with. They wrote that some of Venables' business activities had been unlawful. Alan Sugar also wrote, saying that Venables had broken the rules about agents, but as virtually everyone broke the rules about agents at that time, it was a bit spurious and what concerned me more were the far more serious allegations.

Understandably, Terry would not contemplate a trial period after one or two people had suggested a probationary period of six months. We were approaching the draw for the European Championships which was to be held in Manchester and Bert Millichip had raised expectations by saying that it would be a marvellous publicity exercise if we could have the new coach in place by then.

Sugar said that if we exonerated Venables and gave him the job, we would have to clear Spurs too. He rang me suggesting quite forcefully that he would have his lawyers look at the situation very carefully, if we appointed Venables and then charged Spurs subsequently. I told him I was not afraid of his threats and whatever we wanted to do, we would do.

We held another meeting of the sub-committee at the County Court Hotel south of Birmingham. Jim summarised the position on Terry Venables, Gerry Francis and the then outsider, Glenn Hoddle.

Noel White was now firmly opposed to Venables, but the majority, including Sir Bert, who had initially said Venables would only be given the job over his dead body, remained in favour. The next day Jim and I met him in London to sort out the contractual details. Terry agreed to use reasonable endeavours to clear up the litigation he was involved in against Spurs in six months and to divest himself of his business interests. He was involved in a book which he wanted to finish. That was not a problem.

We wanted him as coach rather than manager, in the continental mode. He was quite happy with that title. There was a short delay caused by the funeral of Sir Matt Busby and one or two of the International Committee members claimed that the sub committee did not have the powers to make the appointment. I had to point out that authority had indeed been given to us – by them!

We held a press conference at Wembley on 28 January to announce Venables' appointment. We had games coming up in the spring against Denmark, Greece and Norway, all at Wembley, and Terry brought back Don Howe, put Middlesbrough's young manager Bryan Robson in as coach, specifically with the FA's blessing that Robson should be groomed as a potential successor. We were happy to see Bryan get that experience. It also seemed a good move when Terry teamed Ray Wilkins with Dave Sexton for the Under-21s.

It was only some years later that Rick Parry concluded that there was a bung paid to agent Frank McLintock over Teddy Sheringham's move to Spurs from Nottingham Forest, the case which had started all of our worries.

The only difficulty I had with Terry up to the time when we were trying to persuade him to stay was when he wanted to bring in his friend Ted Buxton to oversee the scouting and to protect his back. Terry was concerned about young players choosing to play for other countries. Stephen Froggatt was a case in point, coming under immense pressure from some of his Villa team-mates to represent Ireland before eventually committing himself to England. The International Committee, led by Peter Swales, were very much opposed to Buxton's appointment and it took a good couple of months to ease Ted in, while Terry became increasingly irate that Graham Taylor had been allowed to bring in Lawrie McMenemy, whereas they were blocking a fairly modest level of appointment for him.

Terry wanted to stay with the BBC to do his punditry until after the World Cup in the USA. He said he would welcome our help in settling the dispute with Sugar. He assured us that the original *Panorama* programme contained 83 inaccuracies. His appointment provoked an early complaint from the Premier League and David Dein and Ian Stott when, owing to a previous commitment, he was involved in the PFA Chat Line. Clubs saw this as competition for their own Club Call operations. I had to tell him to drop that.

There was a fascinating contrast between Terry Venables and Glenn Hoddle, the man who was to replace him. Terry seemed to have 75% of the press on his side and cultivated them, while Glenn came into the job cold and realised pretty early on that he needed to be more open with the media. But what happened to that realisation, I do not know.

I remember discussing it with Hoddle and he said that he dealt with them but treated them all alike, not having some for and some against, the way Terry had. But, in the end, he managed to get them all against him, even big supporters such as Henry Winter from the *Daily Telegraph*.

After the agreed six months, I went to see Terry on how he was progressing with his 'reasonable endeavours.' He told me then that he wanted to switch from BBC to join ITV, something we had no problem with. He said he had discussed Scribes, the club he owned in London, with his wife, and might be in a position to put it on the market in the near future. But on Alan Sugar he had failed in a bid to mediate through one of the Spurs directors. He was still claiming he had a good case against the Spurs Chairman.

Terry was also in the middle of a dispute with Council member Paul Kirby, the English-based New Zealand representative and formerly his close friend. I asked him whether he was writing about Kirby in his book because if he did, it would not look good if he was seen to be taking on one of his own directors from the FA. He took the point and made the necessary adjustment.

It was a pity I did not ask him at the same time not to mention Alan Sugar in the book – that would have saved another writ, but I suppose it would have removed too many pages!

He was certainly not backing down in his war with his former Chairman and he made it quite clear that he wanted the right of reply to what Sugar had said about him during their long and bitter dispute.

The second *Panorama* programme appeared in October 1994 and there was a further obstacle at Spurs because Sugar wouldn't let him go to White Hart Lane whilst he was, to quote him, 'Suing the arse off me'. Sugar brushed aside the criticism, saying that the England coach could watch the players away from home and would gain more benefit because it was tougher for them away from home.

I offered to arrange a discreet visit to the club but Sugar would not have anything to do with it. Terry tried to force the issue by making it clear that players' international futures could be jeopardised if he was unable to watch them perform. Sugar immediately climbed on his high horse, saying that Terry's comments were despicable, like dragging children into a messy divorce.

On 29 September 1994 Sugar telephoned me to tell me that he and fellow director Tony Berry were issuing writs against Venables over chapters eight and nine in his book. When I tackled him again about banning our coach from White Hart Lane, he then pointed out that Venables could watch Spurs games on television and that, in any case, he had never seen him at any of Spurs' away matches, adding that he did not think he could be that bothered.

By the time October rolled along Sugar had seen Venables' England contract as part of the discovery process in their various disputes. Sugar wrote to me on the 7th of the month and said that Terry had no intention of complying with his obligation to extricate himself from the court case within six months.

I issued a statement after the second *Panorama* programme, saying that it did not affect his ability to do his job. Terry's response was that this programme also contained many mistakes.

Spurs manager Ossie Ardiles gave a ray of hope when he said that Terry Venables would be welcome at Spurs, but Sugar promptly poured water on the idea and scorn on his own manager by replying that Ossie was in cloud cuckoo land. I immediately asked for clarification: could he go to White Hart Lane or could he not? In fact, he never went back until the Worthington Cup semi-final in 1999. When he did it was probably galling for him to see how much the club was worth, having had a hand in rescuing it from insolvency in 1991.

I saw Sugar once more in an attempt to resolve the disputes. Nic Coward, Raj Parker of Freshfields and I went for a meeting at Herbert Smith and Company, his solicitors. I asked why they did not agree to some form of mediation to stop the case dragging on as it was now moving towards its third year. But he was not giving much away. He claimed that Venables had caused him all sorts of problems with the media after his dismissal in May the previous year.

Venables still owed him the costs of the first case, which he had lost. Sugar wanted paying up, he also wanted Venables and his cronies to stop sniping at him in public and he wanted an apology for what had been written in the book. He suggested that Freshfields should examine his claim because, he said, Venables must be overestimating what he was going to win if he carried on with the case.

Venables had alleged in his book that Sugar had tampered with board minutes, had paid a £20,000 bribe and had defrauded his Amstrad shareholders.

Throughout these exchanges Sugar clearly thought that I was discussing the case with Venables when, in truth, we never discussed it at all.

Sugar thought Venables had shopped him in the loans case which had resulted in Spurs becoming embroiled in a dispute with the FA about the deduction of points and the FA Cup ban.

He promised me that Venables would be in court during the build-up to Euro '96, so we had better think about persuading him to shift his position. We thought we might go back to Terry and set out the position following the meeting, but we never did it formally.

Mihir Bose in the *Daily Telegraph* and Harry Harris of the *Daily*

Mirror constantly highlighted Terry's business problems; Charlie Sale in the *Daily Express* and Jeff Powell, a long time friend, in the *Daily Mail* were equally steadfast in their advocacy of his coaching expertise.

In October 1995, before a friendly with Norway in Oslo, reports filtered through of an offer to Venables from Inter Milan. Bert Millichip and I had a chat with him in Oslo when he admitted he had some reservations about continuing in the job, but told us that he had turned down the Italian club. One of his worries was the uncertainty about what would happen with his contract at the end of 1996. We said that we would not announce it, but would open discussions before the end of the year.

Bert, as was his wont, duly released the information on our return to England when he was asked about Venables' future at the fateful Luton airport carousel, the curse of the FA. It was the place where you could not escape the probing and the questions as you waited for your bag, usually in the small hours of the morning. That baggage hall spawned more FA exclusives than anywhere else.

Just before we were due to discuss the issue again, Terry suffered an embarrassing court verdict. He was being sued by a man called Jeff Fugler over an unpaid invoice and the judge, in summing up the case, used the word 'wanton' in relation to Terry's evidence, adding he did not find it awfully reliable. Terry claimed that the word he used was 'wanting', not wanton, a big difference in legal speak. I never really got to the bottom of that one. Members of the committee expressed concern when the judge made his comments and awarded Jeff Fugler £15,000, although Terry said this was only part of the claim and the story.

I went to the draw for Euro '96 in Birmingham on Saturday 16 December after the Aston Villa–Coventry game and fell into conversation with some Coventry fans who offered to give me a lift into town. When we reached the parked car we discovered that it had been vandalised and consequently we had a chilly ride to the Hyatt Regency where I bought them a round of drinks and awaited the arrival of Terry, whom I knew had been very upset by press comments emanating from FA members following the judge's remarks.

We had by then appointed a legal mediator to try and resolve the dispute between Venables and Sugar, and I opened the meeting in Terry's hotel room early that evening by saying that I wanted to give the mediator another month to try and resolve the dispute. I assured Terry that we still thought that he was the right man for the job but he had to understand our worries with all the adverse publicity. He understood, but he did not agree with the concern which was being expressed.

He observed that, whatever happened, Noel White would be quoted in the press, adding that he could not fight insiders as well as people who were sniping at him from outside. He felt he was a sitting target as everybody wanted to have a go at the England coach. This was true because much of the interest waned after he left the job.

He set me aback when he went on to say that he had discussed the situation with his wife and that he no longer wanted a new contract after Euro '96. He assured me that he would do everything he could to help whoever took over but was adamant that he would not stay.

I asked him to confirm that he had decided, or was this just his intention and could he be persuaded? He stressed that he could not be persuaded. He still wanted to see Noel White about the matter and I arranged a meeting with Noel and Bert on the day of the draw.

By the time we met on the Sunday, Bert had already been quoted in the Sunday papers, saying that he wanted Terry to carry on after Euro '96 because he had the team playing the way Bert had always wanted to see them play. This took me by surprise because these comments had been made two or three days earlier after a UEFA Executive meeting but had not surfaced until that day. Bert's comments provoked disquiet amongst other members of the International Committee who were not aware that we were discussing an extension to the coach's contract.

We had the showdown in my hotel room with Bert repeating what he had said to the papers, adding that he had neither seen nor heard anything which worried him and he wanted to extend Terry's contract until 1999. Noel White said that clearly there were matters to be considered before a new contract could be considered, something which he had also said in the press. He had said that we had been concerned about the allegations made against the England coach.

Terry said bluntly that he was concerned about the lack of internal support, to which Noel responded that he had given him his support – up until 1996. But Terry persisted and told them that he was unhappy about Noel's comments to the papers and couldn't continue unless he had 100% support in the long term. He wanted an apology from Noel and for him to insist upon a correction if he had not made the remarks.

Terry pointed out that other countries changed their coaches and announced it before finals. Indeed Richard Moeller Neilson had already agreed to go to Finland even though he was coaching Denmark in the finals that summer.

The strange thing was that Terry did not actually tell Bert and Noel that he had already made his mind up to go, and the meeting ended with us asking him to go away and think about it.

I had six meetings in all with him, including that first one, in an attempt to resolve the situation, but Terry was adamant that he had made up his mind. I tried to float the idea of a one year extension as a compromise which might satisfy those who were worried. He thought it was too woolly and he was probably right. I had not even been given the authority to put the idea forward, but I thought it was worth sounding him out to try and find some way of keeping him while all the problems sorted themselves out.

Eventually we had to announce his resignation. He said that he did not want to carry on because he would be in court for long periods in October 1996 with Alan Sugar and would not be able to give the job his undivided attention. Then, when talking to the Sunday press, he admitted he could not continue if his own people were becoming 'wobbly'.

Ian Stott, one of the doubters, who had asked who had the right to give Terry a new contract, pulled in his horns and said that he was only querying the procedure of extending the contract and not his ability to do the job.

I told Terry when his resignation was announced: 'At least, you can't sue us.' He replied, 'There's still time!'

What I liked about the man was that he knew what he was doing. He had the confidence of the players, he was resilient and he had the ability to compartmentalise things. He was embroiled in all this nonsense with Spurs and yet when he put his England tracksuit on, the team was the only thing on his mind. He successfully brought young players like Steve McManaman, Jamie Redknapp, Gary Neville and others through and I thought it would be crazy to jeopardise the progress we had made for the last two years, albeit that we had not been tested in real competition. That was Noel White's argument, that Venables had not only not proved himself in any competitive matches but also had all these problems. He wanted to know why Sir Bert should be so anxious to extend his contract. My response was to get it sorted sooner rather than later and not leave it until after the Euro finals. That would not be good business for the FA because we could not be negotiating from a position of weakness.

Elements of the press had consistently highlighted Terry's off-field problems. On 1 December Ian Stott had been quoted, after stories that Venables owed VAT, as saying that all of it was not doing English football any favours.

After the Panorama programme it was claimed in the *Sunday Times* that I was losing confidence in Terry Venables. There was no truth in that at all and whoever supplied the information, if anyone, was being malicious. Nevertheless, it should be recorded that Terry was eventually banned from acting as a company director.

It was certainly never dull or boring under Terry Venables and just before the European Championships there was another rumpus after the return flight from Hong Kong on a Cathay Pacific 747. What can you say about something that happened while you were asleep? I had not known what had happened on the aircraft but I was annoyed that the airline had alerted a national tabloid before discussing the situation with me.

I was, naturally, unhappy with any trouble caused by England players when on duty with for the Football Association. I told Terry that I wanted to find out exactly what had happened and who the culprits were. It quickly became clear that those responsible were not going to own up and that the other players were going to protect them through collective responsibility. Terry, while not condoning the vandalism which occurred, thought it was exaggerated. But we came in for a lot of flak because immediately following the statement about collective responsibility, we had the dentist chair pictures of heavy boozing in a Hong Kong night club. Someone again sold photographs to the same newspaper and put Terry on the defensive.

I sometimes wonder at the stupidity of the players. They know they are under the spotlight and yet they do things in public which are bound to come out. Certainly they didn't learn from the Paul Gascoigne episode in Hong Kong, because Teddy Sheringham was caught in licensed premises at an odd hour, when he should not have been, before the World Cup. My admiration for a superb playmaker was not increased by his wooden delivery of a public apology.

Terry, like Bobby Robson before him, was another coach to bow out after a glorious failure on penalties against Germany. What is it that makes history keep repeating itself with the England team?

Alex Ferguson thought enough about the England team at that time to predict that he thought that they would win the World Cup two years later.

At the end of the match against Germany I went down onto the pitch to thank Terry for everything he had done, to commiserate and wish him well. I actually went to Scribes for the first time that weekend on the night before the Final. We had a reasonable evening, but it was very much clouded by the fact that Terry had lost his best friend, the former Fulham player Bobby Keetch who had passed away earlier that day. Behind his brash smile and ready laugh, Terry had a deep sensitivity about the close relationships he cherished most. He was really badly affected by the deaths of mother Myrtle and father Fred.

I was sorry to see Terry go. I was reconciled by that time as we had had a successor lined up for a couple of months; nevertheless, I regretted that we would not be working together any more. Perhaps many would see it as an unlikely friendship but he had modified his views of the FA for a while before they swung back again before his departure, and again when the job became vacant and his return was blocked by Noel White and others. I certainly learned that you cannot judge a book by its cover.

CHAPTER THIRTEEN

Glenn Hoddle

A lex Ferguson might well have become the first Scot to coach England but for the determination of Manchester United to keep him at Old Trafford.

It was in February 1996 when we first became aware that the United boss was interested in the England job. The initial approach to Alex had been made by Jimmy Armfield, who was our 'undercover operative' charged with sounding out potential England managers. Alex initially mentioned the Technical Director vacancy to Jim, but it soon became clear that he was interested in succeeding Terry Venables as England coach.

When I spoke to the FA committee they were fairly evenly split. They were interested in Ferguson, but I do not think Chris Willcox wanted a Scot while Keith Wiseman was slightly easier with the prospect of Glenn Hoddle than Ferguson. It transpired that the two were the main contenders for the vacancy.

I went to see Manchester United's Chairman and Chief Executive Martin Edwards on 13 March and told him that Ferguson was in the frame and asked whether we could interview him. He thanked me for coming and said that he doubted they would release him, but he would put it to his Board. He revealed that they would be offering Ferguson an extension to his contract in the summer and he promised to let me know fairly quickly.

Edwards rang back on the 19th and said that the Board would not release Ferguson. He still had a year on his contract and he was invaluable to Manchester United's future. I thanked him and told him that I was not surprised.

At a League Managers' Association Annual Dinner in May held at the Sopwell House Hotel, I happened to be sitting next to Alex Ferguson after the dinner. During our conversation, he made it clear to me how disappointed he was at not having had a chance to discuss the England post with me, the Manchester United Board having already barred him from applying. He added that his brother, who was chief scout at United, was keen for him to have a go at it.

Obviously we were stymied. How could we take this any further with him once Manchester United had said no? It was impossible. We were now down to a shortlist of one.

There had been the usual pattern of managers ruling themselves out. Kevin Keegan had just signed a ten-year contract at Newcastle United; Gerry Francis said he was not interested; and Bryan Robson was coming to realise how difficult the job would be, having worked with Terry Venables in the England set-up. Bryan was coaching Middlesbrough and discovering that it was a full-time job in anyone's language, and I also had the impression that he was thinking of giving up his England duties after Euro 96 to concentrate on proving himself as a club manager.

There were the customary letters of application from unknowns for me to acknowledge. One lady, Pamela Sharp, wrote a saucy application, saying she would kit the players out in lycra. Although I told her not to give up her day job, Pamela, a student of the media, achieved the publicity she was seeking and she has since recruited me on behalf of her employers, the charity MIND. She knows a soft touch when she sees one.

We had the usual sub-committee to discuss the England vacancy with Bert Millichip, Keith Wiseman – in for the first time for Ian Stott as Premier League representative, Chris Willcox – Vice-Chairman of the FA at the time, Noel White – Chairman of the International Committee, Jimmy Armfield, and me.

Our first meeting was on 15 January 1996 when all expressed reluctance in contemplating a foreigner for the position, whether Scot, French or whatever. Two weeks later at the second meeting, we were down to the nitty-gritty and discussed all the likely names, including the three who had ruled themselves out.

Kevin Keegan was out of the equation. We recalled having had our fingers burnt with Keegan before Venables was appointed. Newcastle

Chairman Sir John Hall had become quite irate when we mentioned Keegan's name back then, before hedging his bets by suggesting a part-time appointment.

The committee did not want to go back either for former manager Bobby Robson or for Howard Kendall, whose star had dimmed somewhat.

There were rumours that Kenny Dalglish was interested but, as far as we were concerned, it was never more than speculation and was taken no further.

Hoddle's name was now predominant and appearing in the newspapers, prompting Ruud Gullit to say on behalf of the players that Chelsea did not want him to go, while Terry Venables thought it a job for an older, more experienced man. But, more importantly, the committee were all happy with the prospect of Hoddle.

On 18 March Hoddle's agent Dennis Roach rang and asked how much the job was worth. Well, he would, wouldn't he? Hoddle was approaching the end of his contract with Ken Bates at Stamford Bridge at the time and he wanted a week to come back and talk again. That was no problem as we were in no rush.

I met Glenn at the Hilton Hotel at Heathrow on 26 March and he seemed very keen. We discussed the possibility of a four-year contract before getting into a rather esoteric conversation about the relative values of reflexology and spiritual healing without realising the significance of it at the time – I wish I had! I also explained to Glenn the terms of reference for the role of Technical Director, explaining that we wanted someone who would spark a revolution in the necessary development of players. Bobby Robson was one name we mentioned, but it was not taken any further.

Glenn felt that all England teams, from youth level through to the senior side, should play the same tactical formation, citing the case of Michael Duberry who had come through the youth system at Chelsea and graduated to the first team without any difficulty. The only negative mentioned was the fact that he had a young family, with three children aged thirteen, ten and five, and he was concerned about the time spent away from them.

We ended our meeting with a promise to meet again to discuss the England job further.

In the meantime another agent, Jon Smith, was keen for Ruud Gullit to come and see me and discuss the post. Gullit was not a name we had considered, but there was nothing to lose by talking to him and I agreed to meet him. The only problem was that he never actually made it from Chelsea's training ground to Lancaster Gate. It certainly seemed that he had set out because I received a message from Jon saying that the traffic was bad, another that he was on his way, then he was in Hyde Park and just around the corner. But Gullit never arrived for our meeting and I heard nothing more from him on the subject. Very strange.

Not that it mattered, for it was now clear that the post of coach was going to Glenn Hoddle and I went off to meet Roach and Hoddle on 18 April to talk terms for a four-year contract. They seemed reasonably happy and I reported the fact to the sub-committee a week later when they approved the appointment and said we should notify Chelsea and Venables at the end of the month before holding a press conference.

I had the final meeting with Hoddle and his agent at Roach's office in Dorset on 29 April when we finalised the contract. Roach agreed to share his commission on Glenn's outside activities (except for television work) with the FA. Then we had to speak to Chelsea. Hoddle had spoken to Colin Hutchinson and I rang to tell him that Glenn would be leaving at the end of his contract. He accepted that was the way it was, even though Ken Bates was not awfully happy. But Glenn was keener to tell Matthew Harding than Bates, Harding having made a last-ditch but vain attempt to keep him at Stamford Bridge.

I talked to Glenn about the Technical Director position. He was keen on Arsene Wenger and promised to call him in Japan to see if he was interested. His other choice was Trevor Brooking, as nice a man as you could wish to meet, but I did not see him cut out for that particular job as he had his media, business and Sports Council interests. The Technical Director would be faced with a massive task and it was a full-time job.

On 2 May we held a press conference with Glenn Hoddle and Terry Venables together at the specific request of David Davies. Glenn was asked whether the prospect of daily vilification concerned him. It did not. I was then questioned as to whether I had checked for any skeletons in his cupboard. I was able to say that there was only his pop record with Chris Waddle, as far as I knew.

The first non-football problem to arise for Glenn was in November 1996 when Paul Gascoigne admitted to beating his wife Sheryl. He told me that he had spoken to the player three times and that Paul was having counselling. They were both aware of his problems and Glenn was impressed with Paul's determination to sort himself out and so picked him for the squad to go to Georgia.

This was a tricky one. There was a public outcry against the player and a strong lobby for him to be left out of England's plans. It was not our position to interfere with selection of players by the England coach. Bert Millichip had said throughout the years that the coach had a free reign unless there was a disciplinary problem and then the FA reserved the right to rule a player out of selection.

In this case it went rather wider than football discipline. It was a decision for both the coach and the FA to assess together. I went to see Glenn at Marlow to talk it through with him. Glenn clearly wanted to keep Paul in the squad and give him a chance and as far as Keith Wiseman, now Chairman, and I were concerned, we wanted to give Glenn his head so early in his tenure and not be seen to overrule him.

I personally thought it was a difficult situation. I am not sure that I would have ruled him out, but the climate has changed since then and if the same thing had happened today, Gascoigne would have found it difficult to keep his place. On pure footballing terms, my heart says I would love to see Gascoigne back in the England team as his is a talent we have not been able to replace. Indeed, Kevin Keegan would appear to have that same view. But my head says he would not be able to recapture that golden vein of form that so endeared him to us all.

Keith wrote to the Executive Committee explaining our support for Glenn. There were doubts cast over Glenn by certain sections of the media over the Gascoigne incident, mainly away from the back pages, but on the football front he appeared strong, even after the home defeat by Italy at Wembley. That did not create any doubts in our minds, either, and he still had our total backing. In fact England, at the time, were playing much better away from Wembley, counter-attacking with pace and style and winning their matches.

The test of this was surely in Rome in October 1997 where England needed at least a draw to clinch a place in France the following summer and consign Italy to the play-offs.

We were not involved in Hoddle's pre-match planning; what he did about players' fitness, tactics and team selection were up to him. We were not privy to his little white lies to the press about who would and who would not be fit in a bid to disrupt the Italians' preparations. Managers' mind games was not an area we interfered in.

We were far more concerned about security after what had

happened in Dublin and at recent club matches in Italy. The Italians are always very difficult to deal with because the Italian FA and the police will say yes, yes, yes, or no, no, no, giving whatever answers they thought we wanted to hear, particularly over the indiscriminate selling of tickets and segregation. But when it comes to the crunch, they always mix the tickets and affect the segregation; it is the same story over and over again.

The goalless draw was a great triumph on the pitch, one of the best nights of all, to deny the Italians in Rome. The drama was incredible as we almost snatched a win when Ian Wright hit the post and then almost lost it in the last heart-stopping moments when Vieri's header flew inches wide.

The occasion was somewhat spoilt afterwards when, some time after the final whistle had blown, the interviews were completed and the convoy with players, officials and police was ready to leave for the airport, we discovered that many of the England supporters were still caged in at the stadium. It was unbelievable that there was no one capable of giving an answer as to what was happening.

Staying with the team before the game, I was impressed with the build-up. There was a quiet professionalism about the place, they knew what they had to do and what they had accomplished. It was all a massive plus for our coach Glenn Hoddle and we were understandably delighted with our appointment.

The next problem facing Glenn was to pick his squad for the World Cup and, as usual, the biggest headache of all was whether or not to take Paul Gascoigne.

Even his selection in the initial group of players had caused an uproar with the usual 'should he, shouldn't he' arguments being voiced. To be truthful, Gascoigne did very little to convince anyone in the warm-up match against Morocco in Casablanca, where he limped off early. He was obviously off the pace and far from match fit.

As usual I was not part of the selection process and I was unaware that it had been announced that Gascoigne had been left out on the Saturday evening before departure. I had travelled back from Morocco, and when I heard the news I could not help but support the decision. Even so it came as a bombshell, mainly because once he had been picked in the original squad, I had not expected him to be left out of the final 22. It was a brave decision by the England coach.

I knew nothing of Gascoigne's reaction until I read his 'exclusive' in the *Sun*. It was only later that I heard about his behaviour in the hotel leading up to the decision. There was no reason for me to have been informed of him missing the team bus and his drinking escapades unless it had become public. That is all part of delegation and it is up to the coaches to instil the discipline and take the necessary action unless it gets out of hand. In this instance, Glenn dealt with it in his own way.

In the build-up to the Italian game, the usual arguments surfaced about bonuses both for players and for coaches. It is always difficult, with the coach feeling that he was the meat in the sandwich between the FA on one side and the senior players' committee of Tony Adams and Alan Shearer on the other. Shearer's attitude was that the FA were going to make lots of money out of France 98, but he did not realise that, with the increase to 32 finalists from 24, the amount received per match did not rise. For the tournament as a whole, the FA were not going to take much more than £2.0–2.5 million.

The players' attitude was that they had earned that money and should be rewarded. My answer was that it was a gross figure, and not net, and there were a great many expenses to be paid out. The cost of running the international team is immense these days, with every last detail looked after and attended to. We took on Sir Brian Hayes to look after the security; we had our own chef and our own policemen to look after the team. The squad took over a top-class hotel in La Baule which was to cost about £500,000. Police spotters cost over £100,000. If there was a profit at the end of the tournament, it would be used to develop the game, and it was certainly not lost in the FA's coffers.

Glenn wanted some of the administrative staff included in the bonuses, but I told him that if they were going to receive a bonus, it would be separate and nothing to do with the team operation. We always had this dichotomy of whether the staff are working for the team or the FA. Those who are working their socks off at Lancaster Gate when there is a surge of interest tend to get overlooked if all the perks go to those fortunate enough to be with the team. We had a policy whereby, if there were extras or bonuses, all the staff participated to some extent, not just those lucky enough to be travelling.

It could be argued that working with the team was a bonus in itself. Fans would give their right arm for a job like ours, being involved with the World Cup from the inside.

The other side of the coin was that it was very demanding. We would

241

be away from home, hopefully for only a month but maybe even longer if the team did well.

It is not a nine-to-five job when you are away with a football team, more like from the time you wake up until you go to bed. Glenn, for his part, not unnaturally liked to think that everyone in the team hotel was part of 'his team'. He argued that they all played a part in the success or otherwise of England. On the other hand, staff who manned the England Members' Club offices in France had an equally difficult job which was crucial to the success of the players. It is always a difficult one to resolve.

The bonuses for the coaches were even more difficult. They were not settled until the night before the first match on Sunday 14 June in the Sofitel at Marseille airport when I was given authority to push the figures up a bit for John Gorman, Ray Clemence and Peter Taylor. Glenn helped by reducing his own bonuses slightly.

The players were by this time sorted out, but it had been quite tough. In the end, Finance Director Mark Day had to tell them that what they saw was what was on offer and to remind them that they were playing for their country for what we thought was a very fair figure. The 22 players stood to share a sum well in excess of £1 million, had we won the World Cup. It is ironic that, for the finance people, the optimum result is not to win the Championship, because bonuses eat into the final figure allocated by FIFA. But, of course, the subsequent spin-offs from winning would have been immense.

Another bone of contention was over the wives and girlfriends. They were going out to each game and we appointed someone specifically to look after them, but Glenn wanted the partners of *everyone* to be invited and not just those of the players and coaches, opening up the same debate again. Why, for example, should the travel manager Brian Scott have his wife flown to France for the games when it is his job to be there? I found it hard to follow this line of thinking.

Glenn's viewpoint was that he did not want long faces about the squad, he wanted people to be happy and smiling and if that meant bringing the loved ones out, then so be it. We eventually conceded the point to Glenn, so anyone who was there had the right to send someone on the plane to the matches, though not everyone took advantage of the FA's offer. It was sometimes difficult to argue with Glenn because he had experienced the World Cup Finals as a player.

I had made the decision that, because of the security problems and the focus of attention in the venue city, that I would stay with the team until two days before the game, at which time I would move off to the venue city to be prepared for any problems which arose.

Many of those in the French Organising Committee did not have a football background, which made dealing with them a little more difficult than it might have been, provoking a situation whereby you would ask a serious football question of the Organising Committee and they could give no answer.

The decision to move the teams around from venue to venue was probably helpful as it turned out, because it meant that England supporters did not tend to gather together in huge numbers, although with the time before the games there were still a great many of them in Marseille and Toulouse prior to the matches being played on the Monday.

We were disappointed with the number of tickets allocated to us. We made repeated representations to FIFA and the French but finished with just under 4,000 for each of the games. Just before the tournament we were given an extra 2,000 category one tickets for Marseille and just 250 extra tickets for Lens. We accepted them gratefully, allocating them as fairly as we could. The French asked us to keep quiet about it, but no sooner had we sent them out to our members than the French announced that they had given us more.

We finished with 7,300 for Marseille; 3,300 for Toulouse and just under 5,000 for Lens. It was not, of course, representative of the true numbers inside the stadiums with 25,000 in Marseille and 20,000 at both Toulouse and Lens. It was a total fiasco and everybody connected with the tournament came in for criticism. We had done everything in our power to gain a fair allocation but ended up with minuscule amounts, leaving the true supporters to be ripped off by the touts. It was a system which encouraged a flourishing black market as local authorities and sponsors were allocated a great many tickets, while national associations around the world were not blame-free as we often found tickets coming back from that particular source identified by the country name printed on the ticket.

The Home Office spent £1 million on an advertising campaign to discourage supporters from travelling without tickets. It was a total waste of money, especially with the French Tourist Board inviting everyone to come over and join in the festival of football!

We went on the offensive after Marseille and said we had to thank the people who came to watch. There were 25,000 English supporters inside the stadium and not a whiff of trouble. In fact, there was no trouble at all inside the grounds and I was further convinced that those who caused trouble in the streets were not true supporters.

By and large we were very pleased with the genuine supporters and there were a lot of them. I spent a lot of time talking to English people, especially in Marseille and Toulouse, but not so much in Lens because you couldn't get near the place.

Lens was the most unpleasant atmosphere of all the venues I visited. It was with some cause after the running fights in Marseille before our game and, more to the point, the fact that a local policeman had been trapped, cornered and beaten near to death with an iron bar by some German thugs there.

I visited Vimy Ridge battlefield on the way from La Baule to Lens. It was a moving experience, to think of the staggering number of soldiers who lost their lives in one day when the Canadian and Allied troops took this important vantage point. I went on to the game between Spain and Bulgaria that night. It was a surreal day altogether with Spain winning 6–1 and still failing to qualify, while the Bulgarians sulked throughout the game.

My World Cup had started much earlier with the opening match between the defending champions Brazil and Scotland in the brand new Stade de France. I travelled out to Saint-Denis early to sample the atmosphere on my first visit. I was very impressed with the transport system costing around £1 for a fast ten-minute ride from the centre of Paris right to the stadium concourse. The atmosphere outside the ground was fantastic with the Scots fans being their predictable selves. I can quite categorically state that, as it was a breezy day, they do not wear anything under their kilts and are not the least bit shy about it. The Scottish fans even queued for the toilets!

I received a friendly reaction from them, in fact probably better than from some of those who claimed to support England. I tried to find out whether there was any prospect of them returning the crossbar they borrowed from Wembley in 1977 after the England–Scotland home international. I always said that I was more popular outside the country than I was in it, and the banter confirmed my belief.

The Scots put up a brave performance but could not pull off a result. I dashed back into Paris on the final whistle to catch the fast train to Nantes. I bumped into BBC reporter Rob Bonnet on the train and got a lift from him to La Baule, getting lost en route. The atmosphere in the England camp was good when I joined the players, but I did not stay long as I had to fly down to Marseille the following day and meet the various FIFA officials based in the city. Purely in the line of duty, while I was there I also met model and television chat show host Melinda Messenger, a pleasant young lady who was on the *Sun* bus which I visited, and enjoyed a can of Tango while listening to the Sheffield Wednesday band, part of our official entourage.

I heard about the team selection for our opening game against Tunisia and was surprised that David Beckham had been left out, but not as surprised as the rest of the world at the omission of Liverpool's brilliant young teenager Michael Owen. I did not question the decisions as I had faith in what Glenn was doing. I had watched Michael Owen come through the ranks, scoring goals for the Under-16s against Northern Ireland, but Teddy Sheringham and Alan Shearer were a tried and trusted partnership, established back in Terry Venables' reign. I felt that a bit of experience would not go amiss going into a World Cup campaign where nerves would be jangling because of the importance of that first game.

The Manchester United striker Sheringham was cause for some discord in our household as my dear lady wife moans like hell about his international qualities and I have to tell her that she doesn't understand the finer points of his game, his vision and his skill. She responds that he is too slow and I remind her of what a man said to her when we were entering Manchester Cathedral in February 1998 for the service to mark the 40th Anniversary of the Munich crash. We were dashing up the steps past all the people unable to gain admittance and one disgruntled man, clearly upset at having to stand outside in the rain, said aloud: 'What does she know about football?' If it had not been on church property, she would have decked him. Romayne does not take any more kindly to that sort of remark than she does when car park attendants patronisingly call her 'Love!' Being the holder of an PSV licence, she is perfectly capable of getting a car into any space quite comfortably.

I was more surprised that Beckham had been left out, because he had seemed to become an integral part of the team. I thought he would be critical to supplying the ammunition for Shearer to shoot the goals and couldn't understand the logic behind his omission.

I generally liked to find out the team so that I could make sure that the travelling committee members were fully in the picture, but I did not always go seeking the line-up because I know how sensitive the coaches are to leaks and it reached the stage where I didn't really want to know so that there would be no slip-ups. It became a regular routine that I would learn the team on arrival at the stadium from one of the FA staff members, or occasionally one of the players might mention in conversation who was in and who was out, but even that was difficult if they were under Glenn's usual three-line whip to tell nobody.

Knowing the team sheet was always a useful point of contact with the players at somewhere like breakfast, as we were from different cultures and different age groups, and it was particularly important to have a topic ready to discuss when sitting next to Spurs' huge defender Sol Campbell, whose meals can turn into a lengthy process as he rarely makes do with just one plate of food.

The players like their food and I remember them moaning like mad on one trip in Eastern Europe because the doctor had put them on diabetic jam with their toast – apparently sugar does not go into the system at the right speed – and made other alterations to their fare. It is a strange life that boils down to eating, sleeping and playing football.

Because I was not travelling in to the grounds with the team I made use of public transport or walked, often stopping to have a discussion with a fan or, just occasionally, a row with a yob. Most were surprised to see me on a bus rather than in the back of a private limousine. The reality was that we had a couple of cars made available to us, but with 45 people accredited they were always fully in use. We argued for the number to be increased from the original 40 to 50 to include the extra security people and the observers Howard Wilkinson wanted to take out. Howard was very angry that he did not get accredited himself in the end. It was my decision and it was made simply because there were not enough cars to go around. I had to choose between him and Sir Brian Hayes who was working on the ground. Brian needed access to the pitch, whereas Howard did not.

There were plenty of lifts available, but I wanted to spend some time with the fans, seeing for myself what was happening on the build-up but missing out the night before matches because there was too much aggravation. We held a big press conference after the trouble in Marseille and I just wanted to walk part of the way back and experience the full event and every aspect of the day. I stayed in Marseille overnight rather than returning to headquarters because of the threat of hooliganism, struggling to find a hotel room. In the event it was all fairly quiet and there was no problem about my leaving early the following morning.

I flew back to London the next day where we had a special meeting of the Council on the Wednesday to discuss the National Stadium. Work did not stop because of a World Cup and it was not until Thursday that I rejoined the team and then flew down to Toulouse on Friday for the game against Romania.

The majority of the time seemed to be spent with TV and radio as there were quite a lot of requests for interviews in the build-up to that game, and I tried to emphasise how well the supporters had behaved in Marseille, particularly in the ground after the initial trouble on the streets.

There was no trouble in Toulouse, with plenty of space for the fans to move around down by the river and lots for them to look at. I thought the street entertainers were fantastic and the England supporters really seemed to enjoy the festive spirit. On the pitch, though, we threw away a game we should have won. Kevin Keegan, commentating on television, remarked after England's equaliser from substitute Michael Owen that there was only going to be one winner, and it was not going to be Romania – who promptly went on to snatch the game through Dan Petrescu's injury-time goal. A bit worrying that this was the man the FA turned to in their hour of need after Glenn Hoddle!

We flew back to La Baule that night and the atmosphere was very down. The players were depressed at losing a game they should have won. I did not spend a lot of time in the camp, probably no more than three or four days in total because of the need to be in the venue cities and because of the trip back to London. It was while I was there that I appreciated just how strong a young man Michael Owen was and what an immediate impact he had made. The players were lounging around the pool, with the captain Alan Shearer searching for volunteers to speak to the press. Owen flatly refused, not in a nasty way, but just yelled: 'I'm not doing anymore. I've done everything so far. It's someone else's turn.'

Shearer raised his eyebrows at the response and carried on his search but it displayed the fact that Owen was not afraid to be assertive even at that early stage of his development.

Lens had a particularly unpleasant and oppressive atmosphere after the problems with the Germans, but the players saw little of it. It was all very threatening, particularly around the traffic island on the way from the station to the ground, but once again the atmosphere in the stadium was tremendous and the real supporters gave their team invaluable support. After the disappointment of Romania it was an excellent night against Colombia as David Beckham, restored to the side, scored from a superb free-kick, adding to the earlier goal from Darren Anderton, who fully justified his return to the team.

The players went back to the chateau with the wives and families who were staying overnight with them before departing on the Saturday evening. I set off for St Etienne where we were to play Argentina in the second stage, arriving at about 5 pm and immediately taking a call from a relieved Doug Hopkins, the policeman attached to our security team. He had seen a battered Jaguar with a British registration on the autoroute and feared it was mine.

For the game against Argentina we did not expect quite the same number of England fans to travel and in the event there were about 12,000, well outnumbered by the Argentinians who knew well before we did where the game would be played and had time to prepare.

It was disappointing that we had such a tough route to the Final having failed to win our group, and it was clearly going to be a difficult game against Argentina. Had we beaten Romania we would have been in a totally different section where, for once, Germany might have proved to be the best opponents.

We could and should have beaten Argentina. We were certainly good enough to win on the night, despite the brilliant free-kick rounded off superbly by Javier Zanetti of Inter Milan. It was more than equalled by Michael Owen's goal which I have watched so many times, confirming that he had just five touches on a very long run. It was all movement, pace and direction, taking him away from various defenders trying to get a foot in. Clinical finishing by a nerveless youngster for whom the one goal must have made many millions of pounds.

It was devastating to go out, particularly on penalties once again. It was also depressing the way the game and the luck had gone against us. Technically you could not argue against the decision to send off Beckham, but it was such a trifling incident, no more than a petulant gesture of frustration. While you do not like to see that on the field, the mountain England were left to climb playing all that time with ten men against Argentina seemed out of all proportion to the offence committed. Add to that the handball that was not seen in Argentina's penalty area in extra-time and the disallowed Sol Campbell goal and I certainly felt, if not cheated, certainly harshly treated. The decisions made by Danish referee Kim Milton Nielsen had gone against us.

I tended not to enter the dressing room very often because, once you start going in, you have to go all the time. There is no point doing it only when the atmosphere is euphoric. This time I went in to commiserate with the players and understandably there were a great many tears and a lot of silence. A dressing room is an awful place after elimination from a competition, and it left a very vivid memory; the atmosphere remains with you, just as it did at Italia 90 after we had gone out by those dreaded penalties, this time at the hands of the Germans. It is just very, very quiet. No one wants to say anything, no one can make any difference but the realisation is that you are on the way home while others are preparing for the rest of the competition. I know how I felt, so imagine what it does to the players involved with the hopes of the whole country dashed.

Sepp Blatter said it was the best game of the entire World Cup, but that was small consolation. He was there and enjoyed the drama, but then he was neutral.

Sol Campbell was a colossus that night and, indeed, in all four games. It must have been all those breakfasts. Sol suffered more than most, having scored what we all thought was the winning goal, presenting us with the bizarre sight of three England players celebrating off the pitch and Argentina attacking our goal, something I had never seen before. It was strange for the referee to allow that to happen. I am the last person to condone players running off the pitch, but it was a genuine mistake. On the day I certainly thought it was a goal and it was only in the replays that you see Shearer's offence on the goalkeeper. We were all up in the air – Keith Wiseman, Geoff Thompson, Noel White, David Dein, Jack Wiseman and myself – thinking we were through to the quarter-finals.

It was a short flight back to La Baule but it seemed to be one of the longest ever. Like the dressing room after the game, it was eerily silent. No one was talking as players sat with their headphones on, lost in their own thoughts. On our arrival one or two went into the restaurant for a light supper but not many felt like being sociable and those who did eat returned to their rooms pretty quickly.

The next morning did not become any easier. A few went out to play golf while we arranged travel back in the afternoon. I went to see Glenn about some business matters, but such was the numb state of our minds that neither of us can remember what it was about. It was probably about his contract, but it was not the right time and the discussion was left until we were on the plane later that day. It still was not the ideal moment, but there was that fear in my mind that he would be off on holiday and I would then have no chance to see him for three weeks. I did not want him to disappear without saying anything to him about the terms of his contract which were due to be reviewed on 1 July.

I packed up ready to go home, having decided to fly back to England. I wanted to see more games in the World Cup, but I thought it would be remiss not to travel back with the team. I told Romayne to head south and keep going until she came to water and that I would meet her back in Marseille for the quarter-final on Saturday. Some of my gear was in the car, more in La Baule and the rest in the office in London. I never had the right tie at the right time, but then what's new?

Just before we left I was standing on the steps of the hotel watching the players making a presentation to Doc Crane to mark his final World Cup match when my mobile telephone rang. It was the FA's Personnel Manager Andy Hall calling from London. He said he was sorry to trouble me but he had six fire engines outside Lancaster Gate battling a blaze and all the staff had been evacuated. We were about to fly back so all I could do was ask to be kept informed. I spoke to my deputy Pat Smith and told her to forget about her planned day in the garden because her office was going up in smoke. Her day off was cancelled.

It was quite moving to see the reception that Glenn and the team received at Heathrow when we arrived back on Concorde. Travel manager Brian Scott had made the arrangement for us to complete the formalities at the Sheraton Skyline Hotel at Heathrow, so we did not need to go through the usual controls and we were taken direct from plane to hotel by coach. The difficulty with that was that whilst it is more convenient for the players, who can avoid being troubled by crowds, all the baggage arrives at the same time so that you are working with the slowest common denominator and it was another two hours before I was able to jump into a hired car and head for Lancaster Gate to assess the devastation.

The player most affected by the elimination was David Beckham who, that morning, received the full force of the nation's disappointment. I felt particularly sorry for him as he shook hands and departed as quickly as he could for a holiday. He has this trait of looking you in the eyes while he is talking to you, and he was the one person you thought might want to slink away and hide without meeting your gaze, but he did not. There was little either of us could say other than 'thanks very much' with a firm shake of the hands.

He has since shown his character by overcoming the abuse of the crowds up and down the country and enjoyed his best ever season when many thought that he would escape abroad. He grew up a lot in 1998–99.

I arrived back at Lancaster Gate at around 6.30 pm, by which time firemen were mopping up. There had been two rooms virtually gutted at the back of the building on two different floors. It was suggested that a workman had caused the blaze. The structural damage was not as heavy as it might have been. We were fortunate that the evacuation procedures had worked well and no one had been injured. However, it was clear that an enormous amount of reorganisation was urgently needed if the FA was to be able to deal with the implications of the fire, all the insurance and safety aspects, and also to carry on operating. Thankfully, the disciplinary files were salvaged!

All the telephones were out of order and two-thirds of the building was inaccessible to the staff. After briefly quickly surveying the scene I went along the road to the Park Court Hotel where Pat, after contemplating her spell in the garden, was already chairing a meeting of the members of the management team who were in London that day, together with other key members of staff. I had flown home on Concorde but she had taken a scheduled flight from Lyons and had easily beaten me back.

I rang Romayne late that night where she had found somewhere to stay on the road to Marseille. I told her to turn round and come back home because there was no way I was going to meet her at the quarter-final or even get back at all.

Romayne drove back on the Friday and promptly had an encounter with a mugger at Calais. She had stopped at a hypermarket in the French port to purchase some duty free beer for her sons Ian and Paul who had travelled out to Lens for the Colombia match and discovered that the entire North of France was an alcohol free zone.

She was on her way to the Ladies when a North African youth pulled a knife on her in the corridor. Not one to surrender her belongings easily, she started yelling at the top of her voice, causing everyone around to stop and look. He fled. He was a brave man to start with, to take on my wife, but he quickly realised the error of his ways.

It was not an auspicious week. There had been a series of setbacks and incidents, all in the space of four days. It's a wonder it was not my Jag on the road.

I did return to France, but only for the France – Croatia semi-final in Saint-Denis. Having been to the 1994 Final in the USA, I decided to watch this one on television. It is a massive event and hard to enjoy for what it is, a football match. It is a hassle being allocated tickets and queuing to obtain them. Everyone is running around and claiming the time of the FIFA officials.

Sadly it was a rotten game, a total anti-climax, but I was delighted France won it, for the friends we had made, for my friend Gérard Houllier and for all the work they had put in.

That should have been the finish of it all for a while but it was not. While I was trying to pin down Glenn Hoddle and the International Committee to sort out his contract, the wheels were turning in a strange way with massive consequences to follow.

Who would have thought that, after all the tension and drama of the Argentina match, a woman, a book and a couple of bad results would conspire to remove the England coach, who had been so near to World Cup success?

I was never that concerned about Glenn's friend Eileen Drewery, the faith healer, as I was always of the opinion that if she could help players, as she did with Darren Anderton when he came back from injury with a wonderful goal, then I could not see it doing any harm. I do not profess to know what goes on in the head of a top class athlete or sportsman, but I do know that they have to have their minds right when performing at that level and if this method can contribute half a percent (rather than the 20% which Glenn seemed to suggest later) then I did not see any reason to get upset about it. Rather like a placebo, if the players felt it worked, then why not?

Graham Taylor had used a sports psychologist in John Gardner whom Peter Swales thought was a psychiatrist. Howard Wilkinson also used psychologist Bill Beswick, while the Brazilians have been using them for years.

Billing the FA was never an issue and did not come to my attention until long after the World Cup and neither did the fact that Glenn had joined her company, although he should have sought my permission if he wanted to become professionally involved. I never had the impression that it was a money earner for him and it was never discussed. For me the entire Drewery business, at this stage, was an irrelevance. In the end, however, it was the reason he left the FA. The Councillors did not like her involvement because they felt it held them up to ridicule.

It was, however, clearly in his mind at the time because he mentions it in his book, the controversial *World Cup Diary* which, along with Eileen Drewery, eventually prompted his downfall as the media turned on him.

I had no problem with Glenn writing a book; after all, there had been a precedent with Bobby Robson who wrote his *World Cup Diary* during the World Cup in Mexico, and again in Italy, and there had been no difficulties.

David Davies expressed himself keen to write the book and Glenn's agent Dennis Roach wanted to put the deal to bed quickly. I gave my consent for it, thinking that David would provide the safeguard in that there would not be any fingers pointed by the rest of the press pack as there had been with Bobby and his co-author, even though no confidences had ever been breached. I also felt that it would prevent Glenn putting anything in the book which would rebound on the FA.

In the event, because of the way the book was received, it had precisely that effect. I took the view that he had to stand or fall by whatever was in the book; it was his, and I could not be expected to censor it and wield the blue pencil. We were all grown-ups.

I was asked by David Davies to look at a couple of things, one of them about the Shearer case. I must hastily add that I did not make any alterations and did not ask them to keep anything out of their book in order that I could use it in mine!

Seriously, I did not have the right to veto it and neither did I read the finished manuscript.

But, of course, it transpired that he had been economical with the truth throughout the build-up and in the World Cup itself, and there is nothing that upsets the members of the journalistic profession more than if they feel they are not in the coach's confidence on the inside track. Worse, they felt that they were used to purvey misinformation. That, coupled with what they saw as a derisory claim that Eileen Drewery could have improved performance, meant that it was open season as far as they were concerned. It allowed them to criticise the entire concept of the book. The fact that Glenn claimed he had breached no confidences was like a straw in the wind; no one took account of that and suddenly the players were reported to be losing confidence in their coach. Personally, I do not think that was true. Certainly, Alan Shearer forcefully denied it.

The fact that Glenn did not achieve the results after the World Cup in his three qualifying matches for Euro 2000 did not help his cause as the pressure built up on him. It fuelled the ammunition of those involved who remembered the slights against them, real or imagined.

That was the public battlefield and, internally, there was also a situation before the World Cup when Howard Wilkinson was seeking to expand his role as Technical Director. He wanted, among other things, the Under-21s under his jurisdiction. Normally the Technical Director of a Football Association would advise on the appointment of the head coach and that was how I envisaged it happening, the way it did in France. But in the case of England, Hoddle was there first, and we had to strive to bring in a Technical Director who was compatible with him rather than the other way round.

This was not easy. Howard thought that he should have been involved more in the back-up for France, particularly over the scouting. Glenn thought that Howard was too busy with his Charter for Quality. Howard told me he wanted qualified people to be involved and took a dim view of Eileen Drewery and her role.

In May, he produced a report suggesting, among other things, that we must have a plan for the long term with proper back-up for the coach and that, in future, we must appoint a Head Coach from a cadre of coaches working within the system already in the way Ron Greenwood had set up his hierarchy.

It was not the right time to be confronting Glenn Hoddle with these proposals as he prepared for France and I resolved to speak to him straight after the World Cup.

Glenn's contract said it should be reviewed in 1998, based on the success of the team in the World Cup and on what other international managers were being paid at the time.

I told him while we were on Concorde coming back from La Baule the day after elimination that, if I had an office available, having heard that the FA was burning down, he should come in and see me to talk about matters contractual once the emotion of going out of the competition had settled.

I also explained to Glenn that we needed to sort things out with Howard. This sort of infighting had been the bane of the FA for as long as I could remember and I made him readily understand that he had to work more closely with the Technical Director.

It was not until the end of July that I was able to see him, but he was still not ready to talk about the contract review. He had other things on his mind, particularly with the European Championship qualifying game against Sweden in Stockholm coming up, and we agreed to leave it for a further couple of months.

I actually managed to persuade Howard and Glenn to meet round the table on 26 August to discuss Howard's proposals. Glenn did not concede any ground on the Under-21s, apart from agreeing he and Howard needed to work together more closely. He saw the Under-21s as the last stage before qualification for the full team. He said that players were fully fledged internationals by then and were no longer in the development stage. Development, he said, was up to the Under-18 side, but not for young men of 20.

I told Howard to revise the report and send it to Glenn so that we could have another discussion. I was really trying to get them to work together because I did not want to have a crunch situation with either. I was keen for Glenn to carry on as coach and for Howard to back off a little. He knew that Glenn had the Under-21 situation covered in his contract and could not be expected to give them up just like that, but Howard wanted to press the point.

I had a meeting of the Executive Committee on 1 September shortly after the launch of Glenn Hoddle's book, the *World Cup Diary*. They were unhappy at the storm which had blown up following the serialisation in the *Sun*. I told them that Hoddle's contract needed sorting out anyway and that we should set up a small group to discuss that and the other matters arising.

I met Glenn again two weeks later and he was anxious for an extension of two years on his contract. As Keith Wiseman had said publicly that he wanted to keep him for two years, he was echoing what was already thought in some quarters. He was also adamant that he kept the Under-21s in any extension of his contract.

There was, however, a growing voice within the media that Glenn had let his players down through revelations in his book, combined with his relationship with his favourite faith healer. The pressure was growing when we travelled to Stockholm. I took my seat in the stand an hour before the game to hear the tannoy playing the Dexy's Midnight Runners hit 'Come on Eileen'. I could not believe it, but it was scarcely a coincidence, more a display of Swedish humour.

We did not see a lot of humour in what followed as England lost: Paul Ince was sent off, our fans were wrongly accused of racist chants and a nasty hooligan element caused damage in the stands in an incident which could have had much more serious consequences.

It was not the result wanted by Glenn for a number of reasons, not least because of the discussions on his new contract. We had a preliminary first meeting of the sub-committee on 16 September with

Keith Wiseman, Dave Richards and Noel White. They were happy to extend to 2002 but Dave Richards said only with conditions, pointing out that there should be no more books, no more faith healers and limited payment if we had to pay him off (liquidated damages). He also had to work with Howard Wilkinson.

That was strong enough but Noel White was against any extension at all, presumably because he was still undecided at that time. He had seen the World Cup as not an unqualified success and we had just lost in Sweden.

Richards and White agreed on one thing; they did not want Roy Hodgson to take over. This came up because the press campaign to be rid of Hoddle was growing stronger and names of likely successors were already being put forward. Richards wanted Trevor Francis.

The first proper meeting took place on 18 September when Geoff Thompson had been added to provide a little balance and to maintain the tradition of involving the Vice-Chairman. We also wanted one other, with the choice between David Sheepshanks and David Dein. I suggested it would probably be better to have David Sheepshanks, who would bring a broader perspective, being the Chairman of the Football League, and Keith Wiseman agreed.

We reached the conclusion that it was too early to consider an extension until we knew whether we would qualify for the finals of Euro 2000. The committee also reiterated that they did not want any more books and that Glenn should restrict the use of Mrs Drewery. Generally the committee were in favour of Howard Wilkinson's proposals and it was thought that Glenn might agree to give up the Under-21s as part of the negotiations on his salary. Clearly they did not know the man too well, but I kept my counsel even though I did not think it at all likely.

By this time the situation with the Under-21s was being talked about outside, with Joe Melling suggesting in the *Mail on Sunday* that the coach might walk out if he lost control of that team. To be fair, there was no talk of him losing that control during the remainder of his contract, but he continued to make it perfectly clear that he felt so strongly about it that he would be unlikely to sign any new contract which did not continue his authority over the Under-21s. He believed any such change would be wrong in principle.

I had a further meeting with Glenn's agent Dennis Roach on 22 September who assured me that his man wanted to stay and offered the fact that he had turned down the Spurs job as evidence. I told him that there were still two major issues which worried the FA, the book and Eileen Drewery. He said that Glenn understood the position about having to prove himself and therefore he was no longer looking for an immediate extension to his contract.

Roach rang a couple of days later from France and said Glenn wanted more money than we were offering. He said that Glenn understood the need for compromise and would try hard to reach a working relationship with Howard Wilkinson.

There was a six-figure difference between our offer and what Glenn wanted, a fairly large gulf by anyone's standards, so we had another meeting of the sub committee on 28 September. Noel White told us that he had telephoned all the members of the International Committee by then and only one of them wanted to extend Glenn's contract, although he was not prepared to say who. They were also still keen on Hoddle making concessions to Wilkinson. Howard, though initially suspicious about the machinations of the FA Committee structure, was proving adept at internal lobbying, whereas Glenn preferred to leave the committees to me and concentrate on his football.

Dave Richards was upset about David Davies telling him what to do. Presumably David had stuck his oar in, telling him that in view of the press interest it needed to be settled sooner rather than later, and Richards had taken umbrage, rather like Peter Swales had done earlier.

The committee decided to increase the bonuses payable to Glenn on his current contract, thinking it might help negotiations.

Eileen Drewery was beginning to feature more prominently in these discussions, just as she was in the media. There was a major debate as to whether the FA should continue paying her or whether the players should consult her at their own expense. They did not quite get to the bottom of that, but they decided unanimously that they no longer wanted her at the training camp at Burnham Beeches where she had been on previous occasions to save players having to queue to see her at her home.

The instruction sent out to Glenn was that he must help us to help him and that Eileen must not darken the FA's doors again because the situation was holding them up to ridicule. If that was not a strong enough message, they also stood firm against the increase in salary that he wanted.

Keith Wiseman had been quoted in a strong defence of Glenn in the press to the effect that he did not care if Glenn consulted *Merlin the Wizard*, provided it got results. This prompted Geoff Thompson to complain of blasphemy.

Roach clearly indicated the next time I spoke to him that they wanted the higher salary figure, rather than the extra bonuses, and when I went to see Glenn at Burnham Beeches on 7 October before the game against Bulgaria I told him of the upset the book had caused. He could not understand the fuss, he said, because it was him and not the committee who was being criticised. I conveyed the views of the committee about Eileen, asking him to protect them, but he was unrepentant and rejected any criticism of her, saying that she had helped Paul Merson tremendously.

He said that the committee did not understand the work she did and offered to bring her along to meet them! I told him not to call me on that one, I would call him. Or perhaps not. I was beginning to feel that I might need her services myself, the way things were going.

Progress was certainly limited as he was disappointed with the financial offer on the table. We were talking about the bonuses, but he was not happy with the base rate and wanted to talk about it more. His position was not unreasonable the way he was putting it, but I thought that there was little chance of convincing the committee. He thought the FA were underestimating the difficulty of the job.

After the problems over Alan Shearer before the World Cup and the way the meeting had progressed, it was with some trepidation that I told him of our plans to charge Paul Ince for the 'V' sign in Stockholm. This time he was in tune and, indeed, promised to speak to the player himself about his behaviour.

An additional spanner had been tossed into the works with the Manchester United complaint over the injections that the players had received during the World Cup. Glenn claimed that they had it all wrong and that neither Paul Scholes nor Teddy Sheringham had been injected, but we still had to write to the club and promise to tell them whenever anything like this was being planned in the future.

The rift between Howard Wilkinson and Glenn Hoddle appeared to be widening and in Birmingham, where I attended the FA Coaches' Association Annual Conference, Howard further alienated the England coaching staff of John Gorman, Ray Clemence and Peter Taylor in the audience by expounding the virtues of the flat back four as opposed to the system used by Glenn in the World Cup.

While I was there I took a call from Dennis Roach. He hit the roof when I again refused the upper figure they were demanding, saying that it meant that the FA did not really want his man.

Fate certainly seemed to be conspiring against the new Hoddle contract when England contrived to draw with Bulgaria at Wembley, dropping two more valuable points and putting a huge question mark over qualification.

In Luxembourg for our group game I had discussed the situation with Noel White, whom I had kept up to speed with all my dealings on the matter, and again he suggested increasing the bonuses further to try and resolve the situation.

This eventually did the trick and on 27 October Glenn and Dennis came in to see Keith and me. Glenn did not want the contract reviewed again until we had our fate for the European Championships decided. The point the Hoddle camp had been making was that his salary had been outstripped by Premier League managers and other international coaches, but our argument was that having the title of England coach offered a commercial opportunity that others did not have. We successfully stuck to our original figure.

Two days later Howard Wilkinson attended the committee meeting with Noel White, Geoff Thompson, David Sheepshanks and myself. He went through the entire story of how Ron Greenwood had appointed a number of established coaches; referred to the need for databases and backup and said that he was not Technical Director, merely Director of Coaching for the time being. He wanted to have the authority to implement the proposals in 2000 and continue the dialogue with Glenn in the meantime. Noel White promised a policy decision which would fix a date when the proposals would come into effect. After Howard had departed I pointed out that if they made the planned announcement they would effectively be sealing the departure of Glenn Hoddle at the end of his current contract. What would happen, I asked, if he embarked on a run of success and won the European Championships and we had already alienated him by taking the Under-21s out of his control? Sheepshanks appreciated the argument and I suggested they should listen to Glenn's argument for retaining the Under-21s.

In the meantime we had a lot more anti-Hoddle press. In the *Sun* Brian Woolnough, acting, we suspected, on the tip-off of an agent of a London-based player, alleged Shearer had rounded on Hoddle in the dressing room after the Luxembourg game.

Glenn Hoddle successfully elicited an apology from the *Sun* but he felt that the support of the FA had not been what it should have been. I had said that we would help him in gathering all the necessary witness statements but he had wanted us to help with the legal costs. I was never too keen on doing that. Glenn felt very strongly that the dressing room should be sacrosanct and that once that line had been breached it would affect the FA in other ways, in committee rooms and the like. He received his apology, but I said we would not pay the costs. We would merely look at the principle for the future.

I felt great relief when, on 18 November, we beat the Czech Republic 2–0 in a friendly at Wembley and I thought that on the England scene there would be a quiet three months in prospect before the next game. Some hope.

Behind the scenes the row over the Under-21s continued to dominate and it became clear at the International Committee on 1ᵃ December that, while the sub-committee were in favour of Howard's proposals, others were not and both Ray Kiddell and Ray Berridge of Bedfordshire took the line that Glenn should retain control of the youngsters' team.

Six days later Glenn met the sub-committee and explained his position to them. Howard had suggested that Glenn ran the full England team and the 'B' team, but Glenn thought that the 'B' team was a waste of time and he would rather have Peter Taylor develop the young players in the Under-21s on the same lines as the full England team. He and Peter worked side by side because the players needed to learn quickly between the ages of 19 and 20, trying to get the habits right for the full team. He also said that he would accept and welcome a consultant, someone in the mould of Bobby Robson.

Glenn was asked why Premier League players could not play the same way as Glenn wanted England to play. He patiently explained that managers would not conform, and as an example he pointed out that West Ham United manager Harry Redknapp wouldn't allow central defender Rio Ferdinand to go forward with the ball in case the team lost their shape. All in all, it was a good meeting and they took in a lot of what he had to say.

This was the only time that they ever had a meeting with Glenn outside the formal meetings of the International Committee, which were definitely not a forum for discussions of this nature. He was very strong in what he was saying about Howard's proposals, but he did not categorically say that, come 2000, he would not sign a new contract if he did not have control of the Under-21s, although I always had that impression from my talks with him.

Eight days later I left the FA and he went shortly thereafter! Within weeks Howard Wilkinson had jettisoned Peter Taylor and had taken over control of the Under-21s. He had his own way at last and time may prove him right.

Without doubt the FA hung Glenn out to dry after his controversial interview appeared on the Saturday morning, 30 January 1999, in *The Times*. I still believe that, however upsetting his comments will have been to disabled people – and I sympathise very much with the hurt they will have felt – he did not need to lose his job for personally-held opinions.

Certainly he could have apologised more fully and he could have explained his comments more succinctly. I am still not clear exactly what he did mean and he could have given assurances for the future that he would not talk in public about his spiritual or religious beliefs and allow those beliefs to intrude on his statements as England coach.

I noticed that after the furore in the media, David Davies immediately began referring to him as Mr Hoddle, whereas previously it had been Glenn. When the Prime Minister Tony Blair entered the fray on the Monday morning, Glenn's fate was virtually sealed. He had spent 48 hours digging a deeper hole for himself, threatening to sue *The Times* and telling a different tale with every interview. In my opinion, he had brought a lot of the problems on his own head.

It is rumoured that he was asked by the FA to give up Eileen Drewery altogether and I believe it was his use of this faith healer, coupled with mediocre results, which was the cause of his downfall. It was not because of his unwise comments about the disabled – that was merely the excuse.

It was ironic that he had initiated his own departure by embarking on a conscious effort, on advice, to build bridges with the press. He had previously given a lengthy interview to Joe Lovejoy of the *Sunday Times* without incident.

I spoke to him on the Monday evening, the day before he resigned and had a general chat about the situation he found himself in. I felt a very great deal of sympathy for him. I had grown to like him very much. He was a decent person who ultimately was unfairly treated by the Football Association. And he was tactically astute.

I was not surprised that the FA went for Kevin Keegan to succeed Hoddle. I had said publicly that I thought Jack the Ripper had a better chance of getting the job than Terry Venables, many people's choice once Glenn had gone. The FA were just not going to re-appoint him whatever Noel White or anyone else said subsequently. They did not want him.

Howard Wilkinson had obviously vastly increased his sphere of influence at Lancaster Gate with the departure of Glenn Hoddle. Peter Taylor's fate was sealed long before his eventual leaving, notwithstanding his impressive record. He felt he was in the way of Wilkinson's intentions; Howard contended that Peter didn't want to work in the new structure. Obviously there was no meeting of minds and Peter soon went off to manage Gillingham.

The FA were bitterly criticised over Keegan's appointment as a part-time coach, and it was only the high regard in which Kevin was held that got them off the hook. The FA had been impressed with him since he took temporary charge of the Under-21s and he made a very big impression on members of the International Committee in the way he handled the whole England set-up. He had also worked for the FA at the annual all-party parliamentary dinner where his speech was warmly received by members of both sides of the Houses of Parliament.

Tactically, at the highest level, Keegan still has to prove himself, as was demonstrated in the disappointing draws with Sweden and Bulgaria in two key Euro 2000 qualifiers back in June. His enthusiasm is one of his greatest assets, but in the pressure-cooker world of the England job, that emotional aspect to his make-up may prove to be his Achilles heel. Time will tell.

CHAPTER FOURTEEN

Sleaze

The Football Writers' Association Awards Dinner in May on the Thursday before the Cup Final was agog with the news that Terry Venables was to leave Spurs.

What emerged over the coming months and even years was the biggest bust-up to hit football for a long time.

The saga began back in June 1991 when Terry Venables and Alan Sugar joined forces to defeat Robert Maxwell and buy a controlling shareholding in Spurs from Irving Scholar and Paul Bobroff.

It lasted until that spring of 1993, when the mud started to fly and a falling-out between Venables and Sugar appeared inevitable. Sugar was unhappy at certain payments made to the agent Eric Hall and Terry Venables' employment of an undischarged bankrupt, Eddie Ashby, on Spurs business. The use of agents was to feature strongly throughout this story. Aston Villa had been disciplined for using the services of an agency, First Wave, to sign Mark Bosnich. Halfway through the case the Midlands clubs demanded of the FA a deal or they threatened they would reveal all about the activities of agents and other clubs. The FA refused to be blackmailed and Aston Villa were fined.

Spurs had a longstanding policy whereby players were given loans not authorised by the football authorities and in 1991 Anthony Grabiner QC advised that the loans, which were never repaid, should be notified to the Football League. They never were.

A year later the Inland Revenue went into White Hart Lane where

Financial Director Colin Sandy disclosed that Irving Scholar had had scant regard for financial controls. The murk at the bottom of the pond had been well and truly stirred but the details were not sent to the FA Premier League until 29 November 1993.

The full impact was not felt until Terry Venables sued, following his removal from Spurs. Alan Sugar's affidavit in reply said that Venables had told him that Nottingham Forest manager Brian Clough 'liked a bung', and he (Sugar) refused to pay a bung in the transfer of Teddy Sheringham from Nottingham Forest. It later transpired from the Premier League report into the matter that Alan Sugar had signed the cheque for cash for £50,000 which had somehow disappeared in the direction of Nottingham.

The Premier League said that when signing the cheque Mr Sugar's customary acuity had deserted him. Brian Clough denied any involvement after it had been said that he received the money in a motorway rest area in a carrier bag. The colourful Clough claimed that the last time he had used a motorway cafe was to have a pee.

I recommended to the Executive Committee that we set up an inquiry ourselves at the Football Association, but Sir Bert Millichip was not prepared to countenance this because of the litigation going on at the time between Sugar and Venables.

Venables was subject to a scathing attack in a programme broadcast by the BBC *Panorama* team on 16 September 1993. He then wrote to the FA, asking for an inquiry to investigate what Alan Sugar had said about bungs. I told Terry to provide whatever information he could and send it in to us.

Sugar invited Rick Parry and me to visit him to discuss the irregularities he said he had found since Venables left Spurs. Rick and I went to Sugar's company Amstrad in Brentwood and the following month Parry set up a Premier League Inquiry comprising of Robert Reid QC, a deputy High Court judge; Steve Coppell, Chief Executive of the League Managers' Association at the time; and himself.

The starting point was the Sheringham transfer and Paul Gascoigne's move from Spurs to FC Lazio in Italy. Rick Parry said that he was aiming for a short, sharp exercise which would produce recommendations for new transfer rules; any disciplinary matters would be passed to the FA.

Little did he, or anyone else for that matter, realise how long it would take. There was a lot of pressure from outside, particularly from the press and from certain Members of Parliament who were calling for an independent inquiry. Parry started collecting evidence and at the end of 1993 there was a Granada *World in Action* programme which revealed details of the unauthorised loans.

The loans were very similar to the previous case which had resulted in Swindon being demoted by the Football League. We could see right from the start that there was going to be an outcry one way or another. The Premier League could not deal with it because the loans had taken place before the Premier League's formation, leaving the FA to charge Spurs with the full approval of the Football League.

It transpired that these loans had been used to induce players to sign; in effect they had cheated other clubs by disguising the full remuneration to the players thus causing the compensation fees to be lower than they would have otherwise been.

It represented widespread abuse of the rules going back to 1985. Peter Leaver QC had advised, contrary to Anthony Grabiner, that the loans should not be disclosed as Spurs were no longer members of the Football League. There was a difference of viewpoint in the Leagues. Parry did not regard the case as too serious and did not think we would demote Spurs. The League, with their Swindon experience, probably did. Personally I did not think that a fine would act as a deterrent and we decided to charge Spurs as soon after the 1993–94 season ended as possible.

Lawyers had met Sugar to discuss the dispute he was embroiled in with West Bromwich Albion over the move of manager Ossie Ardiles to Spurs and he told them he wanted to have the loans case dealt with as soon as possible.

He rang me following some what he regarded as horrific stories in a Sunday newspaper. He suspected Eddie Ashby was leaking documents which he had acquired while he was working for Terry Venables at Spurs. He said he wanted to co-operate, adding that they had a lot of information at the club. I replied that I was not sure that we needed any more information at that stage. He requested that I keep him informed. I promised I would and he said 'All right, mate!' All very friendly – but it was not to last.

On 12 May we charged Spurs with 40 offences and they immediately admitted over half of them. Alan Sugar thought that we had deliberately chosen the moment because that was the day Venables' company Edennote wound up in court. It was, of course, not the case as we had always planned to issue the charges straight after the end of the playing season. I had no inkling of the Edennote hearing.

I was away in the USA at the World Cup when the disciplinary commission, comprised of Keith Wiseman, Jack Wiseman, Ray Kiddell, Frank Pattison and John Reames, was held on 14 June. They deducted twelve points from Spurs' league total, banned them from the FA Cup, fined the club £600,000 and ordered them to pay the costs of the hearing.

Herbert Smith and Company, on behalf of Spurs, tried to obtain a ruling that there had been no dishonesty and they also requested a smaller points deduction. Spurs were most surprised at their banishment from the FA Cup. Sugar was also unhappy that Terry Venables had not helped them to defend the case.

Sugar went ballistic and suspected collusion between Venables and the FA. It was, of course, total paranoia, complete nonsense. We never talked to Venables about the case at all. Sugar was claiming that there was a vendetta against him, because the FA thought he was a bully who needed to be stopped. He expected to lose three points, having reported the breaches of regulations himself. He suggested that the FA believed he was trying to disgrace the England coach. He said that Terry Venables and Jonathan Crystal had promised to take care of the notification of the loans, but had not done so.

Gordon Taylor had his say. He announced that the punishment was too severe and that it should have been a bigger fine. That is all very well, but what does a big fine mean to a large club? If they can buy their way to success, they can buy their way out of trouble. It is like a rich man paying a fine to save himself going to prison.

Spurs appealed and, on their behalf, Rick Parry went along and told the Appeals Board that Spurs had fully co-operated with the Premier League. The punishment was changed to a six points deduction; the fine increased to £1.5 million and the Cup ban stayed. This time it was Bert Millichip, Chris Willcox and Geoff Thompson who made the decisions. Sugar decided not to be legally represented and, instead, presented his own case. He said they had not intended to deceive anybody and that the previous commission had given him no inkling of how seriously they regarded the case; the wrong people had been punished and it should have been a financial penalty only.

Spurs, having won a partial victory, pushed their luck when they then asked for time to pay the fine. I was adamant that they could not have that. They promptly threatened legal action. Sugar demanded to see Bert Millichip and me but I refused in view of the fact that he was threatening to sue us.

We were eventually advised that we should arbitrate the case by our own legal people. We did not want to end up in court with eight members of the FA Council being on the witness stand, along with Terry Venables; that could have been extremely embarrassing. We agreed to arbitration within fairly narrow parameters and after weeks of haggling we drew up an agreement which only allowed the arbitration panel to remit the case to a new commission; they could not actually vary the decision themselves.

The arbitration panel of Sir Roger Parker, Donald Findlay QC, who in 1999 resigned as Vice-Chairman of Rangers for serious misjudgment of singing anti-Catholic songs, and V V Veeder QC eventually sat on 24 and 25 November. They thought it was a unique case and that the FA did have the power to deduct points. Spurs had admitted to making inducements, but they said the officials responsible for the breaches wouldn't be affected and that the current officials were blameless. They accepted that the offences were serious but that it was irrational to impose any penalty but a fine. They thought the £1.5 million on its own was enough.

I was bitterly disappointed at this setback: not only had we been forced to climb down to Alan Sugar, but also the term 'irrational' proved to be particularly damaging. When used in this legal way, the word has a fairly standard meaning; it does not mean completely lacking in reason as the dictionary would indicate. It was the only serious case I lost in my entire time in football. I did not think that the arbitration panel could possibly reach the decision they did.

There was a very small chance of an appeal against arbitration but we quickly ruled that out. What really went wrong was that the original commission should have given reasons why they had dealt out such a stiff penalty. This would have given us much more chance of resisting any future challenge. What I could not understand was that if it was a serious case and we did have the powers they said we had, why was it not appropriate to use those powers in this case?

Our QC muttered darkly about the unfairness of it all. We then had to go to a new commission on 13 December 1994, but it was no more than a formality as they confirmed the fine.

That was not the end of my difficulties with the Spurs Chairman. He said that he had given *World in Action* information about the loans to divert them from attacking Ossie Ardiles. I told the press conference after the final commission that the loans had only been disclosed via *World in Action*, i.e. disclosed to the authorities by the media and not by the club.

Sugar said I was arrogant, dogmatic and ignorant and demanded an apology for what I had said at that press conference. But it all widened into a much bigger scandal as there was widespread publicity about alleged bungs and irregular payments. Rick Parry said that clubs were providing reports to the Inland Revenue and getting a clean bill of health, not because they had anything to hide but because they wanted to avoid dawn swoops and to clear matters up first. He actually tried to avoid getting any details from the clubs which he would have had to pass on to the FA. He did not want to help the clubs sort out their tax affairs and then be accused of snitching to the FA. He tried not to know very much about what they were discussing with the Inland Revenue.

The Premier League then introduced new rules on agents, and clubs had to provide audited certificates to the effect that they had observed football's rules relating to transfers and agents.

I thought we should call for information from the clubs, but the Executive Committee were persuaded by Keith Wiseman that we should not stir up a hornets' nest at that time. The Inland Revenue will never reveal anything against those who pay up, but they use leaks as a legitimate weapon to nail those who do not.

George Graham was sacked by Arsenal in February 1995 for receiving an unsolicited gift of £425,000. He always maintained that the money from the company of Norwegian agent Rune Hauge was not linked to transfers. The FA Premier League submitted an interim report at the end of February 1995 which reported their findings in the Graham case and he was banned from football for a year, the 1995–96 season, by the FA, and ordered to pay the £50,000 costs of the commission.

It was quite strange that this had taken so long to come to light because a dispute had surfaced originally in 1993 between Brondby and Hamburg. The Germans claimed that Arsenal had paid £1.6 million for John Jensen, not £900,000 as published, and Hamburg wanted 25% of the difference. The dispute went to FIFA where Joao Havelange, the ubiquitous Jacques Georges and Viacheslav Koloskov from the Football Union of Russia ruled that £793,000 had gone to an agent and Hamburg were due 25% of it. However, they never went any further into the case when they could have charged the clubs under FIFA rules for using an agent, an offence at the time. The Premier League inquiry reached the conclusion that George Graham had been involved personally in talks in Oslo over the transfer to Arsenal of the other player involved, Pal Lydersen.

George Graham at one point threatened to talk about other clubs and other cases in much the same way that Aston Villa had done earlier but he, like them, declined the invitation to give details.

The Premier League eventually published its final report in 1997. It ran to 10,000 pages and even then was not particularly clear. So the FA asked Sir John Smith, former deputy Metropolitan Police Commissioner, to report on the way football regulated its financial affairs and we had to submit the Premier League words to our own lawyers for detailed analysis.

Sir John reported that there needed to be much more stringent financial and ethical standards in the game. He added that there should be a code of conduct which set standards for everybody. It was unfortunate that the Premier League and the Football League had not seen fit back in the early days of the financial scandals to act upon a report of the chief officers of the FA, the Premier League, the PFA and the Football League. We advocated that a compliance unit be set up, staffed by independent financial experts to monitor clubs' finances, to provide advice to clubs and in serious cases to instigate breaches of regulation procedures.

Unfortunately the Premier League, in particular, did not see the need for what they regarded as an expensive bureaucracy. They argued that, as listed companies in many cases, the clubs were already subject to increased regulation. This was not an adequate response to the growing concern about sleaze. I went to White Hart Lane for a match just after the Premier League report came out and Alan Sugar urged me to charge Terry Venables, saying: 'I could go out with a shot gun, come back with millions of pounds, buy Asprilla from Newcastle United and when the police come round I would say that I was doing it all for Spurs.'

After more months of lengthy deliberation we decided to charge Nottingham Forest, not over the Sheringham case, but over the transfer of two players from a small club called Leicester United whom, it appeared, Forest had considerably overpaid.

We reached the decision not to charge Brian Clough because of his failing health, and at the time I was about to leave the FA I was trying to negotiate a deal with Phil Soar where the matter would be put to bed quickly with Forest being subject to a fine.

I am reluctant to damn all managers with generalisations. It is very difficult for them to defend themselves when unspecified allegations are made. Nevertheless, I find it difficult to believe that, at a time when agents were moving money around Europe completely unchecked, George Graham was the only recipient of a 'gift'. Alex Ferguson's subsequent revelations in his autobiography tended to confirm this.

Arsenal were deeply shamed by the 'bung' affair and they suffered further agonies when their legendary skipper Tony Adams bared his soul with a book which revealed his serious problems with alcohol. He was not alone at Highbury, for even worse were the revelations of another favourite son Paul Merson, who confessed to drugs, gambling and alcohol!

It was November 1994 when Merson admitted serious cocaine abuse in the *Daily Mirror*. We had a problem because whilst obviously he was not denying using drugs, he had not been caught under the FA testing regime; nor had it been proved that he had used the drug in any performance-enhancing way. Rather the reverse.

Arsenal put out a statement, saying that Merson needed time away from the pressure of the public spotlight with a view to sorting out the difficulties which he had notified them of. They added that while not condoning what he had done, they would support him all they could through a difficult period. There was no indication that the club had been aware of the problem beforehand.

We called Merson to a meeting at the Hilton Hotel near Lord's Cricket Ground. I said before the hearing that our emphasis would be on treatment and rehabilitation out of concern for the player and his family, and that disciplinary action would be the secondary consideration. George Graham came to the hearing with him, as did Gordon Taylor and Alan Hodson, the Head of Medical Education at the Football Association.

It was a tearful meeting as Paul was in a considerable state. We eventually decided to send him for residential rehabilitation treatment and said that if he failed to last the course, he would be subject to discipline. As it was, he was banned from playing football and was told that he would be targeted for drug tests for eighteen months. Both he and Arsenal would have to contribute towards the cost of the course.

His course covered the Christmas period. During it we received regular reports of his progress and after six weeks he was discharged. We were advised that a point would be reached when to delay his return to competitive football would be detrimental to his progress. He continued his rehabilitation as an outpatient, went back to training with Arsenal and played his first game in a friendly against AC Milan.

I thought that this was one of the best things we ever did during my time at the Football Association, for it showed that we could act in a compassionate and caring way. Merson responded by doing the difficult part and when he came back into the England squad there was no one more delighted than me.

He had many problems but clearly the hard drugs were the unacceptable part to the outside world. It was an addiction problem which he had to overcome.

The drugs issue is causing concern, and I'm often asked about the scale of the problem. If there was a serious drugs problem, I was usually the last to hear, as naturally the clubs concerned would try to conceal such issues. Looking at society today, alcohol and drugs is clearly a worry and the laddish culture has not helped. Funnily enough, foreign imports have helped to change the attitude among young professionals. These players know how to take care of themselves.

Nowadays there are 500 tests per season with still a fairly small number of positive cases but, hopefully, the programme will continue to have a deterrent effect. The anti-drugs regime cost the FA a mere £13,000 per year in 1993 – now the bill is nearer £1 million.

Arsenal, in the circumstances, must have been quite pleased that their striker John Hartson, bought from Luton Town, had moved on to West Ham United by the time he grabbed the sleaze headlines at the end of 1998, posing the FA something of a dilemma.

The Welsh international striker had been shown to strike out in an unorthodox way, his left boot connecting with the head of team mate and Israeli international Eyal Berkovic at West Ham's training ground at Chadwell Heath.

This, of course, happened during a private training session and if the FA took action every time there was a training bust-up, we would never have done anything else. However, it was a particularly severe incident which had been captured by a fan's video camera and transmitted on national television.

Harry Redknapp's protestations were in vain and I felt that there had to be a charge of breach of rules. Hartson was subsequently fined £20,000 and banned, a punishment for Wimbledon who had signed the player for a reported £7 million.

I thought long and hard about it. I could see the point that it was an incident which had occurred on a private training ground. I didn't want to interfere, but neither could I see how we could ignore something so horrific no matter what the background. I felt that there was no alternative but to put the case before a commission.

There were no doubt some nerves at the FA handing out punishment for an incident in such circumstances but, needless to say, there was no adverse reaction from within the game as it would have been seen as defending the indefensible. In the end, I was satisfied that we had taken the right course of action.

I was equally horrified to hear the details of the Paulo Di Canio incident. I had not seen the push on television before I heard about it on the radio. For a player to actually knock a referee to the ground was bad news indeed, although it was not the first time that a player had been in trouble for assaulting a referee. Frank Sinclair of Leicester, when on loan from Chelsea to West Bromwich Albion, had gone tearing up to the same referee, Paul Alcock, could not stop and barged into him. He suffered a nine-match suspension for that indiscretion.

The Di Canio case was one of the easier decisions, as Sheffield Wednesday had already taken it upon themselves to suspend him straight after the game. There is no doubt that he pushed Alcock and although he claimed that the referee's fall was theatrical, I thought: 'So what?' There are some players who know a thing or two about theatrical dives. It certainly did not affect what had happened. He put his hands on him and if we allowed players to get away with that there would be anarchy. He was caught bang to rights. Not that Mr Alcock's comments in the press helped in any way.

Referee Uriah Rennie booked two players for diving in one game in 1999, PFA Footballer of the Year David Ginola and Eyal Berkovic, as the prevalence of diving grew along with shirt tugging after the 1998 World Cup. But the practice had been going on for some time, and back in 1992 Scottish international striker Gordon Durie was suspended for three matches for feigning injury. I charged him as if he had been sent off for foul play himself.

Sometimes the circumstances have to be taken into account in such incidents, as was the case when Manchester United's Roy Keane stamped on Gareth Southgate, then of Crystal Palace, in an FA Cup semi-final replay at Villa Park. We took action because of the whole aura surrounding that tie. A Palace fan had been killed before the first game and a lot of Palace supporters would not go to the second game. It was an eerie sort of occasion until Keane went and stamped on the London defender.

We charged him as much because of the circumstances as for the offence and there was a predictable outcry from Old Trafford. They wanted to know why we were making one match any different from another, but I thought it was a particularly bad situation. He was fined but not suspended. We were not going to make him miss the Cup Final, but it was a point we wanted to get across.

I was pleased when a less fiery Keane came back from a long injury some years later to play such an important role, as captain, in United's push for the treble of Premiership, FA Cup and European Cup.

We once took action against a former referee, Alan Robinson, after Gordon Taylor complained about his opinion, expressed from his position as Public Relations Officer of the national Referees' Association, that many players were guilty of cheating. Even though I ascertained from referees' chief Peter Willis that he was happy for the FA to proceed, I have sometimes recalled the case with some unease. After all, what is deliberately breaking the laws if it is not cheating? It must have been the way the views were expressed and the use of the emotive word 'cheat' which caused offence.

We found it embarrassingly difficult to intervene when, to the fans' disgust, Brighton and Hove Albion Chairman Bill Archer sold the Goldstone Ground and entered into a ground-sharing agreement with distant Gillingham. The supporters could not understand that our lawyers advised us against charging Archer with bringing the game into disrepute. We could only offer exhortations whilst the club was brought to its knees, for the rules did not allow us to intervene in the internal affairs of autonomous limited companies.

After months of deliberations we successfully brought off a mediation by the Centre for Dispute Resolution which ruled that the club would be owned 49% by Mr Archer, 49% by prospective new owner Dick Knight, who had plans to build a new ground, and 2% by Martin Perry, representing the developers. The FA could only exercise the powers granted to it by its constituent members, i.e. the clubs. It was not an independent regulating body.

There is no doubt that clearer and firmer Premier League rules have helped to eradicate the sleaze allegations that cast a blight over the game. However, we in the FA should have taken much earlier action to update rules that had not stood the test of time. The scenario is likely to be repeated as Parliament takes a much closer interest in attempting to regulate such matters as admission prices.

Graham Bean, the Chairman of the Football Supporters' Association, had, like many of his colleagues, impressed me in our meetings with the supporters' organisations and I had no hesitation in accepting Nic Coward's recommendation to appoint him as the FA's first Compliance Officer. It was a step in the right direction. I hope it was not too little, too late.

CHAPTER FIFTEEN

*Who's the B****** in the Black?*

R eferees have never been under so much pressure. Their every
move and decision is dissected by a dozen cameras from different
angles and by analysts, commentators and experts, many of whom do
not know the laws of the game.

Modern technology has changed the game completely for the man
in black. Decisions he has to make in a split second are slowed down
to be viewed at leisure before the finger is pointed at both him and his
assistant.

There were some referees in the past who would have relished the
spotlight. One such was Welshman Clive Thomas, who was one of the
best ever and certainly the most controversial. He changed his style of
refereeing twice, going from 'Clive the Book' to becoming the players'
confidant and friend and then back to the book again. He was superb
– and he knew it.

He was accused by the late Don Revie of kicking Leeds United
striker Allan Clarke during a game, a most unlikely scenario providing
League Secretary Alan Hardaker with his biggest dilemma, not
knowing who to support out of two men he despised. In the end he
could not bring himself to support Revie.

They had a few ding-dongs, did Hardaker and Thomas. Clive felt
that it was part of his duty to sell the game. He wanted to be a star, a
promoter and a spokesman. He would meet the sponsors before the

game, make presentations to the player of the month and generally involve himself in areas that displeased football's headquarters. The Football League did not like personalities dressed in black. He was summoned to explain himself to Alan Hardaker and Bob Lord one time. Insults were traded as both sides became irate, but Thomas was sufficiently composed to be able to recall the discussion word for word for subsequent publication.

Clive once disallowed a goal for Brazil in the World Cup when the ball was in flight as a corner was taken, a clear breach of the 18th law, the use of common sense! Then he found himself refereeing in the Third and Fourth Divisions for a spell. He complained to the referees' overlord George Readle who was powerless to do anything about it. The orders came from above and the instructions were to tell Thomas that there were some very difficult games in those lower divisions which needed a top referee to control them.

He was probably the first rebel referee and always outspoken, with retirement not affecting him one jot; he still has a quote and a comment for every occasion. One year he made a brilliant presentation to the annual conference of the Association of Football League Referees and Linesmen (AFLR and L), covering everything from encroachment to dissent. He spoke for an hour in one of the best talks I have ever heard.

It is said that there are not the characters around amongst the officials that there used to be. The Leicester schoolteacher Gordon Hill was another to fall foul of the Football League for allegedly swearing back at the players. Then there was Roger Kirkpatrick, who ran backwards, more quickly than anyone I knew. And Freddie Nicholson, who drove a big, flash car and suffered the humiliation of having his wig blow off during a match. Not all of them were as good as they thought they were, but Jim Finney of Hereford was a referee who, whilst technically adroit, controlled the game more by force of personality.

For many years the training and education of League referees was handled by the Association of Football League Referees and Linesmen which eventually became a registered trade union and subsequently fell out with the Football League about National Insurance contributions. Relations suffered for a while when they became very militant.

There was a big referees' clampdown in 1971 when Alan Hardaker and George Readle began to take away discretion from the referees for the first time. All of a sudden there were bookings everywhere, the name-taking escalating as the League gave instructions to tighten up on the application of the laws of the game, especially dissent, time wasting, encroachment, and foul tackles from behind. They were waging a war against the cynicism that had crept into the game. Ken Ridden, the Refereeing Director of the FA, always argued that you could have common sense or consistency but you could not have both. Commonsense was no longer good enough as the stakes rose. It allowed too much inconsistency and unfairness.

The trend was confirmed in an article written much later by the talented Leeds United midfielder Johnny Giles in which he freely admitted that, at the height of their prowess, the Leeds team used to stretch the laws of the game to the absolute limit. He admitted that he deliberately went over the ball in certain circumstances to protect himself.

This period also saw the start of the assessment system. Former referees were appointed to watch every game and report on the performance of the officials in charge. The referees themselves saw it as a necessary insurance against the vagaries of the club marking system where an irate manager might give them a low mark. The managers saw it differently; to them it was jobs for the boys.

It was from this time that there grew up a gulf between the officials and the playing side of the game which has never been properly bridged.

Old-timers like Jack Taylor, who awarded a penalty in the first minute of the 1974 World Cup Final, faded from the scene. He never became involved in any aspect of refereeing at a national level although he came back to the Football League in a commercial role much later on.

His type were replaced by a breed of referees whom managers considered were unduly influenced by the need to please the assessor in the stand.

I became involved with Gordon Taylor in a bid to improve relationships with referees. We had a number of regional meetings with players, managers and officials and, following that, instigated the forum known as the liaison panel where regular meetings took place at national level between Football League referees, managers and players. With the advent of the Premier League this came under the chairmanship of the FA.

The refereeing question featured large in the first seminar of the

Football League chairmen in October 1980 when ways were being sought to make the game more attractive in the wake of falling attendances. In addition to the decision to award three points for a win, Jimmy Hill persuaded the meeting to make some revolutionary changes to the way the game was handled. Many commentators over the years regarded Hill and Sepp Blatter as meddlers in their attempts to keep the laws of the game one step ahead of the more cynical coaches. I prefer to think that by their efforts they contributed more than anyone to the more open, cleaner game we enjoy today.

Ernie Clay, the Fulham Chairman, wanted to declare UDI at the seminar and other representatives supported him when he suggested that the Football League should play under their own rules if the changes they wanted to implement could not be brought in by the International FA Board. The International Board is a body which meets every year to consider amendments to the laws of the game. It comprises England, Scotland, Wales, Ireland and four further representatives from FIFA. A three-quarters majority – six votes – is needed to effect a change.

In the event the chairmen set up a special committee, falling back on their old reliable maxim 'if in doubt, set up a committee'. But this was a committee with a difference as it consisted of three former players – Jimmy Hill, Sir Matt Busby and Bobby Charlton – who comprised the influential Football League Advisory Committee which met in 1981.

The Management Committee of the Football League, of which Lord Westwood was the President, was sceptical about the new committee. Nevertheless, I joined the three wise men in a mood of some optimism as we sat down to frame some recommendations about the way the game could be improved.

Before the meeting began Jimmy Hill complained bitterly about not receiving the standard £5 fee which substitute linesmen received after he had stood in for an injured official at Highbury some years earlier. I promised him I would look into it.

The International Board was very conservative at the time; changes to the laws of the game and the way the game was refereed were few and far between and the FA, as the International Board's agent, reflected that caution.

One of our first recommendations was the four-second rule for goalkeepers holding the ball. That took fifteen years to be implemented, coming in at last in 1997 when referees were told to allow five to six seconds for goalkeepers to get rid of the ball. Even then it caused some problems because in the World Youth Championships in Malaysia in August of that year, David Will, chairman of FIFA's referees committee, told the teams that the five seconds started from the moment the goalkeeper played the ball and in effect included the time when the ball was at the keeper's feet.

I thought Gérard Houllier had gone crazy when he told me that. I remarked that it was not the rule change we made, but he assured me that was how they had been instructed to interpret the new law. It was not at all popular, as it was so hot, and the players had no time for a breather.

I thought Jimmy Hill's suggestion was new in 1980, but I later discovered that Sir Stanley Rous had floated the idea much earlier, although he thought it would be a problem if the referee stuttered.

We also recommended that the back pass to the goalkeeper be outlawed. I personally was not very keen on that, but it came in during the next decade. I thought that it would lead to players kicking into touch more and conceding more throw-ins which, to me, were never a great attraction to the game. But what actually happened was that goalkeepers became more adept, better footballers. It was one case where I was quite happy to have been proved wrong. It certainly adds to the tension if the forward is charging in, but is it fair to the goalkeeper when the ball bobbles in front of him? Whether it is good from the purists' point of view, I do not know, but it has increased the excitement and speeded the game up.

Glenn Hoddle came up with an interesting idea when he was England coach. He suggested that goalkeepers should be restricted to their penalty areas with the result that the game would be stretched more, again adding to the excitement with a goalkeeper unable to retrieve a desperate situation just outside the box. Glenn thought it would lead to the re-emergence of the sweeper system, as opposed to the goalkeeper acting as the last line of defence. But he did not go as far as suggesting a stick like they have in Subbuteo.

The North American Soccer League had a similar proposal designed to open up the game more and reduce the congestion in midfield in the early 1980s. They were using American Football pitches for soccer which were narrower and they found themselves afflicted by some negative European tactics. The Americans came up with some odd ideas, but one I liked was the 35-yard offside law. I saw it in an international tournament in New York when it certainly reduced the number of stoppages and increased the action in the penalty areas. However, it was never taken up by the International Board, although every year without fail Bert Millichip told them that something needed to be done about the offside law.

Joao Havelange floated ideas about larger goals and four quarters before the USA World Cup, but they were quickly dropped by FIFA. There were counter suggestions of a smaller goalkeeper!

An argument could be made for reducing the number of players to ten to open up the game on the grounds that players are much fitter nowadays. However, with that you would be reducing the opportunities for kids to play the game because two places would be lost to every match. Reducing players progressively during extra-time, to try and rid the game of the dreaded penalty shoot-out, was another idea, but the medical people came out against it very quickly with the prospect of seven-a-side on an eleven-a-side pitch too taxing for the players.

Frankly I do not think that there is a better system than the penalties for deciding a Cup game which is drawn. I am still not convinced about the 'Golden Goal'. I suppose the tension and drama is increased, but there is a terrible finality about a goal from which you have no chance of recovering, especially if it involves a decision which leaves the spectators confused, as in the Final of Euro 96 when Germany beat the Czech Republic.

In 1981 we also recommended that a foul throw be awarded when time was wasted at a throw in; for example a player who walked along the line could easily be penalised by giving the ball to the other team, although the value of a throw-in in most parts of the field is not very high. Sepp Blatter remarked that the game is played with the feet and advocated a kick-in rather than use of hands. But after three seasons of low key experiments in the Belgian Second Division, his idea was quietly dropped.

There was another recommendation for no offside with a ball received from the goalkeeper. That never saw the light of day.

Probably our most far-reaching recommendation in 1981 was to send off a player guilty of the so-called professional foul. This was the denial of an obvious goalscoring opportunity which had become prevalent. Managers, players and commentators were often quoted: 'He had to do it.' We had to find a way of making it wiser for players *not* to do it.

Jimmy Hill suggested a penalty be awarded irrespective of the position of the offence. He thought our alternative, the definition of the professional foul as serious foul play and therefore a sending-off, was second best. He did not believe 10 against 11 was particularly good for either team nor, most importantly, for supporters and in many instances the team benefiting would be the opponents of the culprit's team a few weeks later when he was suspended.

We also thought that the interpretation should include handling the ball. We could not see any reason why a last ditch foul on the edge of the penalty area should be treated any differently from a handling offence in the same place. The FA put the suggestions to the International Board without any real conviction. Some required changes to the laws of the game, the FA were not convinced of the arguments and it was no surprise when the International Board rejected the package.

In 1982 the Football League issued its own interpretation of those changes which we thought could be brought in without amending the laws of the game. We did not think the interpretation of the professional foul as serious foul play was a change in law and we included the handling offence within that interpretation.

We also brought in the foul throw recommendation in the Football League. However, no sooner had the season started than the FA said that handling of the ball could not be regarded as serious foul play; they ruled that serious foul play could only be a physical offence. I thought it was a foul against the spirit of the laws which could be even more reprehensible in certain circumstances.

Then in 1983, after one season, the International Board ruled that the throw-in interpretation was wrong and we would not be allowed to apply it any longer. In fact, they went further and said that only National Associations could put forward interpretations of the laws and not Leagues. It was very frustrating because we really thought that we were making inroads into some major issues in the game.

In 1984 the Liaison Panel decided to give captains an arm band to help communication with referees and give them a little bit of status, because nowhere in the laws of the game or the rule book was the captain of the team even mentioned. He was a non-person, even for the toss-up. Spurs' Danny Blanchflower would have loved to discover that, as one of the best and most famous captains of a team ever, he was just another player.

Two years on I recruited John Goggins to the Football League, a former referee who had become involved in the AFLR and L. He came out of retirement to make a superb referees' officer for the Football

League for many years. The game at the highest level has been very well served by some very distinguished former referees who followed on in much lower profile vein the work carried out by Sir Stanley Rous as Secretary of the FA in the 1930s and 40s. Ken Ridden was another technician on the laws of the game who commanded instant respect from everybody in football, as did his counterpart in Scotland, George Cumming, a former player who became a referee educator. They, together with Michel Zen-Ruffinen, were responsible for rewriting and simplifying the laws, erasing some of the tortured wording that had been introduced as bits had been added piecemeal year on year.

There was a widespread feeling that the Football League did not allow referees to fraternise with managers after games. We always said that they should be prepared to discuss decisions with managers, providing sufficient time had elapsed to ensure that the discussion was a rational and fruitful one.

We also encouraged managers to be more open about the relationship with the referees, but very few actually took the trouble to attend meetings and contribute positively to the problems about which they complained so volubly. Notable exceptions were Howard Wilkinson, then of Sheffield Wednesday, David Pleat, Graham Taylor of Watford and Mick Buxton of Huddersfield Town.

There was considerable controversy about the use of red and yellow cards in the early days, because the FA felt that they led to an increase in cautions, believing that referees were tempted to pull the cards out too quickly. The FA even banned them at one time and then re-introduced them in 1987, but took great pains to say that cards were supplementary to the notebook, and that they were not to be used instead of taking a note and formally cautioning the player as laid down in the laws of the game.

The player's name had to be taken first before the card was shown. It was only many years later that Harrow housemaster and the FA Premier League's leading referee David Elleray proposed that it might be helpful in certain circumstances for officials to show the card before they took the player's name. Situations involving dissent or a confrontation could thus be defused more quickly.

In 1987 Jimmy Hill formed a new committee and this time he had former England manager Ron Greenwood and Arsenal double winning manager Bertie Mee as his partners. This had the rather clumsy title of the 'Improve the Game Committee'. Bertie and I were summoned south to Jim's home at Hurstpierpoint as Ron Greenwood lived in that area. The first thing I saw when going into the house was the cheque I had sent him for £5 for his substitute linesman's appearance after his earlier complaint – it was framed, hung in the toilet and never cashed.

The main aim of this committee was to try and reduce misunderstandings with referees. They had a number of meetings with managers, officials and referees. George Graham, David Pleat, Bobby Robson, Graham Taylor, Gordon Taylor, Howard Kendall, Bryan Hamilton and Gordon Milne all attended one meeting at Coventry City.

We never managed any agreement on altering the offside law, as ever, but put forward the four second rule again. We also agreed to implement an idea which had been started in the World Cup in Mexico in 1986, that of the ball being returned to the opposition if it was played into touch for a player to receive medical attention. It survived 11 years as a mere convention, rather than a rule change. When the Irish FA wanted to put the practice into the laws of the game in 1998, I was one of a number who argued against that at the International Board meeting in Paris. I very much liked the idea of a code of sporting play being followed voluntarily without the need for legislation.

After I left the FA I recalled that meeting vividly when the furore broke out at Highbury in the FA Cup tie as Arsenal scored from a throw-in which, under the code, should have seen the ball returned to Sheffield United. Arsenal players Nwankwo Kanu and Marc Overmars claimed a misunderstanding, with the referee Peter Jones unable to do anything about it. It created such a fuss that, within minutes of the game finishing with Arsenal winning 2–1, Arsene Wenger offered to replay the game. In an historic decision the FA agreed that evening and Arsenal went through after the game was replayed.

This latest committee also met the referees and had a round table meeting with George Courtney, Neville Ashley, David Elleray, Keith Hackett, Ray Lewis, Neil Midgley, Roger Milford, Lester Shapter and Joe Worrall. These referees, by and large, were the most established in the League at the time and they accepted the managers' complaint about the assessment system. They took the point that it was unnecessary for international referees like Courtney and Hackett to be assessed on every single game and so the number of assessments was reduced.

The committee went to see Jack Dunnett, who was no longer

President of the Football League, having been replaced in the new system by Philip Carter, but was chairman of the Referees' Committee. I was not sure what qualification he had for that particular role, but he certainly did not exhibit any great inclination to embrace Jimmy Hill's recommendations. The result was that the four second rule still did not come in!

The 1990 World Cup in Italy, despite England's exciting progress to the semi-finals, was widely regarded as a poor tournament, characterised by cynical, negative and defensive play. The first phase was a League with the second being a knock-out. But the second stage did little to improve the statistics of goals scored. The overall average was 2.21 goals per game and, whilst goal count is not everything, it was certainly a dramatic reduction from 5.38 in 1954. The game had changed out of all recognition in those few decades.

By this time Sepp Blatter was establishing himself as a leading campaigner to make the game more attractive and he also set up a committee to change the game. I was appointed to 'Task Force 2000' along with Peter Mikkelsen, the Danish referee, the former French captain Michel Platini and Barcelona President Jose Luis Nunez. Blatter wanted to bring a fresh approach to the issue and I think it is correct to say that he took a somewhat jaundiced or less compliant view of the refereeing fraternity. He believed that the referees were there as the agents of the law makers and the game's rulers, present to ensure that fair play was observed and that the managers and coaches would not be allowed to frustrate the spirit of the game.

Various recommendations were framed. No longer was a player to be ruled offside when level to the second to last defender; England's stance against the professional foul (including handling the ball) was endorsed and three points were recommended for a win in the League section of the World Cup.

I suggested that if experiments were carried out with the laws of the game, they should take place in established leagues over a longer period. Previously they had been tried out merely in international youth competitions.

Platini said that referees were unable to judge between fair and foul tackles and that tackles should be banished completely. I thought that was rather an extreme view of refereeing problems, and such comments coming from such an eminent international personality did little to help anyone.

The difficulty with the professional foul ruling was one of

definition. It was the denial of an obvious goalscoring opportunity – but what was an obvious goalscoring opportunity? What was obvious to one referee was not to the fan in the stand.

Referees were instructed to ask themselves three questions:

1. At the moment of the offence, was the attacking player moving directly towards the opponent's goal?
2. Where were the other defenders positioned relative to the offence, and could they get back to retrieve the situation?
3. Where was the committed offence relative to the opponent's goal? (The further away from goal, the less likely it was to be an obvious goalscoring opportunity).

The issue of the guidelines did not do an awful lot to reduce the arguments which arose when the season started in 1991 under the new procedures. Managers were up in arms and none more so than Kenny Dalglish of Liverpool who demanded urgent discussions. When a meeting was held, Kenny did not turn up!

In January George Courtney was involved in a controversial incident with John McClelland of Leeds who tripped Andy Rammell when the Barnsley striker was clean through in an FA Cup third round replay. I asked Courtney for an explanation as to why he had not sent McClelland off and he responded that it had never occurred to him to dismiss him. This was the same official who had been the referee in one of the earliest recorded, clear examples of the professional foul when Willie Young of Arsenal tripped Paul Allen of West Ham United just outside the penalty area in the 1980 FA Cup Final.

Then, shortly after the McClelland incident, Courtney sent off Jimmy Case of Southampton for what appeared to be an involuntary trip on Bryan Robson of Manchester United in a League Cup quarter-final at Old Trafford. David Burrows was only booked by Joe Worrall when he brought down Danny Wallace and it was becoming very difficult to establish a clear pattern. In many respects, it boiled down to a question of intent. Courtney was applying a commonsense element to the ruling. He thought that McClelland had caught his opponent by accident and in doing so he highlighted a major problem, because strictly speaking and according to the laws of the game, if McClelland's trip had been accidental he should not have been penalised at all. It should not even have been a free-kick.

Ken Ridden and I decided there and then to push for an amendment to the law. We thought that, if a player was brought down by a reckless or a careless challenge which was just as capable of denying an obvious goalscoring opportunity as a more cynical trip, it should be classed as serious foul play. We felt that to remove the concept of intent from the law would have a twofold effect. Firstly, it would improve the game because defenders would be obliged to tackle more carefully and the more skilful player would be allowed to flourish. Secondly, the new law without intent would more closely reflect what was custom and practice, as referees routinely gave fouls for what were nothing more than accidental collisions. That change was duly brought in a few years later after Ken Ridden and David Elleray carefully re-wrote the law.

One of the saddest moments in my football career concerned linesman Frank Martin who, in 1993, moved a marker cone during his annual fitness test for the following season. It was suggested that it was a prank which went horribly wrong, but the supervisor of the test was very upset as he thought that Mr Martin and his colleague John Griffiths were trying to circumvent the rules. The FA charged the two officials with misconduct and took them off matches following a meeting with representatives of the Premier League and the Football League. The next day Frank Martin committed suicide.

The AFLR and L led by Neil Midgley threatened to strike. They said they thought the two should merely have been admonished, and at a very highly-charged meeting with Midgley and his colleagues at the Hilton Hotel at Manchester Airport, it was eventually agreed to reinstate John Griffiths and hear his case as quickly as possible. The Association called off the strike threat, but the coroner criticised the FA for being heavy handed.

I felt awful at what had happened because we had quite simply wanted to follow normal football procedures, and if someone was ostensibly involved in a breach of a rule there was a charge laid against them. However, the fact of the charge weighed heavily on Frank Martin with the result that he took his own life.

The referees were understandably very emotional about the entire episode and took it very badly at the time. No one could envisage that what was regarded as a routine decision taken on the evidence presented would result in such dreadful consequences.

Sepp Blatter renewed his attack on cynical play for the 1994 World Cup in the USA when instructions were given to referees that were even more stringent than any new law change that had been contemplated so far. Sepp wanted a red card for any player who even attempted a tackle from behind. He had close to his heart the example of the Dutch striker Marco van Basten, who had to retire from the game following an injury caused by such a tackle.

There were a lot of doubts but the tournament was a success with players like Jurgen Klinsmann of Germany and Sweden's Tomas Brolin flourishing as referees were encouraged to err on the side of the attackers on the offside law. They were told it was better to have a dubious goal rather than a dubious offside. It does not sound very good, but that was how it was put and it shifted the balance totally.

There had been a lot of misunderstandings over the offside law for years. Many thought that the linesman indicated the offence and the referee had the discretion to overrule or accept. In reality, while this was technically correct, the position in England had long been subject to a memorandum on co-operation between referees and linesmen whereby linesmen only flagged for the offence of offside, not for the position. They had to put themselves in the same place as the referee and not decide on the position of an offside offence but on whether an offence had actually been committed. The decision in England was the linesman's and the referee would only allow play to go on if there was an advantage to be obtained by the defending team.

There was also another massaging of the offside law in the 1994 World Cup when it was ruled that the concept of active play be introduced. Linesmen became obliged to delay the flag while they assessed the direction, the speed and the trajectory of the ball. There is still misunderstanding to this day when a flag goes up late after a linesman, or assistant referee as they are now called, has taken the time to assess whether a player, for example, running towards his own goal has in fact become involved in active play. Running the line became even more difficult.

After that World Cup it became a clear red card offence for a violent challenge from behind with little or no attempt to play the ball. Referees were told not to allow time to be wasted allowing players to take a breather, and no treatment was to be allowed on the field.

Ken Ridden formulated three exceptions for the English game which no one argued with – a head injury where referees had to call on physios immediately; a goalkeeper injury, for obvious reasons; and an injury to a player for which the opponent received a yellow card. While the referee was cautioning the offender, the injured player could receive treatment.

Many commentators think it is odd for a player to leave the field, only to be summoned back a few seconds later, but it acts as a deterrent to the timewasting which formerly was so prevalent. Moreover, the player can always decline to have the physiotherapist, in which case he can remain on the pitch.

In 1995 we considered the proposal to allow referees more time to assess whether an advantage had accrued. The change foundered on the word: 'immediately' because the law-makers could not agree how immediate it meant. We managed to have the change agreed in 1996 when we explained to the International Board that 'immediately' meant a couple of seconds after the offence. What this change was doing was merely putting into the laws what the good referee, the official with the best feel for the game, was doing already off his own bat.

By and large, managers do not know the laws of the game properly or fully judging by things that are said, particularly when they are acting as expert pundits on television or radio. They often come up with laws which simply do not exist or they often get them wrong.

Everyone talked and wrote about 'ungentlemanly conduct' when Arsenal scored the controversial FA Cup goal against Sheffield United but that phrase does not exist any more. It is now 'unsporting behaviour'.

With the phasing out of appeals against bookings or sendings-off, often used as a tactical ploy to delay a suspension, managers can now only ask for an unfair dismissal to be reviewed from video evidence which means that managers do not put their foot in it so often as they used to do.

The great Scottish international referee Tommy Wharton, who controlled twenty-three Old Firm derbies, told me the story of a player in Scotland who wore false teeth. Tommy, known as 'Tiny' because of his great bulk, called the player over after one incident and, towering over the footballer, said: 'Please don't do that again, or you will be joining your teeth in the dressing room.'

The use of a light touch like that or a little banter can often diffuse a situation and shows a degree of understanding that is often missing from the modern, highly-charged, fast-paced game. However, while the officials take more of a berating now than they used to, I am convinced that they are better than ever before.

They are certainly fitter and quite capable of keeping up with play. I cannot see anything for the experiment of having two referees. There are already three officials involved, and if a fourth were added, the number of referees would be vastly increased. Would there be two tiers with one referee in the parks and two at the higher level? I cannot see the sense in it and there would be a lack of consistency from one half of the field to the other.

As a group, English referees are probably still the best in the world; certainly they are the most respected abroad. It is unfashionable to say so, but I think the referees do a good job. Recent law changes may have made it slightly easier in stretching the play out more with much more penalty box to penalty box action. Before the changes in the offside law and the outlawing of the tackle from behind there was so much congestion in play that it was often like a pinball in some of the less salubrious games and, of course, the more bodies there are, the harder it is to have a good view.

Much the same questions would be asked with the proposed introduction of electronic eyes. Will there be the same laws for the World Cup Final as for the games on Hackney Marshes? One of the attractions of the game globally is the universality of the laws.

I concede that there is an argument for goal-line technology, although it would be very expensive. Perhaps the expense could be justified if it can eradicate the goals that were not the obvious mistakes which occur like the one in the game between Romania and Bulgaria in Euro 96 when Romania had a goal disallowed by Peter Mikkelsen and, as a result, failed to qualify for the next stage of the tournament. It was a wrong decision which had far-reaching effects, but it is unrealistic to expect the referee and assistant to adopt the perfect position every time. Sometimes it is a physical impossibility.

I would go along with the eye on the line, but the referee's judgement with his naked eye is difficult to beat nine times out of ten because he has a feel for the game and he is out in the middle. I do not think a decision by camera is necessarily always the best, even if a player goes down in the penalty area after trying to hurdle a defender. The referee can often be in a better position to judge whether the defender committed a foul or not.

Another change which has come about for the match officials is having one list for the Football League and another for the Premier. I think it would be better to have cross fertilisation and allow a Football League referee to take a low profile Premier League game now and then if there is such a thing. But they are kept very much apart.

The Football League were the originators of the seperation and now the Premier League have, even if subconsciously, created an elite. Because of television they are personalities in their own right and it is no longer Mr Taylor from Wolverhampton but Uriah Rennie, the Leisure Centre manager from Sheffield, who sent off Patrick Vieira last week.

I also think we are heading inevitably towards full-time professional referees with half a dozen whose living is derived purely from officiating football matches. Not that full-time referees are necessarily going to be any better. I am not absolutely sure that to have someone relying on the game to make a living is going to make him any better at decision-making. It may make him more mentally attuned to the game, but on the other hand he is no longer independent and no longer has the freedom to make his own objective decisions.

If the professional official is allowed to mix with clubs and talk to players and managers during the week, it would be a fruitful use of his time. Not that the modern official has much time to do anything else as the increasing number of European and international matches take up a minimum of three days, with even more on the horizon now with the European Super League and two domestic matches a week.

The Premier League chairmen were very sceptical when Philip Don, the former international referee and now Premier League Referees' Officer, made his presentation on full-time officials.

There is no reason why women should not continue to come through the system as Wendy Toms, the first lady to be appointed to the Premier League line list, is no longer even noticeable which means she is doing her job well and not attracting undue attention. More women are playing and watching the game but it will not be any easier to become a League official. It takes a long time and that is one of the reasons, by and large, why professional footballers are not attracted to the job.

Accelerated promotion for them is anathema to other referees. They want everyone to come through the same system, otherwise those who change in a Nissen hut on a Sunday morning will feel unfairly prejudiced. There have been a number of schemes to try and involve players in refereeing, and there was a special course a few years ago. Nigel Clough put his name down but he had to cry off.

It is not easy to combine the two activities. But there is one underlying factor which not even Gordon Taylor will deny, and that is that the average professional player does not have the referee mentality. I am not saying that is right or wrong or making any judgement, but players simply do not see themselves as referees. With the way the game has gone, players at the top level are more like pop stars than sportsmen. You will not sit on a number 19 bus out of Liverpool and find yourself sitting next to Michael Owen.

Until recently, referee appointments in international football and in particular World Cups were made on the basis of football politics and not football performance. For many years there was a quota which was careful monitored with, quite rightly, a number of officials taken from developing countries but it meant that if there were two top referees from one country, one would have to miss out, depriving the finals of one of the best referees.

As the game becomes ever bigger and ever more commercial, so the referees and their decisions grow in importance and significance and everything must be done to ensure that they grow apace with the game. But, equally, there must be renewed measures to ensure that managers and chairmen are no longer allowed to make referees the scapegoats for others' shortcomings. Some of the criticism is ludicrous.

Moreover, the referees must be given absolute and total support. I was astounded when Paul Danson was taken off an FA Cup match between Lincoln City and Sunderland after it was suggested by Sunderland that his presence would cause crowd trouble in view of his having sent off two of their players at Highbury. That should never have happened.

CHAPTER SIXTEEN

Corner Flags and Whitewash

I came to dislike David Mellor even more than Margaret Thatcher. He had been an effective and helpful Minister for Sport, but his populist and patronising outpouring on BBC Radio 5's '606' programme reached such a low that I could no longer bear to switch on. There came a point when his references to 'salt of the earth' fans and glottal stops, deliberately manufactured to convey the 'man of the people' image, reduced me to apoplexy.

It seemed a remarkable choice when Prime Minister Tony Blair selected the former Tory member of parliament to head up a Task Force in 1997. We were asked for a representative from the Football Association and I appointed my deputy Pat Smith because she was better versed than most in the needs of our supporters, having done so much to promote their interests. Then Mellor decided to take more people from within football to form an inner core to travel round the country as a working group to hear evidence from various people.

He especially wanted David Davies to serve on this small committee, but I was not that keen on the idea as I had the feeling that Mellor was just circumventing the fact that I had put Pat Smith on the case.

It looked vaguely as though Mellor was surrounding himself with people who followed Manchester United. There was David, Adam Brown of the Football Supporters' Association and Sir Roland Smith, the chairman of Manchester United plc, who were all invited to join. Why an avid Chelsea fan should do this I was uncertain and I am not even sure he knew. Here he was heading up an organisation supposed to look after the fans' interest, yet he was surrounding himself with people who had a close affinity with the richest club in the world and a club which had been accused of ripping off the fans more than most.

I thought that Mellor was prickly with Pat Smith and he clearly thought that David would be more receptive to him. This was corroborated by Richard Faulkner, the vice-chairman of the Task Force, who virtually admitted as much to Pat.

When the subject came up I was in Jerusalem for a game between Beitar and Sporting Lisbon on behalf of UEFA while Mellor was also away in Germany on holiday. We had a few words and I told him that in the FA's best interests and, indeed, the fans, the answer was to have Pat Smith on board as she had the track record of meeting supporters and had established the England Members' Club involving England members' forums around the country.

But Mellor kept repeating that she was retiring in a year's time and he did not want to take her for that reason. When he discovered that he was not making an impact on my thinking, he became sarcastic and told me that people equally eminent to me had caused no problem. He claimed he had nothing against Pat Smith, but still managed to give the impression that he thought my opinion of her was inflated.

I told him that I needed time to think about it, but he said that it needed a quick decision as he was going to make the announcement in two days' time. In that case, I said, the answer would have to be 'no' as I refused to be pressurised.

His response was that he was going to inform the Prime Minister that the FA had refused to co-operate. I was quite happy to go to Number 10 and explain my position if it was that important.

I changed my mind the following morning, because it seemed to be a pointless battle over a trivial issue. I told him he could go ahead and we both agreed to have a new start in our relationship which had not been good since he had been forced to leave the Government.

He apologised and said he had been going through a bad time. I had no problems in starting afresh for the sake of harmony.

I thought Mellor seriously overstepped the mark when he asked on his Radio 5 Live programme '606' whether Chris Kamara had been sacked from Bradford City for being black. The City Chairman Geoffrey Richmond complained and I was very tempted to take his side in the argument which followed but, unfortunately, there was not a position for the FA to take. Had there been one, I would have been very tempted to have had a go at Mellor for manufacturing an issue out of nothing. Chris was the same colour when he left Bradford as he was on his appointment.

Gordon Taylor and Peter Leaver were particularly upset at the Football Trust helping the Task Force with their administration. The Trust had been under threat and they had promised to look after the Task Force, but both Taylor and Leaver thought it outside their remit. Eventually it became apparent that the Task Force was not going to last very long. The Football Trust agreed to carry on looking after them for the remainder of its life, but not before they reached a decision to appoint MP Tom Pendry to replace Richard Faulkner as the Trust's representative on the Task Force. However, notwithstanding the decision of the trustees, it was Peter Lee, Chief Executive of the Trust, who eventually took over from Faulkner.

It seemed towards the end of the life of the Task Force that David Mellor was losing interest. Its remit had been to make recommendations to the Government on various matters which affected the supporters such as racism, access for the disabled, ticket prices and merchandising policies.

I went to all of the fans' forums that the Task Force arranged up and down the country with the exception of one in Sheffield, but Mellor was more conspicuous by his absence.

It was a problem for football that the Government had appointed someone who had an ombudsman-type high profile in the media. Tony Banks, the Minister for Sport, pleaded that this was a qualification for the job, but I felt very strongly that Mellor's views were in danger of being confused, particularly outside our shores, with those of the Government, as happened with the build-up to the Rome match between England and Italy in October 1997. A lot of dangerous misunderstandings were created as he was making demands on the local police on behalf of the supporters which were not necessarily the messages our Government and police were seeking to get across in their highly delicate negotiations with the Italians.

I was forced to apologise to Tony Banks after one meeting at the Home Office after I had complained about this to the Home Secretary Jack Straw. I had spoken to Banks' official from the Department of Culture, Media and Sport, Colin Jones, to forewarn him on the way into the meeting, but he had not had the opportunity to pass the message on to the Minister and when the Home Secretary sided with me over Banks' protestations it did not need any great foresight to anticipate a volley once we finished the meeting.

I could only apologise to Banks on the pavement outside the Home Office for not raising it fully beforehand, but the opportunity had presented itself to make an important point on behalf of the FA in the build up to France, and when I explained the circumstances we smoothed it over fairly quickly.

The origins of the Task Force were almost certainly contained in an article which Tony Blair wrote in the *Mail on Sunday* before he became Prime Minister when he attacked Manchester United for 'another example of the sport's growing obsession of money making' by changing their strip too often.

Managers operate in a very different environment. They have to control and mould multi-million pound players who, we are safe to assume, at the top of the game are like pop stars rather than sports stars, who earn more than the managers themselves. The manager is subjected to scrutiny, the like of which nobody else will experience in their working day, when the television camera is trained on him every second and every minute. Not even the Queen nor the Prime Minister face that. Sky have a permanent camera trained solely on the manager, waiting for his every reaction after a goal, a miss or a controversial incident like a bad tackle.

It must be very much more difficult to manage at the highest level nowadays with the pressures of agents and the media, than it was in the days of Sir Matt Busby, Bill Shankly and Brian Clough.

Shankly had the reputation of being an absolute fanatic, and in my experiences with the man it was true. I once had lunch in the players' canteen at Anfield with the great man as he actually moved the salt and pepper pots around the table to illustrate a tactical point, bringing in the knife, the fork, the sauce bottle and everything within reach before he finished. He was one of the first managers to be fiercely protective about his players and would never say a word about them in public, but in private he could be quite scathing, sometimes snubbing injured players completely.

Tommy Smith recounts a lovely tale in which he is being tended on the treatment table by Joe Fagan. Shankly enters the room and conducts a conversation with Smith entirely through Fagan. When Shankly leaves, Fagan is obliged to remind Smith that his injured leg belongs not to him but to Liverpool Football Club.

Clough had a problem with timing or geography. When he was manager of Brighton, which narrows it down to a fairly tight time span, albeit longer than his tenure at Leeds, he signed two players,

Ronnie Welch and Harry Wilson, a cousin of my friend Stuart Flynn, from Burnley. In those days the registration had to be in the Lytham St Annes office by 5 pm on Thursday, otherwise the player was not able to play on the Saturday.

Albert Maddox, the Burnley secretary, rang me at 4 pm to say that Clough had just left Turf Moor with the transfer forms for the two players. He called again at 4.45 to see if the deal had been completed and we closed the front door as usual at precisely 5 pm. Brian turned up at seven minutes past. We said we were sorry and to come in for a cup of tea but that he was too late to register them for Saturday. Clough was having none of it and baldly claimed that he was there at 5 pm prompt, looking round the side of the building for the door, and that it was not his fault that the door was closed.

Tongue-in-cheek, I told him that I would refer the matter to Mr Hardaker and if he gave his permission it would be fine with me to play the two players on Saturday.

The friction between the pair was legend and there was never any doubt who was going to be the winner over this one with Clough gracefully retreating, saying: 'Don't bother. Don't waste your time' and the debuts of Messrs Welch and Wilson were duly delayed.

Jim Armfield and I tried to improve the relationship with the League managers. We had meetings with them in 1994 and 1995, while Jim met the League Managers Association when Gordon Milne was chairman and I managed to reduce the public criticism of referees for a short time by appealing to their better nature.

The managers were interested in the Technical Director's job and wanted to know more about it, but the top men were more interested in reducing domestic commitments for our clubs playing in European competition. The French, they pointed out, played only two matches between European legs while we had three, with the League Cup being the problem. Eventually the Football League were prevailed upon to reduce the commitments of the clubs qualifying for Europe, allowing them a bye in the first two rounds.

We discovered that Glenn Hoddle, when manager of Chelsea, had tested all of his players for drugs at Stamford Bridge. It sounds laudable but I was not too keen on that, firstly because it could be an early warning and a way around the official testing and, secondly, a lot of the independent tests lacked reliability.

The managers all seemed to want a mid-season break. The subject came up with great regularity, particularly from Howard Wilkinson which is significant now that he has a position of such influence at Lancaster Gate. On this occasion during our discussions, they suggested starting the season two weeks earlier and finishing in late May.

But my answer then is the same as it is now – when do you schedule a break in an English winter? Have it at the wrong time in a nice December or January and then suffer a terrible February, and the entire season is totally messed up with a backlog of fixtures. What would clubs do if they had a mid-season break? They would play abroad for money, of course!

Another demand by the LMA was to play the international matches at weekends so that they could have their players back at the clubs for a full week of training. They are gradually having their way with that suggestion, as it is happening more and more with the new UEFA schedule for 1998–2000. Not that the fans are pleased when the weekend club fixtures are disrupted.

There was a further meeting organised towards the end of 1995 when we met up with the managers who had been in Europe that season. They were all available as none of them had lasted long that season. There was Jim Armfield, Terry Venables and myself from the FA; Gordon Milne and Olaf Dixon from the LMA; plus managers Frank Clark, Alex Ferguson, Ray Harford, Joe Royle and Howard Wilkinson. The only absentee was Roy Evans who could not make it. It seemed to be an ongoing problem for Liverpool managers.

There was one common theme running through this meeting and that was that there were too many matches and not enough time to prepare their players.

Harford pointed out that Alan Shearer, then with Blackburn Rovers, had already played 27 games for his club and if the internationals were added, it was already over 30.

Ferguson quoted the shrewd old French coach Guy Roux of Auxerre who said he loved to face the English teams at this time of the year because they were always knackered. The central theme was to reduce the commitments on players.

Terry went on to discuss technique and technical issues with them and, all in all it proved to be a very good, helpful meeting. It was felt that players both young and old were not receptive to tactics and that there was a need for football education to be brought in much earlier. Wilkinson felt that foreign players understood the game better and consequently adapted better. It was interesting to listen to the experts and even more fascinating to compare what was said then with what came out of Howard's Charter two years later. He was quite clearly on the same wavelength as the leading managers, wanting more time to prepare players, more coaching time and more quality coaches.

A good relationship was built through these meetings and Jim Armfield was able to negotiate with the Football League on Alex Ferguson's behalf when he played a weakened team against Port Vale. He persuaded the League to take a more relaxed view of it. Alex clearly decided that if he couldn't reduce the number of games, he would increase the size of his squad and rotate the players when he could to give his top players a rest without conceding too much in domestic competitions.

The League still have their rule, but obviously they now take a much wider view with such large squads. How could they or anyone else judge what is the best Manchester United, Chelsea or Liverpool team? Sometimes not even their own managers seem to know what is the best formation!

But sometimes no one can help the managers, no matter how much one wants to. I was astonished when driving home after work on the last Friday before Christmas in 1996 when I heard on the car radio that Middlesbrough had called off their match at Blackburn Rovers.

Because of sickness and injury 'Boro felt that they were unable to put a team out at Ewood Park. Even though they were told that they could not just pull out of a fixture at that late stage they failed to fulfil their fixture. The Premier League set up a commission which deducted three points from them. It seemed to be a fairly clear-cut case, very similar to the incident with Exeter in which I had been involved at the Football League many years earlier.

There had been some problem for the club in making contact with the Premier League officials as neither the Chief Executive Rick Parry nor the secretary Mike Foster were readily or easily contactable, leaving assistant secretary Adrian Cook caught in the middle. Cook it was who had been labelled the most important man in football in a magazine poll earlier because he was identified as the person who compiled the League fixtures for the season. I am sure he wished for some of his omnipotence when 'Boro came on the telephone that week.

Personally I felt that it was a grave error by manager Bryan Robson and his club to have a game called off in such circumstances and it gave them little chance when they threatened legal action.

They contested the case long and loud and, notwithstanding their difficulties in trying to retain their Premier League status, they reached Wembley twice that season, the first time against Leicester City in the Coca-Cola Cup. It was at that game that the walk from my car to the bottom of the steps at Wembley, which normally takes 30 seconds, took me 30 minutes as I was besieged by 'Boro fans chanting for the return of their three points.

Poor Keith Wiseman was invited to be guest of honour by the Football League and walked out to an unexpected crescendo of jeers despite the fact that neither he, nor I, had anything to do with the decision.

I tried valiantly to argue the point with the fans that day, but with a conspicuous lack of success. Then when they reached the FA Cup Final against Chelsea in May, I thought that the mood was likely to be even uglier because by that time they had been relegated. I was right. I took the precaution of going through the back door and making a run for it, the first and only time I did. Discretion was the better part of valour.

When we went out onto the pitch with the Duchess of Kent to be introduced to the teams, the booing started again. Nigel Pearson, the 'Boro captain, was quite embarrassed and made a gesture to try and quieten them down, but to little avail.

Despite the fact that I had nothing to do with the decision, I did not venture back to the Riverside until a friend took me on a spare ticket early in 1999. Apart from one loudmouth, the 'Boro fans were fine.

Bryan Robson has shown a lot of character, the way he changed the team around and bounced back into the Premier Division after being relegated and, while he has not been slow to turn down the chance to become England coach in the past, I think he is an ideal candidate to coach England in the future.

He did not rule himself out because he did not want the job, but because he felt that he was not experienced enough and that was probably right. He does not seem to worry about the skeletons that have rattled out of his cupboard now and again. He is another straightforward guy who looks you straight in the eye. He is one not to be shifted. In 1990 he broke his toe on a bed in Italy, he smashed his nose on the hotel bedroom sink on tour in Chile and suffered more injuries than most of the rest of the England squad put together, but despite his problems he never gave less than 100 %, scored many important goals and was, quite rightly, nicknamed 'Captain Marvel'.

Plainmoor has been on my banned list since the Gary Blissett case.

The closest I came to going back to Torquay was when I went to a game at Plymouth. They are a loyal lot down there and a man who sat in front of me turned round and told me I was not welcome. I decided then not to take my holidays on the English Riviera.

Gordon Taylor, the voluble and energetic leader of the Players' Union, has always been central to my story, it seems. Gordon, a good winger with clubs like Birmingham City and Blackburn, always has a genuine regard for the game and really cares about it as well as his players. But like any good trade unionist he has an eye for a main chance and is an opportunist insofar as seizing a platform is concerned.

He often seemed to upset the League, particularly when he criticised them for demoting Swindon. I could not agree with him when he said that financial penalties were appropriate for financial misdemeanours because there will always be clubs who can buy their way to success.

I also had to differ with him in 1998 and before, when I said that I did not want to attend the PFA's annual dinner because it was a men-only affair. I do not like single sex functions. It received more publicity that year because of the MCC business when the members of the venerable club caused an uproar by voting against admitting women, a vote which was to be overturned a year later. But the PFA Dinner remained an all-male bastion.

By and large though, Gordon always manages to convey a true feeling and love for the game, and for that I can always bury any differences of opinion that may surface. Maybe new Sports Minister Kate Hoey will smash the sex barrier in the new millennium!

CHAPTER SEVENTEEN

Visions of the Future

Football in England has never been in a better, healthier state than it is right now. The Premier League stadiums are full, the money pours in from television and commercial contracts, and there is no more popular televised football around the globe than ours. Now is the time to consolidate but, instead, there could be a massive power struggle developing from the direction of the powerful Premier League which would threaten the entire fabric of our game.

In the time since I have left the Football Association I have been able to take a step back and look at what is happening and some of it frightens me.

Before I departed from Lancaster Gate I set up a series of meetings with Peter Leaver, Chief Executive of the Premier League, and Richard Scudamore from the Football League, with the aim of agreeing common objectives for the whole of football.

We were trying to ensure effective competition within each League and we did not want any financial barriers to clubs being promoted. We wanted to promote the concept that we should all move forward together. Perhaps that is why two of the three of us are no longer helping to run the game!

Sadly Peter Leaver and his Chairman Sir John Quinton followed me into limbo, forced to resign by the Premier League in bitter circumstances in March 1999 after the clubs passed a vote of no confidence in them by 19 votes to one. The clubs were angry that they had given the go-ahead to a deal with two former BSkyB executives

Sam Chisholm and David Chance, to advise on a new television contract for the League.

It is increasingly important that a sense of realism is injected into all levels of the game and the best people to do this are the independent executives who have no personal axes to grind.

Since we went into nirvana there have been indications that English football is uniting – but the impression given suggests this unity is being forged under the leadership of all-powerful Premier League chairmen.

This is definitely not what I had in mind. The FA needs to take very great care that the new-found togetherness is not illusory or transitory but, indeed, that sensible steps are taken to progress the game in the widest interests of clubs at all levels.

I was disturbed when the Premier League appointed the stand-in Dave Richards as chairman for another year. I do not believe that the League is best served by having a club chairman as their own chairman. I think the old system was better with an independent chairman and chief executive. I can only assume that the appointment of a club representative is part of a concerted push for power by the Premier League within the Football Association.

This was further evidenced when they drew up plans to pay £12 million a year to the FA. All very well, but the game will not be best served by a split into professionals and amateurs. The new structure, which was promised after I left, needs to reflect properly the whole game.

The signs of Premier League influence were there when Sir John Quinton was not nominated on to the FA Council. Five club representatives were nominated to sit on the Council, demonstrating a clear move away from the concept of independence. I believe this is dangerous. Taking a hypothetical situation, say Martin Edwards, Chairman of Manchester United, criticises referee David Elleray over a particular incident – would it be the FA who should take action under their rules? Who would take action in the Premier League? It is not practical to have one chairman hauling up another. That is what happened in the bad old days thirty years ago.

It is nothing new. Top clubs, in my memory, have always wanted more power. They have often resented the authority of the Football Association, but they never seem quite sure why; never quite sure of just what it is the FA prevents them from doing.

As far as I am concerned it is too much of a coincidence that Leaver,

Quinton, Wiseman and myself were removed in such a short space of time. We all exercised independence, Sir John was totally unbiased and Wiseman was no longer recognised as a Premier League representative on the FA. He was concerned to look after the interests of clubs at all levels.

The more I thought about the entire situation, the more I was led to the inevitable conclusion that there was a conspiracy. I found it astonishing that so many uncontroversial, middle-of-the-road, typical FA people on the Executive Committee went down such a highly controversial and emotive road to remove Keith Wiseman and me. Many of the ordinary Council members have subsequently asked me why I didn't stay and fight the issue.

The coming together of ambitious people with a common agenda was all part of the story. David Dein, David Sheepshanks, Geoff Thompson and Dave Richards are those men in power who must have led the move to be rid of us.

Why did an old campaigner like Ted Powell, an ordinary guy like Barry Bright from Kent, or Ray Kiddell, who wrote to me afterwards, allow themselves to be led down the controversial road? That is something that still baffles Keith and me.

It is clear that there has to be a streamlining of the structure. The way it is set up at the moment, the amateur game has a large majority on the Council and so there is a fundamental imbalance which leads to impatience, frustration and suspicion. Not only do they need to establish a modern management board comprising representatives of all areas of the major areas of the game, but the FA also needs to become more representative of the game it seeks to govern.

At the moment the ruling body is little more than a loose collection of football clubs of all sizes. If it is to be regarded as the true force for progress, it needs to be much more inclusive; it must include representatives of players, managers, referees and supporters.

It is anachronistic that the Council still has representatives from Australia, New Zealand, Cambridge University and Oxford University when the part played by such organisations is so much less than when they were originally accorded representation.

There are claims that government legislation will be introduced to enable an independent regulator to control admission prices and the cost of replica shirts. This is the last thing that football wants or needs. But in order to resist it, the FA must take on more of an independent nature so that it is not so patently acting at the behest of the clubs all of the time.

There is little doubt that had Keith Wiseman and I remained in our posts at Lancaster Gate, we would have forcefully opposed the significant and dangerous changes proposed by the chairmen of the Premier League, notably their so-called 'Golden Share'.

After we had been ousted, the interim leaders at the FA were quick to announce to the football world that they would seize the opportunity to usher in a new dawn with the modernisation of the venerable old body.

The proposals came to light immediately prior to the Council meeting in Chester in June when they met to elect the new chairman and his deputy, with Acting Chairman Geoff Thompson, the secretary of the Sheffield and Hallamshire FA, challenged by Old Etonian David Sheepshanks, the chairman of Ipswich Town. David Dein agreed to stand down from the vice-chairman's poll in favour of Dave Richards of Sheffield Wednesday, who was thought to have too much clout for rival Ian Stott.

But many of the Council members who voted in Thompson for Chairman swung behind Stott for Vice-Chairman after recognising right at the last moment the full significance of the recommendations for re-structuring. Buried deep in the small print was a recommendation that the Premier League should be given a 'Golden Share' in the FA's constitution.

This would effectively give them the right of veto and would oblige the ruling body to seek prior written consent of the Premier League for any rule change which affected either the Premier League or the Football League.

The Football Association was ready to sell itself for £12 million a year and give away the principle which it has jealously and rightly guarded for 136 years: that is, the authority, confirmed only a few years earlier in the High Court, to govern football in the widest interests of the whole game at its absolute discretion.

The Premier League are also claiming five of the six seats that are to be allocated to the professional game on the new fourteen-man Board of Directors who will become the Company Directors of the FA in place of the Council.

What does the FA receive in return for handing over the power and running of the English game? The sum of £12 million a year for the development of grassroots football, a modest investment by the League's standards for something which it had a moral obligation to undertake in any case!

I could not understand why the Council did not demand a delay on the new appointments until the re-structuring proposals were settled. How much better it would have been to appoint a respected national figure to pilot the new plans to completion, to allow the elections to take place under more appropriate and realistic circumstances.

As it is, the dangers to the future of football are stark and very real, with the major concern being that the interests of the Premier League will rarely coincide with the broader interests of the game in general.

They have, in the past, adopted short-term solutions to problems which directly affect them. They are scarcely renowned for thinking in the long term and for the good of others apart from themselves. We have the very real prospect that every decision facing the game will go the way the twenty Premier League chairmen want it to go.

What will happen, for example, to the age-old confrontation between club and country? The clubs are always whingeing on about meaningless friendlies taking their international players away unnecessarily and the call on their younger players for FIFA-organised tournaments in-season. If they are given the ultimate power of veto, the Premier League could wipe out England friendly matches at a stroke. Perhaps they should talk to the fans, for supporters know full well that Kevin Keegan needs those games to build a team to challenge for the World Cup and European Championships.

The confrontation between club and country took on another slant in the close season with the furore over Manchester United's non-participation in the 1999–2000 FA Cup due to their commitment to play in the newly-created World Club Championship in Brazil, a tournament which clashed with the 4th round of the FA Cup scheduled for January 2000.

I find this whole situation riddled with ironies. It was clear that it was a desperate situation requiring desperate measures. Indeed, with the close involvement of Tony Banks, it looked as if Banks was running the FA at one time! New Labour's media management skills are well known and it is ironic that they and the FA appear to have misjudged the depth of feeling of Manchester United fans and of other clubs and the media.

It's interesting to see that the FA were later saying they would consider any solution when, originally, they claimed they had exhausted all the options. England's bid for 2006 was at stake, and the FA were worried about alienating friends they had made all over the world if they had turned their back on the World Club Championship tournament. It's clear that most of the 2006 Euro votes would be siding with Germany, so England felt they needed all the votes they could get.

The FA should have given more thought to staging the tournament in this country, which would have given a boost to England's cause in the bidding process. I felt strongly that Manchester United should be involved in the FA Cup.

The final irony is that when the Premier League was formed back in 1992, all Premier League clubs were obliged to be involved in the FA Cup. Now, in 1999, here were the FA instrumental in encouraging a Premier League club *not* to take part.

Another area that worries me is the more serious question of 'bungs' and the like. If the FA were to seek to impose firmer financial regulations for the better interests of the game, they, too, could be blocked by the Premier League's golden share.

There is, therefore, a great burden of responsibility on the shoulders of new FA Chairman Geoff Thompson and Vice-Chairman Ian Stott. Thompson, according to a description in *The Times*, is small, bearded and balding, a Justice of the Peace who has been chairman of the Disciplinary Committee, he is a very effective chairman of the many meetings he conducts. He is thoroughly conversant with the complexities of FA administration after twenty years on the Council, although it worries some people that he drops his Sheffield accent when he speaks in Council.

He and Ian Stott should work well together, as there is no inherent clash. But the position of vice-chairman still remains something of an anomaly as successive incumbents have mentioned.

In fact, Geoff Thompson complained to me that he wasn't involved enough as vice-chairman shortly before I left. He clearly had itchy feet at the time.

But I cannot see Stott stand by doing nothing, waiting for the call to arms when Thompson absents himself for one reason or another. He is simply not that sort of person. He will push himself forward, just as he did when he was kicked off the International Committee after Oldham's relegation. He complained so bitterly that Sir Bert Millichip immediately had him reinstated! He will certainly not harbour a grudge silently.

He is, however, an amiable man, not unpopular. People tend to react reasonably warmly to him although not so much so that he would have won the vote without the protest element. Nobody would accuse him of being self-effacing, but he has a good sense of humour, which can redeem a lot of faults. He is very experienced in the ways of football administration and has always been keen to put himself forward for office. He was on the Executive Committee of the FA for a spell when Oldham were in the Premier League and he served on the Football League Management Committee from 1986, so he is well qualified for the position, even though he came through on the rails.

The Board of Directors needs to be prepared to delegate authority to the senior management personnel augmented by the Chief Executives of the Football Association, the Premier League, The Football League and possibly even the Professional Footballers' Association and the League Managers Association.

The distinctions between League and Non-League and professional and semi-professional should be removed and clubs allowed to reach their own level, determined by their market.

The FA should take on a group of financial experts who would visit clubs, promoting sound financial arrangements and management and monitoring their compliance with regulations.

Each league and division should be allowed to conduct its own central marketing operation, but it should be a cardinal principle that a certain proportion of revenue should always trickle down to the league below, so as to promote effective competition and remove, or at least reduce, the risk of stagnation with its resultant lessening of interest.

I could not understand why the Director General of the Office of Fair Trading took exception to the central negotiation by the Premier League of the television contracts. It was always a fundamental principle in English football that such rights were handled by the organising body concerned. I was pleased the Premier League won. How could the OFT not see they were encouraging monopoly by their action?

I also campaigned against the proposed takeover of Manchester United by BSkyB on the grounds that the main player in the broadcasting of the sport should not be allowed to own the most commercial club. Notwithstanding the alliance between the Football Association, the Football League, the PFA and the supporters' bodies, I was very surprised when the Trade Secretary Stephen Byers threw out the deal on the recommendation of the Mergers and Monopolies Commission.

The last contract negotiated by Rick Parry for the Premier League in 1996 provided for a massive £643 million flow of cash into football over five years. Rick had been keen to ensure that at least a portion of all this new money should be devoted to the good of the game generally.

Whilst it was true that some did go to player development and ground improvements, the vast bulk of it merely served to fuel wage inflation throughout the leagues, as clubs lower down the scale struggled to keep up with those in the higher leagues. Threatened insolvencies were not confined to the smallest clubs, as Portsmouth, Crystal Palace and Oxford United all experienced severe financial pressures .

It is difficult to say where it will end. There is certainly no sign of a decline in interest at the moment and there seems little doubt that Rupert Murdoch and Sky will push the boat out again when their contract ends. Any other decision would be illogical, especially as in the spring of 1999 they suddenly decided to give away £3 million worth of digital boxes. Thus we have to assume that they will go to the limit again to retain the rights which have been so critical to their business.

Whether the clubs will ever agree to some form of salary cap, as Tottenham Hotspur Chairman Alan Sugar advocated in the early days of the Premier League, is doubtful in the extreme. Certainly I believe that nothing will stop the inevitable widening of the gulf between the top four or five big city clubs and the rest.

Every development in the game over recent years has sharpened the focus between those who have and those who have not. The prospect, sadly, of any club outside the top few winning the Premiership is remote.

At least pay-per-view television does not, at the moment, look as though it will be yet another instrument to widen that gap even further, as it appeared when first mooted. It is going to be interesting to assess the effects of the gradual introduction of pay-per-view television to matches where the capacity has been low and the visitors were particularly well supported, such as Sunderland's visit to Oxford in their 1998–99 promotion chase. It is going to be a useful addition to the marketing of football used selectively, but I doubt whether any major effects are going to be felt for a good few years to come.

It is difficult to envisage, at a time when there is a major match on television almost every night of the week, that the advent of digital systems will mean that there will be ever more football available to the viewer and listener.

If football maintains a strong negotiating position, this is likely to result in the Sky stranglehold on televised football being relaxed and also that of the BBC in radio. Not only will the viewer or listener have more choice how he or she watches matches, for example from behind the goal, but there will also be a vast choice of matches to select from. Football's trick will be to exploit these new markets whilst maintaining the attendances at the grounds, something they have managed to do particularly well over recent years.

My resolve for a Premier League of 18 clubs lessened when I realised how much the supporters wanted to retain the existing number of matches. Discussions reached the point with the clubs where only Arsenal and Manchester United were interested in a reduction. However, with the new format for the European Champions' League, the debate for a smaller top division in England will inevitably be revived.

When the FA campaigned against the proposed European Super League in August 1998, we said we were not averse to changes in the structure of European Cup competitions, providing three conditions were observed.

1. That the existing hierarchy in football, e.g. FIFA, UEFA, etc, be maintained.
2. Participation in the new format be decided on merit rather than by invitation.
3. That the domestic football programme be unaffected by any change.

The first two conditions were observed but, in retrospect, the third seems little more than a pipe dream. Immediately there were threats, successfully withstood, that FA Cup replays would have to be scrapped, although semi-final replays were abolished. With the 17 dates required for success in the new Champions League, the fixture compilers were trying to squeeze a quart into a pint pot.

Moreover, the increasing importance, some would say self-importance, of the biggest clubs and their European aspirations means the future of international football is being jeopardised. Powerful chairmen and influential managers are increasingly using the term 'meaningless friendlies'. The standard of international football will fall if international coaches are not allowed adequate opportunity for preparation. The sooner the FIFA, on behalf of the entire world game, is able to lay down a standard international fixture programme which balances the needs of international and club football throughout the world, the better.

This applies to international football at all levels. The FA made no friends when they sent a weakened England team to Nigeria for the World Youth Championships; however, it was equally remiss of FIFA to allow tournaments to be staged when League championships in much of Europe were reaching their climax.

It is important that young players are exposed to international competition at the earliest opportunity without the experience conflicting with their domestic club commitments.

It is better not to go at all, rather send an under strength side. It is unfair to all concerned. The Premier League is shooting itself in the foot, if they claim to be the best and yet are instrumental in England sending a below-strength team to a prestigious competition on which the eyes of the world are focused. We have seen how Spain, Portugal and Brazil and, to a lesser degree, Turkey have used these tournaments for the development of their top young stars who have subsequently made it to the full national team and become better players for the experience.

It is becoming increasingly significant as clubs turn their attentions to the development of young players. While not every club can be expected to emulate Manchester United in investing funds in youth development, it may be that the development of the nursery club concept is one way forward for clubs at lower levels.

Hitherto fans have resisted the idea of being a mere satellite of a top club. However, closer links between clubs at different levels must be one way of ensuring the continued survival of these important breeding grounds.

Undoubtedly, clubs in England will watch closely the Ajax of Amsterdam experience of merging two clubs in Cape Town, South Africa. Certainly Africa and the Far East are potentially lucrative areas for investment by bigger clubs. Indeed, if they are contributing to the development of the game in other countries it will be very worthwhile for all concerned.

What they must guard against, of course, are charges of exploitation. It has been all too easy for some European clubs to take youngsters from other continents and cast them onto the scrap heap when they fail to make the grade. The question of qualification for international football is also relevant because by using qualification periods you could find players from South Africa playing for Holland instead of their own countries, thus upsetting the natural development and balance of international football.

I doubt whether, with Scotland and Wales setting up their own political assemblies, there would ever be a united British team. If there was a British contender to support, like Tim Henman and Greg Rusedski in the Davis Cup, people will follow them, but the British football supporter values national identity far too much to allow it to be submerged into one team. We may have to reconcile ourselves to the fact that, like George Best before him, Ryan Giggs will never appear in the World Cup Finals. This makes it even more important that the English game recognises its obligations to its neighbours and helps them, out of the vast television fees it receives.

Former Sports Minister Tony Banks's renewed call for a British representative in the Olympic Games and then, once more, for an integrated British international team, was always going to fall on deaf ears – until the 'Golden Share' reared its ugly head and threatened to put the decision in the hands of the Premier League chairmen.

This is a possible outcome if the autonomy of the four British Associations is threatened by the introduction of the two giant Scottish clubs, Rangers and Celtic, into the Premier League.

This is neither so far-fetched nor so distant as it sounds. The game is commercially led and it is a question of how long the two Glasgow teams can continue to operate financially and feasibly within the Scottish set-up. There will be Premier League chairmen casting envious eyes across the border at two huge clubs operating so close and generating so much money and television interest around the world.

The obvious conclusion would be for an invitation for Rangers and Celtic to join with the likes of Manchester United, Liverpool, Arsenal and the rest in a reshaped Premier League.

I think it is inevitable because of commercial reality and once it does happen, FIFA will happily step in and reduce the four British votes on the decision-making body.

What future for English football then?

Index

INDEX

Silver, Leslie 223
Sinclair, Frank 272
Sinclair, Michael 90
Smart, Lionel 81
Smee, Roger 126
Smith, Alan 123, 161, 220
Smith, Arthur 208
Smith, Chris 70
Smith, Jill 186
Smith, John 144, 155
Smith, Jon 72, 237–8
Smith, Pat 14, 18, 39, 41, 57,
  59–60, 64–5, 72, 74, 80,
  83, 102, 162, 183, 186,
  250–1, 292–3
Smith, Sir John 55, 149, 161,
  164, 206, 207, 269
Smith, Sir Roland 292
Smith, Tommy 295
Soar, Phil 269
Souness, Graeme 77
South, Sir Arthur 146, 147
Southgate, Gareth 272
Sprengers, Dr Mathieu 45
Spurs, loans scandal 263–8
Squires, Michael 56
Staves, John 119
Stephen, Sir Andrew 134
Stephens, Tony 191
Stott, Ian 59, 87–8, 153–5,
  196–7, 219, 223, 227,
  232–3, 236, 304, 306–7
Straessle, Leon 102
Straw, Jack 294
Stubbs, Ray 66
Studer, Marcus 104
Sugar, Alan
  considered for FA
    Chairmanship 63
  dispute with Venables 224,
    226, 227, 228–30, 232,
    263–6
  Intertoto Cup 102, 104
  salary cap proposal 308
  spoof awards 125
  Spurs loans scandal 263–9
Sugar, Daniel 102
Swales, Peter 54, 68, 87, 101,
  147, 215, 218, 220–5,
  227, 252, 257
Swindon Town, illegal
  payments 81, 82

Taylor, Barry 58
Taylor, Ernie 112
Taylor, Gordon 29, 55–6, 75,
  82, 88–9, 91, 95, 107,
  122, 141, 149, 154–5,
  162, 192–3, 198, 200
  Cantona incident 195–6
  criticisms of Armfield 223

criticisms of FA 224
  Kelly's opinion of 300
  Merson's addictions 270
  referees 273, 277, 283, 291
  replacement of Bobby
    Robson 215
  Spurs loans scandal 266
  Task Force 1997 294
  Wright/Schmeichel incident
    204
Taylor, Graham
  appointed England manager
    215, 217–19
  appointment of McMenemy
    212, 219, 227
  FIFA role 34
  managerial tactics 74
  personnel changes as
    England manager 219
  Premier League negotiations
    89–90
  press advisor 173
  press criticisms 219–20
  press relations 65
  relationship with
    McMenemy 212, 219,
    220
  relationship with referees
    282, 283
  resignation as England
    manager 212, 222
  tactical errors 219–21
  TV documentary 221–2
  use of sports psychologist
    252
Taylor, Jack 277
Taylor, Lord Justice 179
Taylor, Peter 123, 242, 258,
  260, 261
Taylor, Tommy 114
Teasdale, David 65, 173, 175,
  221
Tedin, Manolita 163
Thatcher, Margaret
  dislike for football 170
  football hooliganism 172–6,
    178
  identity cards for fans 159
  resignation 179
Thomas, Clive 275–6
Thomas, Norman 130, 131
Thompson, Daley 121
Thompson, Geoff
  Cantona incident 196–7
  Cash for Votes scandal
    10–13
  Clough disciplinary case 200
  FA Chairmanship elections
    22, 60
  FA Executive Committee 53
  FIFA Presidential elections

44–5
  future of FA 304, 306
  Grobbelaar match-fixing
    charges 207
  Hoddle's contract
    negotiations 256, 259
  negotiations with Welsh FA
    28
  ousting of Kelly 303
  Premier League negotiations
    90
  refusal to support Welsh FA
    deal 27
  replacing Millichip 63
  Spurs loans scandal 266
  World Cup 1998 249
Thompson, Jim 179
Thompson, Sir Harold 57–8,
  137, 149
Titcombe, Adrian 57
Tomlinson, Ellis 116–17
Toms, Wendy 290
Townsend, Cyril 149
Tracey, Richard 175, 176, 177
Turner, Andrew 99
Tyson, George 201

UEFA
  ban on English clubs 174,
    177–8
  bids to stage World Cup
    2006 32–40
  conflict with FA 102–4
  expansion of powers 105–6
Uzzell, John 208, 209, 210

van Basten, Marco 287
Veeder, V V 267
Venables, Fred 234
Venables, Myrtle 234
Venables, Terry
  allegations of shady business
    practice 225–6
  allegations of unauthorised
    loans 224–5
  appointed England coach
    224–7
  appointment of Hoddle as
    England coach 238
  banned as company director
    233
  departure from Spurs 263
  dispute with Sugar 224, 226,
    227, 228–30, 232, 263–6
  dissatisfaction with
    Hoddle's contract 212–13
  doubts about England job
    230–2
  Dublin riot 182
  establishment of
    Shearer/Sheringham

319